TWELVE HUNDRED MILES BY HORSE AND BURRO

Twelve Hundred Miles by Horse and Burro

J. Stokely Ligon and New Mexico's First Breeding Bird Survey

Harley G. Shaw and Mara E. Weisenberger

The University of Arizona Press • Tucson

THE UNIVERSITY OF ARIZONA PRESS

www.uapress.arizona.edu

Library of Congress Cataloging-in-Publication Data
Shaw, Harley G.
Twelve hundred miles by horse and burro : J. Stokely Ligon and New Mexico's first breeding bird survey / Harley G. Shaw and Mara E. Weisenberger.
p. cm.
Includes bibliographical references and index.
ISBN 978-0-8165-2861-5 (pbk. : alk. paper)
1. Bird surveys — New Mexico — History. 2. Ligon, J. Stokley.
3. Birds — New Mexico — History. 4. New Mexico — Description and travel.
I. Weisenberger, Mara E. II. Title.
QL684.N6S53 2011
598.09791 — dc23 2011025183

Manufactured in the United States of America on acid-free, archival-quality paper and processed chlorine free.

16 15 14 13 12 6 5 4 3 2

CONTENTS

ILLUSTRATIONS

Unless otherwise noted, photographs are from the J. Stokeley Ligon Papers in the Western History and Genealogy Collection at the Denver Public Library and are reproduced courtesy of the library.

PREFACE

Many naturalists arrived in New Mexico before J. Stokley Ligon: some perhaps accomplished more, many left better records, and several attained greater renown. Only one, Aldo Leopold, became an icon, but others, such as C. Hart Merriam and Florence Merriam Bailey, were honored posthumously with biographies. Florence Merriam Bailey, like Ligon, was awarded an honorary Ph.D. by the University of New Mexico. Some—such as Bailey's husband, Vernon, and his contemporaries C. Hart Merriam, E. W. Nelson, E. A. Goldman, and Alexander Wetmore—are better known than Ligon because of the volume of their literature. Others, such as Elliott Barker and Homer Pickens, claimed modest renown by ascending in state government and writing their own stories. Ligon lived during the careers of all of these individuals, but he remained largely behind the scenes. Nonetheless, he held their respect, and they all called upon him for his knowledge of southwestern wildlife. He is unknown to the general public, as well as most present-day wildlife biologists.

Ligon sustained a lifelong interest in birds and, as his ecological understanding emerged, forgave even the largest raptors their predatory behavior. He was among the first to seek laws to protect them. Although he came from a west Texas ranching family, he recognized early in his career that some southwestern habitats, especially the river drainages and the high montane country, should not be heavily grazed. Yet he participated directly in the elimination of the grizzly and the wolf from Arizona and New Mexico. He came to regret the demise of the grizzly in his later years, saying that maybe a few could have remained in the high country. According to David Jackson, who wrote his obituary (Jackson, 1961), Ligon late in life also expressed regret over the disappearance of the wolf.

This book is not a biography but rather a story of Ligon's first job as a wildlife biologist: how he acquired it, and how he carried it out. I became acquainted with Ligon's work early in my career, using his 1946 monograph on Merriam's wild turkeys as my "bible" when I carried out research on that southwestern subspecies. Over time, I heard stories of Ligon's first trip through New Mexico in 1913, wherein according to one account, he criss-crossed the state six times. Because of Mara's discovery of his 1913 diary and breeding bird report that give details of this trip, we now know how and where he traveled. Telling the story here gives an early picture of the man at a time when he was transforming from an enthusiastic amateur toward becoming a respected early professional in the field of wildlife management.

Ligon moved to New Mexico in 1907, when he was twenty-eight years old and single. He worked as a windmill repairman on the Bar Cross Ranch, which then took in the southern half of the Jornada del Muerto area. In June 1913, he was hired by the US Biological Survey to reconnoitre New Mexico waterfowl. With a horse and two pack burros, he traversed a loop of some 1,200 miles. Many of his survey records were incorporated into Florence Merriam Bailey's *Birds of New Mexico* (F. Bailey, 1928), but his diary and handwritten report have lain in the files of the Smithsonian since it was submitted at the end of the survey, rarely cited.[1]

Those of us who have been lucky enough to do intensive field studies of wildlife might envy Ligon's assignment; it paid him to camp under open skies and ride horseback fifteen to forty miles daily, encircling much of the fledgling state that would come to be known as The Land of Enchantment. Relative to modern forms of travel, on horseback he moved slowly, was exposed to the elements, and had ample time to view his surroundings without the noise of vehicle engines, air conditioning, or heater fans to mask natural sounds. While he had a specific objective—surveying breeding migratory birds—he learned, as if by osmosis, much more about the landscape he traversed, as well as its wildlife and human inhabitants. While his brief diary about the trip describes some of what he saw, it reveals little about his thoughts as he crossed the still-unfenced wildlands of New Mexico, on horseback and alone. In a sense, it was a vision quest for the young Texan, expanding his geographic horizons; testing his self-reliance, biological knowledge, and communication skills; and teaching him to meet diplomatically the demands of the emerging federal bureaucracy.

The survey Ligon carried out was one of the last of the "long rides" by explorers and naturalists. It was by no means the longest or most arduous. Alexander von Humboldt, Charles Darwin, Lewis and Clark, Zebulon Pike, Stephen Long, James Abert, A. W. Whipple, Joseph Ives, John Wesley Powell, George Wheeler, and others covered larger and less-settled areas of the American continents. The same year Ligon encircled New Mexico, Teddy Roosevelt was struggling through the Brazilian jungle (Roosevelt, 1914). But none of these individuals traveled alone, and their purposes were of a general exploratory nature, gathering information on wildlife, archeology, anthropology, and geology. Later, the more focused naturalists—Elliott Coues, T. S. Palmer, C. Hart Merriam, Vernon and Florence Merriam Bailey, Edgar Mearns, E. W. Nelson, and E. A. Goldman—ranged over the already explored landscapes, collecting specimens of all living things and frantically describing new species. They traveled in smaller groups, at times alone or with local guides. Ligon, however, was one of the first assigned to carry out a specific biological survey of a narrow range of species—to establish, as it were, a baseline that might be used for monitoring future change. He was also one of the few who covered so many miles alone, and he was one of the last to do it entirely on horseback.

In reading his diary and unpublished report, I wished that he had written more reflectively in the way of Darwin, Thoreau, or even Mearns. Some evidence exists that he maintained private journals in addition to the small government diaries upon which I'm basing this book. Parry Larsen, who worked at Ligon's bird farm in Carlsbad in the 1950s, thought he remembered diaries neatly shelved over Ligon's desk. In addition, a sprinkling of pages from larger, bound notebooks exists at the Smithsonian, apparently remnants of more extensive notes. In a document accompanying Ligon's camera, David Jackson wrote: "He was a note taker, keeping journals of his observations, and he was a real nature observer."[2] I have searched the Peabody Museum database and spent considerable time trying to locate any such diaries in other locations, with no success. During the course of my search, I heard one second-hand report from an individual who claimed to remember finding Ligon's diaries rain damaged and unreadable in one of the open bird pens at the Carlsbad farm, sometime after his death. An effort to follow up on that report ended with no confirmation. More recently, I found a letter from Ligon to E. W. Nelson of the US Biological Survey written in 1928 stating that all of Ligon's old records had been stored in the family vault at Fort Stockton, Texas.[3] Upon discovering this letter, I called David R. Ligon, Ligon's nephew, who indicated that everything in the vault had been cleared away when the family ranch was sold, and most of the materials hauled to the dump. Because these diaries have not surfaced at the Smithsonian, in the Ligon files at the University of New Mexico, or at the Denver Public Library, I fear that they were discarded. Yet I harbor faint hope that they might reside in some attic in Fort Stockton or Pecos or Carlsbad.

In the 1913 diary, Ligon, because of his tendency to judge wild species by human moral standards, seems a bit quixotic. His horse, Gila Red, and his burros, Albert and Smokey, enhance the image. If we could substitute a local Sancho for one of the burros, and a lance for his shotgun, the image would be complete. But Ligon was not an aspriring knight going forth to battle. He saw himself as a freelance naturalist, photographer, and writer. In a 1913 letter to E. W. Nelson, he wrote: "While I expect to do the greater part of my work in my home state—Texas—I want to do general work in surrounding regions, broaden my knowledge, in general, of a wider range. My intention since a boy, has been to make a study of Texas birds, with the object of writing a complete history of them, their habits, distribution, and especially their economic value."[4]

By 1913, when he was thirty-four years old, he clearly planned to become active in southwestern wildlife conservation. For someone raised in a large west Texas ranching family, such a goal seems unusual. We have little insight regarding either literary or personal sources that provided inspiration. Ligon was not mad like Don Quixote, but we might guess that his Texas family and cowboy peers on the Jornada del Muerto thought him a little odd.

I hope to write more than a tale of one man's long ride. The diary does that without my help, even though Ligon's entries are all too brief. His notes and report provided a guide that I used to traverse New Mexico, attempting to envision it as it was during the seminal year of 1913—a year when things were changing very rapidly—and compare that vision with the present. I felt that I needed to see the same landscapes to understand how wildlife habitats and wildlife numbers have changed over the past century. To place Ligon in the context of his time, I have provided a brief history of the Ligon family and events leading up to the survey.

My handling of the 1913 diary and breeding bird report needs explanation. The diary is mainly a brief itinerary, written in a government-issued pocket notebook, and submitted to document his labors. The report compiles his observations, providing more detailed descriptions of key areas he visited and detailed notes on bird species observed. I quote the diary and annotate it with my thoughts and observations that emerged while I was crossing the same landscapes that Ligon traveled. I excerpt the landscape descriptions from the report and insert them amidst the diary quotations, thereby improving our ability to see what Ligon was seeing and compare it with present conditions. I have drawn from the bird species accounts in my commentaries on the diaries and have placed them in their entirety in the appendix at the end of the book, hoping that they will be useful to some future ornithologist. Thus, in the text, I shift between quoting the diary and quoting portions of the report, and identify the quotes as either "from the diary" or "from the breeding bird report." To avoid cluttering the text with scientific binomials, except where they occur in the diary or report, I've listed these in appendix table I, and I have used this table to compare Ligon's nomenclature with current nomenclature. In quoting both the diary and report, I have retained Ligon's spelling, abbreviations, and punctuation, feeling that these provide important insights into the level of his professional development in 1913.

ACKNOWLEDGMENTS

Perhaps it is unusual to place a coauthor in the acknowledgments. Initially, Mara Weisenberger's name occupied the place as the individual who had contributed the most to the senior author's efforts on the book. She initially spotted the Ligon diary and report on the 1913 breeding bird survey. She later checked photographic records in the Denver Public Library and photographed all of the pages of Ligon's two photographic notebooks there. She located the Ligon photograph albums at the University of Texas Library and acquired copies of the Ligon correspondence and specimen records from the US Biological Survey and from the Smithsonian. Finally, she reviewed and helped rewrite the text at various stages of development. At some point, it became obvious that the amount of work she had volunteered and her high interest in Ligon merited more than an acknowledgment. This has led to what may be an unusual circumstance—a book written from the first-person point of view of the senior author that has a second author who remains essentially invisible in the finished product. But Mara's work is present throughout the book, and she fully deserves to have her name on the cover.

We are grateful to many others who have helped. Paul Polechla of the University of New Mexico has a long and ongoing interest in Ligon. He traveled with me to Denver on one trip and contributed to our efforts to survey and catalog the Ligon photographs. Paula Martin of Denver spent time at the Denver Public Library, sorting, listing, and organizing Ligon's prints. Each of these tasks saved me time and travel.

Mary Markey of the Smithsonian helped Mara locate the Ligon documents there, and she was consistently helpful in quickly answering questions as the project progressed. Coi Drummond-Gehrig of the Denver Public Library maintained a high interest in the project and helped in every way possible to make the Ligon photographs and files available. Nancy Brown-Martinez of the University of New Mexico Library provided copies of the Louis Blachly interviews of Ligon. Janice Sabec of Trinity University Library, San Antonio, kindly located and researched early catalogs and registrar records for the time Ligon attended that institution. Michael Campbell photographed the pages of the Ligon report and diaries at the Smithsonian, and he was kindly gentle in billing us for the job. Steven Albert located the place where Ligon photographed the Tres Dedos near Ramah, New Mexico, and provided a current photograph of that location. Colleen Flannery and Marilyn Poitras provided genealogical information on the Ligon family and helped delineate more clearly L. A. Renick's relationship with Ligon. S. Smith from the Reference Service Branch of the National Archives and Records Administration helped us locate correspondence and records pertaining to Ligon.

John Hubbard of Espanola, New Mexico, knows more than any other living person about Ligon's specimens, which are scattered among a variety of museums and institutions. He has been willing to provide lengthy and detailed answers to questions regarding the history of biological exploration in New Mexico.

Dave Anderson of the White Sands Missile Range worked with Mara in organizing our trips to Sulphur Canyon, El Paso Canyon, and the Malpais. He has also helped with our understanding of ranching history for the Jornada del Muerto area and San Andres Mountains.

David E. Brown of Arizona State University and Jerry Wallace of the University of New Mexico reviewed the manuscript prior to submission. Their comments greatly improved the content and the style. They also sent materials they discovered during their own research regarding Ligon and his contemporaries.

Writing a book such as this requires the help of many people. To some extent, I wrote it too late. The few people alive who remember Ligon at all—Rollin Baker, Horace Burke, Bill Huey, David Jackson, Gale Monson, Jim and Seymour Levy, and Roy Tomlinson—all knew him late in his career. Each of these individuals gave us insights into Ligon but, as is the case with most accomplished people, finding information on his later life is relatively easy, while tracing his beginnings is more difficult. Here we followed Ligon on his first job as a wildlife biologist, showing how he worked and how he became involved in the field. As a result, we've had to draw upon many people for small tidbits of information, each adding insights into our subject. These include the following individuals, in no particular order.

Marty Frenzel and Dan Williams of the New Mexico Department of Game and Fish provided access to Ligon's camera and, more importantly, have seen to its protection. Jim Enyeart contributed his expert knowledge of the history of photography in assessing the camera as well as Ligon's photographic methods. Tom Myers flew me over the upper Gila River, helping me unravel Ligon's travel routes in that area. Claudia Oakes contributed comments on prairie dog distribution and ranch history. Trish

Griffin of the White Sands Missile Range coordinated trips to Sulphur Canyon. Dave Griffin reviewed historic bird records. Craig Springer provided history of the White Sands pupfish and native species in the Gila River. Rollin Baker, Jim Boykin, Mike Connealy, Randy Gray, Embree Hale, Kevin Hansen, David R. Ligon, Vicki Ligon, Jerry Lutz, T. J. McMichael, Gale Monson, Stewart Perea, Ann Rayroux, Bob Shufelt, Linda Sweanor, Tom Waddell, Frank Walker, Marsha Weisiger, Sandy Williams, and Dale Zimmerman all responded to specific questions. Bryan and Barbara Bartlett provided transportation to Denver for one critical trip. Allyson Carter and Scott de Herera of the University of Arizona Press have guided me through the agonies of manuscript preparation. I'm sure I have left out some individuals, and I apologize for any ommissions.

And, of course, there are those who have contributed on a daily basis—Patty Woodruff, my wife, who endures my weird sleeping hours and my piles of references; who was my companion on trips to Carlsbad, the Pecos, and Stinking Lake; who kept our home life on track during the periods I intellectually disappeared into the manuscript; and who did a final scrutiny of the manuscript for typos and spelling errors that inevitably creep in. Joe Truett provided a willing ear and recommendations for appropriate references. Jan Haley and Steve Siegfried were walking companions, who listened to my latest "discoveries" as I rummaged through the literature and other files.

TWELVE HUNDRED MILES BY HORSE AND BURRO

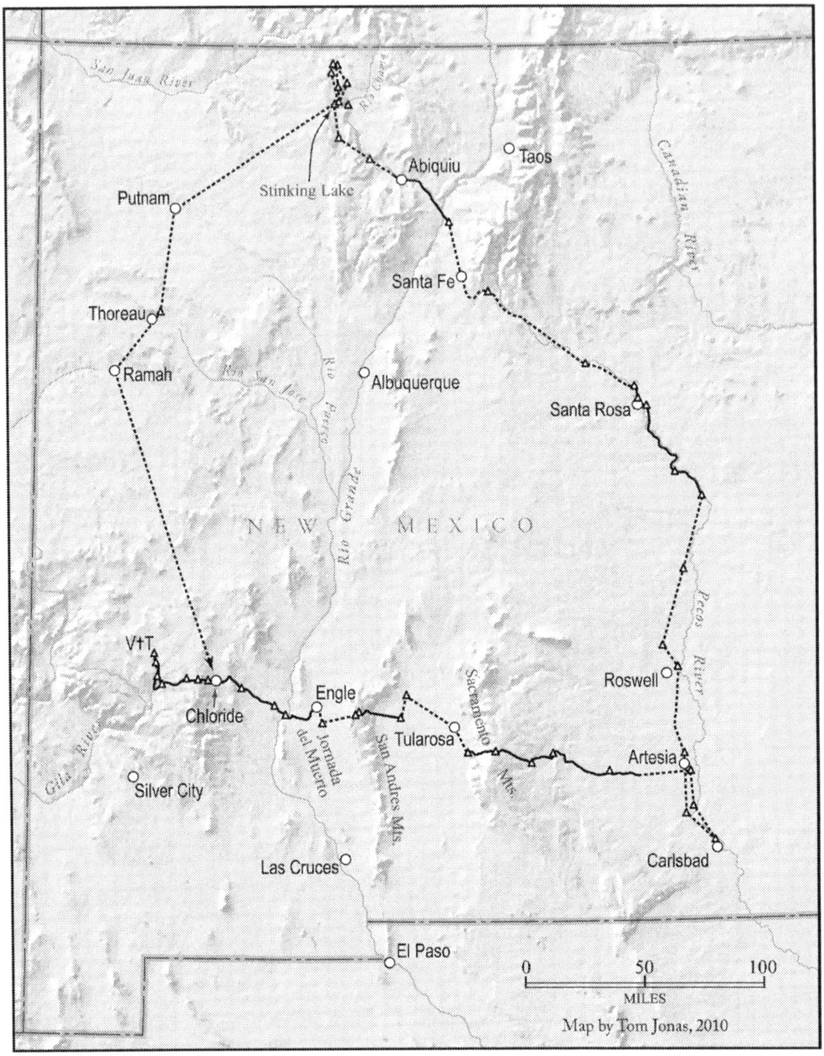

Ligon's ride. (Map by Tom Jonas, Southwest Explorations)

Introduction

In October 1961, David G. Jackson eulogized James Stokley Ligon, calling him "the gentlest of mountain men." Jackson described Ligon as standing "only" 5'8" and weighing less than 150 pounds. But Jackson praised Ligon as a pioneer ornithologist, biologist, oölogist, conservationist, author, and senior citizen of New Mexico.[5]

Stokley, or "Stoke" as he was known to friends, was born in Hays County, Texas, in 1879. He died in Carlsbad, New Mexico, in 1961. His grandparents were slave-holders who moved from Virginia; his father worked briefly as a drover to Dodge City. Stokley became interested in wildlife, especially birds, at a very early age, and as a young man left the family businesses of ranching, freighting, and well drilling to pursue a career as a naturalist, photographer, and writer. The skills with horses and machinery that he acquired from his upbringing served him well in his chosen occupation.

In an interview conducted when he was seventy years old (Blachly, 1952), Ligon credited his mother for his early interest in birds:

> I can remember spring mornings these Meadowlarks singing down at the field gate . . . one of the things that interested me first was trapping or trying to trap the Bob-white Quail. Of course we used an old figure-four trap and the first Bob-whites I trapped my mother was sick at the time and I brought 'em in and I told her we'd make a soup out of those birds for her. I put 'em down in the hallway and after a little went back and the cat had gotten the Bob-whites and that, of course, that made me sick. And after that . . . I was particularly interested in birds and trapping them and studying them and quail always fascinated me very much. And the first little quail that I remember seeing, my father . . . took me with him going up in what we called the mountains. . . . And we were driving along this old brush fence and . . . the old quail and a bunch of little ones . . . flew over this brush fence . . . about the same

J. Stokley Ligon at Monument Park in the Black Range with his burros Smokey and Albert and his horse Gila Red, October 1913. This is the pack outfit Ligon used in doing the breeding bird survey.

time we stopped to go up on what we called Lone Man, it was just a little hill but we called it a mountain. And all I can remember about that walk up on the hill is a dove nest under a little bush. The dove flew off the nest . . . opportunity means a great deal in things like that and . . . my mother . . . would encourage things like that. . . . My father had a few sheep and it was my job and my brother's to herd those sheep. Of course we let the sheep herd themselves most of the time and we chased birds and rabbits. . . . And from that on, why my interest was . . . with nature and it was just a question of opportunity to carry out that interest. . . .

. . . an inherent interest . . . applying your abilities and . . . intensifying them . . . being a close observer. . . . The more you're out . . . the more opportunities you have to learn. . . . In the early days you got very little encouragement because there were very few biologists . . . at least. . . . I didn't come in contact with them . . .

My first knowledge of birds . . . was obtained from Arm and Hammer Brand Soda cards. There was one card in each package of soda and that card had a little description of a bird.

. . . I think geography and natural history go hand in hand. . . .

> you've got to know geography to learn about birds and their habits and habitat. . . . Arbuckle Coffee . . . had a card that showed the map of different countries. . . . And from those I learned my geography.

Stokley was more or less in the middle of the family, with older sisters and one older brother. None of his siblings drifted as far as he did from the family tradition of ranching or ranch-related businesses. Ligon's early interest in quail continued throughout his life and ultimately brought him certain renown. An early awareness of ornithological literature led him to worry over the dwindling numbers of the masked bobwhite in Arizona. In a 1913 letter to E. W. Nelson of the US Biological Survey (USBS), he wrote: "Another line of study I have devoted much time to, is the Quail of North Amer. The principle [*sic*] object in view, the best methods of propagation. . . . I think some day before long, I shall make a search in Southern Arizona and Sonora, for the Masked Bobwhite."[6]

He did, in fact, make such a search but not until years later. He located a population in Mexico and trapped birds from this population, transplanting some in Arizona and New Mexico and using others to establish a penned breeding population. He and his wife, Rose, devoted much effort throughout their lives to propagation of this rare bird, now nearly extinct in the wild. Surveys made by a team of quail experts during the summer of 2008 failed to turn up masked bobwhites in what had once been considered their remaining habitat in Sonora.

Ligon exhibited an early sense of adventure and curiosity. In 1900, he and two brothers floated two homemade boats from the vicinity of Pecos, Texas, down the Pecos River to the Rio Grande, then down that river to the mouth of the Devil River. Unfortunately, we have found no written account of that trip, but a collection of high-quality photographs still exists. This trip and the photographs are, perhaps, symbolic of Stokley's vision of leaving the family trade. He had already purchased a field camera that used 4" × 5" glass plates. The quality and attention given to the subject suggest that Stokley had publication in mind. Photography with such a camera was time consuming, and care of the plates demanding. I have to think he must have written a narrative of this trip, but if so, it seems to have been lost to posterity.[7]

Ligon attended Justice Academy in San Angelo, Texas, in 1898 and 1899.[8] He then spent two years (1900 and 1902) at Trinity University in Waxahachie, Texas. Stokley spent his first year at Trinity in the "Academic Department," which was considered to be a college preparatory curriculum designed for students without high school diplomas.[9] Both Stokley and his brother, Earl, were enrolled in the academy in 1902. Earl was five years younger than Stokley.

Ligon therefore studied only one year at the college level. In the Blachly

Ligon's "Black Beauty" camera, along with his major publications. The netting in the background is a drive net that Ligon developed and that he used to capture prairie chickens. (Courtesy of the New Mexico Department of Game and Fish)

interviews (1952), he states that his principal interests at Trinity were biology, botany, and zoology. Trinity's catalog for 1898 (Trinity University, 1898) notes that the natural history curriculum was intended to teach the student "to have the power to make individual investigations, where necessary, so that he may see some things for himself and appreciate the beauties of nature as they are." As to zoology, it said, "This course . . . will include both Vertebrate and Invertebrate Zoology. . . . A study of such animals will be made as will illustrate the various classes of the animal kingdom with special attention to their gradual development." No course in ornithology was available.[10]

We know little of Ligon's activities between 1903 and 1907. Family tradition says that a party of Ligons, including Stokley, hunted the San Mateo Mountains of New Mexico as early as 1903. F. Bailey (1928, 31–32) states Ligon visited the Jornada del Muerto various times after 1905, but in his interview with Blachly, Ligon says he first came to the Jornada in 1907. Whatever the case, by 1907 he was a "windmiller" on the Bar Cross Ranch. The position of windmiller was a common one on the larger ranches of the era, although their exact duties might vary.[11] Mainly, a windmiller routinely checked and repaired the windmills around the ranch, assuring that livestock would have water. The work included climbing the towers to oil the "engine" of the windmill and/or to repair the fan blades. More than one windmiller or cowboy was injured or killed by being swept off the tower by a gust of wind that suddenly moved

One of the Ligon brothers atop a new windmill installed at the Summerford Ranch on the Jornada del Muerto, 1912. This is now New Mexico State University's Jornada Research Ranch. The photo was taken September 18, 1912, by Ligon from atop an adjacent well-drilling rig. Note "Ligon Bros." and the year in the lower corner of the vane. Ligon's early windmill work may explain his comfort in climbing trees and cliffs to collect eggs.

the fan, or by an unconscious misstep (Hilliard, 1996, 44). Ligon's experience as a windmiller undoubtedly contributed to his calmness later, when he climbed trees or scaled cliffs to collect bird nests and eggs.

Exactly when or how Ligon began communicating with the USBS remains somewhat of a mystery. So far we've found no correspondence between him and members of the USBS before 1913. However, an unpublished report in the Harry C. Oberholser files at the University of Texas, Austin, document bird collections by Ligon in Texas between 1900 and 1908.[12] He was probably freelancing and selling specimens to the USBS through this period. At the beginning of his 1913 survey, his diary indicates he had already collected seventy-three specimens. These may be the same specimens noted by Oberholser. It seems certain, therefore, that employees at the USBS were aware of Ligon; twice in 1908, Vernon Bailey visited Engle, New Mexico, near where Ligon was working, and E. A. Goldman was in the area in 1909. However, the diaries kept by both Bailey and Goldman during this period give no evidence that either of them were aware of Ligon, even though both authors mention natural history observations by other residents of the area.[13] Seemingly they would have noted someone as knowledgeable as Ligon had they met him at that time. More likely, Ligon may have initially corresponded with Wells W. Cooke (F. Bailey 1928, 15–36), who maintained correspondence with a nationwide network of professional and amateur naturalists. Included among Cooke's New Mexico correspondents were Dr. Elmer P. Blinn, living in Chloride during the 1890s (M. Brown, 1967), and Miss Fanny Ford (1911) and Professor Dayton Eugene Merrill at the agricultural college (now New Mexico State University) in Mesilla. Cooke used this network of correspondents to begin the book that became *Birds of New Mexico*, ultimately authored by Florence Merriam Bailey (1928). Cooke died in 1916, with the book partly finished, and Bailey completed it in 1928 (Kofalk, 1989, 163).

Biologists from the USBS were not the only field scientists active in southern New Mexico by 1913. New Mexico State University had been founded as an agricultural experimental station in 1889, and E. O. Wooton, an accomplished botanist, was teaching there and studying southwestern botany by 1890. He traveled and collected widely through New Mexico and Arizona between 1902 and 1904 (Allred, 1993). In 1911, just two years before Ligon's survey, the Jornada Range Reserve, later to become the Jornada Experimental Range, had been set aside for rangeland research by presidential decree. Also by 1900, geologists were actively exploring the White Sands area and the Tularosa Basin (Herrick, 1900; Meinzer and Hare, 1915).

The year 1913, the year after New Mexico statehood, was a period of dynamic transition. During his survey, Ligon passed through landscapes busy with human activity, a fact that, with few exceptions, he hardly acknowledged. Boosters in Alamogordo, Las Cruces, and El Paso were promoting economic growth and tourism in a region that until only recently had been best known for wild Apaches, the Lincoln County War, Billy the Kid, the Albert Fountain murder, and Pat Garrett. Elephant Butte Dam had been under construction for two years. The region was becoming known as a haven for "lungers" seeking the warm, dry climate to recover from tuberculosis. The Wild West remained just out the front door of townspeople, but the Indian wars were over, and the days of hired gunmen and range wars were coming to an end. The railroad and automobiles were beginning to replace the horse as means of transportation.

CHAPTER ONE

Family History

J. Stokley Ligon's father, Seddie Ligon, was born in Virginia in 1851. When Seddie was nine months old, his family, along with four other families, moved to Texas. They were accompanied by seventy-nine slaves, forty-two horses, ten wagons, and five carriages (Flores, 1999). Texas became part of the United States in 1848, and it was considered a slave state. The increasing unrest and sabre-rattling over slavery as well as the presence of fresh, fertile, and cheap land made Texas attractive to slave owners.

The Ligons were among many families from the eastern seaboard that moved westward during the 1850s. Frederick Law Olmsted, approaching the Louisiana-Texas border in 1855, described passing typical emigrants:

> We overtook, several times in the course of each day, the slow emigrant trains. . . . Several families were frequently moving together. . . . Before you come upon them you hear . . . the fierce cries and blows with which they urge on their jaded cattle. Then the stragglers appear, lean dogs or fainting Negroes. . . . An old granny, hauling on, by the hand, a weak boy—too old to ride and too young to keep up. An old man, heavily loaded, with a rifle . . . the wagons jerking up and down as they mount over a root or plunge into a rut, disappearing, one after another, where the road descends. (Olmstead, 1857, 55–56)

After their party reached Texas, it broke up, and the Ligons moved on to Hays County near what later became Buda. In 1871, Seddie Ligon married Rebecca Louise Barton, and by 1873 he was driving cattle to Dodge City. Rebecca's first child, a daughter, lived only four months. In

1886, the couple resettled ten miles northwest of San Angelo. Over time, their family grew to ten children, of which Stokley was the fourth.

In 1892, they lost two daughters to typhoid; other Ligon children caught the disease but survived. We do not know if Stokley was among those infected. The drought of the 1890s and the winter of 1896 forced the Ligons to sell their livestock, and they began hauling supplies to surrounding counties and bringing sheared wool back to San Angelo on return trips. Their freighting rig was made up of two wagons pulled in tandem by eight horses or mules. Stokley was eleven years old and undoubtedly began learning many of his skills with horses at this time.

In 1898, Seddie and his oldest son, Arthur, bought a steam-powered well-drilling machine. Seddie and Arthur ran the drill while Stokley, now nineteen years old, along with other sons, cut firewood to feed the boiler. The family drilled water wells in Tom Green, Irion, Upton, Crockett, and Pecos counties, often hauling their equipment across the unpredictable sands of the Pecos River.

In 1903, Seddie bought a ranch in Reeves County and turned the business over to his sons, who by then were drilling wells throughout western Texas and southern New Mexico. Seddie and Rebecca raised cattle and watermelons until the 1920s, then retired to Fort Stockton. Rebecca died in 1933; Seddie lived until 1940. The three younger sons served in World War I, and all except Stokley continued in the businesses of ranching or well drilling.

CHAPTER TWO

J. Stokley Ligon, 1900–1912

We may never know what brought about J. Stokley Ligon's decision to move to New Mexico. Perhaps Stokley simply didn't want to partner with his brothers, or perhaps it was just a natural time to make a break and pursue a personal dream. By 1907, when he moved, he had ten years of experience in well drilling and maintenance, as well as a background in ranching and freighting. However, he had studied biology in college, and he was driven by his interest in birds and other wildlife. He was proficient with a large-format camera, having documented his float trip down the Pecos River in 1900, as well as multiple windmill and well jobs done by his family. Such a combination of skills and education must have been unique in New Mexico, where reputations were based more upon one's ability to shoot, drink, fight, sequester land, and raise hell. Quietly competent people like Ligon, peacefully going about their business, have never captured the American imagination.

Stokley worked on the Bar Cross Ranch, which encompassed the entire Jornada del Muerto area between Engle and Las Cruces. The Bar Cross still exists, although it now covers a smaller area. In 1907, New Mexico and Arizona were still one territory, but the two geographically distinct entities were vying for independent statehood. The railroad had been extended to Engle in 1879 and to El Paso in 1881, and Engle became a major shipping point for cattle driven from surrounding ranches.

Ligon was not the only Bar Cross hand who moved on to more scholarly endeavors. A year before he moved to the Bar Cross, another cowboy, Eugene Manlove Rhodes, had departed the Jornada. Like Ligon, Rhodes had interests beyond hard cowboy labor. He carried literary classics in his saddlebags, reading while he rode. Rhodes's passion for reading, like Stokley's passions for birding, photography, and exploring, had been en-

A house at Aleman Well on the Jornada del Muerto, ca. 1910.

couraged by the commerce of the day—in Stokley's case, bird and geographical cards; for Rhodes, classical books acquired through mail order using coupons from packs of tobacco. Rhodes began publishing poems and short stories in Charles Lummis's *Out West* magazine in 1902. In 1906, he followed his new wife to New York, where he lived for the next twenty-three years and wrote longingly about the ranch life he had abandoned (Hutchinson, 1956).

On the Bar Cross, Ligon brought his many skills into focus. Store-bought parts were probably scarce, so windmill maintenance required blacksmithing abilities. A windmiller's wagon probably carried a forge and no doubt an array of wrenches, screwdrivers, pliers, and an assortment of tongs, hammers, and files for shaping and fitting parts. It was rigged for camping, with a rear kitchen much like a traditional chuckwagon. The only record of Ligon's time on the Bar Cross resides in his photographs, in his records of photographs taken, and in brief comments made during the Blachly interviews.[14]

We know little of how Ligon worked on the ranch. A quiet man of medium height with a pleasant demeanor and a twinkle in his eye, he must have been popular, keeping windmills working and bringing news

The Ligon brothers' wagon in Ash Creek camp near La Luz, New Mexico, August 23, 1912. Note the portable forge in the foreground. Stokley's brother Ed is standing at the wagon.

from headquarters. He made spurs, bits, and other tack for the ranch cowboys. Such work provided time for him to observe birds and other wildlife and collect bird specimens and eggs, some of which he sent to the Smithsonian and other institutions. It also allowed him to photograph ranch life.[15] Ligon's arrangement with the Bar Cross allowed him to explore widely when not drilling wells or maintaining windmills. He collected specimens in the San Mateo Mountains in 1908, 1909, and 1910, and by 1911, he was exploring the Black Range and using the remote mining town of Chloride as a base.[16]

Ligon left the Bar Cross Ranch for good in mid-1912. He visited his parents near Pecos, Texas, and then, accompanied by his brother Ed, he drove a new wagon to New Mexico, possibly purchased for his uncle, L. A. Renick, or for the Bar Cross Ranch. Stokley and Ed explored the Sacramento Mountains en route. Upon reaching the Rio Grande, they were joined by their father, another brother, and Renick. After installing a windmill at the Summerford Ranch, now New Mexico State University's Range Research Station, the group took pack burros to the San Mateo Mountains for an extended hunting and trapping expedition. After this trip, the other Ligon men returned to Texas, leaving Stokley to roam

A Ligon family hunting party in the San Mateo Mountains. This is one of the earlier hunts, possibly in 1903. The man at the far left is Bela Birmingham. Later photographs by Stokley show Birmingham as a younger man. According to Nancy Coggeshall, long-time friend of the Birmingham family, the name Bela was given to men in successive generations of the family. The older man second from left is Stokley's father, Seddie. The two younger boys third and fourth from left are probably Earl and Ed Ligon. The identity of the man at the far right is unknown.

the Black Range with his burros, Albert and Smokey. Until at least 1918, he lived in a simple camp that he could pack on the burros.[17]

The timing of Ligon's final departure from the Bar Cross job is, in itself, interesting. By 1908, the railroad spur from Engle to the Elephant Butte Dam site was being surveyed, and activity in the area increased. Materials for the dam were hauled by rail to a siding named Jornada, seven miles south of Engle. They were then transported to the dam site by wagon and truck, or by train along a special railroad spur serving the dam. Engle and Cutter had a combined population of 158 people in 1910, but they, along with Hot Springs and Elephant Butte, were changing rapidly (Sullivan, 1994, 80–90). By 1911, dam construction had begun, and it was well advanced by 1913. Ligon was young and strong. He had handled large teams and freight wagons; he was a blacksmith and mechanic; he was already a skilled photographer; and he had attended

A hunting party headed for the San Mateo Mountains, 1909. The individuals shown are Pat Birmingham, Bela Birmingham (second from left), Charles Shaw, Bee Steele, Walter Pinkerton, and Stokley Ligon (third from left). The Bela Birmingham in this photograph is apparently the son of the man of the same name shown in the photograph of the Ligon family hunting party in the San Mateo Mountains. (Courtesy of the Harry Ransom Center, The University of Texas)

college. Labor was in short supply in New Mexico, especially skilled labor. Had maximizing income been Ligon's goal, seemingly he could have had his choice of jobs, perhaps even supervisory jobs, at the dam. Yet he moved to Chloride to study and collect birds. What makes this all the more significant is that Ligon does not mention in his interviews or diaries anything about the coming of the dam, although he stopped to take photographs when passing the site.

From January to May 1913, after the family hunting trip, Ligon collected specimens at Haut [Hoyt] Creek (thirty miles west of Chloride), V + T Ranch (now Slash Ranch near Beaverhead Ranger Station), the upper East Gila River, Chloride, Black Mountain, V + T Ranch again, Fairview (now Winston), Cuchillo Mountains, Willow Springs, Cottonwood Spring (twelve miles west of Elephant Butte), and Beaver Creek (appendix, table 2). From all appearances, he was already expecting his June appointment to the US Biological Survey (USBS).

One record of Ligon's activity in Chloride prior to the USBS job is

The 1909 hunting party entering the San Mateo Mountains. On this hunt, the young men walked from Engle to the base of the San Mateo Mountains with the pack string of burros. They hunted both the San Mateos and the Black Range during the months of October and November. (Courtesy of the Harry Ransom Center, The University of Texas)

provided by Raymond Schmidt, who was a boy in 1913. Schmidt was born in 1897, making him eighteen years younger than Ligon. His family moved to Chloride in 1905, when he was eight years old. In the spring of 1913, Ligon would have been thirty-three years old and Schmidt sixteen years old. In his small book, *New Mexico Recollections*, Schmidt (1977, 39–41) recounts a trip he made with Ligon. In this story, he places Ligon in Chloride in 1911 and his own age at "about 13," both of which are possible, depending upon the time of year the camping trip occurred. I quote Schmidt's story in its entirety here.[18]

The Time I Camped with Ligon

Its [*sic*] hard to believe, unless one has associated with James Stokely [*sic*] Ligon, the many talents the man possessed . . . professionally an

Chloride, New Mexico, ca. 1909. This became Stokley's base for the 1913 breeding bird survey and subsequent ramblings. (Courtesy of the Harry Ransom Center, The University of Texas)

ornithologist, he was talented with all that goes with it. I am fortunate and proud to say that I camped with Mr. Ligon. I feel elated now that I write some of the instances which occurred while in camp . . . hunting bird's nests, eggs, etc.

I believe it was in the year 1911 when Mr. Ligon came to Chloride, walking, driving two pack burros. I was a boy of about thirteen years, only lad in Chloride at the time.

Ligon would come often on his bird study. He said one time he was going to hunt some quail for mounting purposes, invited me to go along. We were only a short distance from town when we saw quail. In three shots he got three birds. Next day at camp he mounted them. They were life-like! We also had quail for noon hour, fried in olive oil. Delicious!

I was trapping some. He showed me how to set a trap for a fox . . . we had a fox next morning. I was anxious to get a black skunk but had not been successful so far. It happened one night that I did catch one. I was elated that I would get a good price for it, but it turned out different. Stokely mounted the skunk pelt and kept it. He showed me how to dispatch a skunk without odor, like this. . . . He slowly approached the skunk with a stick upraised and hit it across the back. He pressed the skunk's heart with his powerful hands for a minute, and the skunk was dead.

Meantime, he told me to dig a small hole. Then he turned the skunk's rear end into the hole until all the scent was gone. There was no scent left on the skunk.

Later we made a camping trip to Monument Park. I had no idea what his plans were, but in two days we were back in Chloride after doing the following.

We were saddled up, the two burros moved right along ahead, well-trained. Stokely had just gotten his mail and as we walked along, he walked easily, reading it. Suddenly he stopped and said, 'There is a blue bird's nest in that box-elder across the creek.' Then goes there and gets the eggs in just a few minutes. Then he would say, 'Do you hear that verio [*sic*]?' which I could not. So we stop, and he goes and gets the nest and eggs. And so it goes until noon. We had reached the bluffs in the Chloride Creek Box Canyon.

Stokely unpacked the burros, turned them loose. We had a snack he had prepared earlier, then we started up the bluffs with a long rope, some cans, a light pole . . . all of which really had me guessing. After arriving at the top, we looked down on Chloride Creek, some five hundred feet below, the bluff leaned over a hundred foot drop.

Stokely tied one end of the rope to a sturdy bush. Then with his cans and rod, the rope tied securely about himself, he went hand over hand, out of sight, down alongside of the precipice. He had lowered himself to an eagle's nest. He climbed part way up and handed me the cans with eggs and rod, then he came up hand over hand on terra firma again. I was afraid for him, but he was very calm, as if an every day event.

We proceeded back to camp, packed up, getting more kinds of eggs on the way. One hawk nest was high in a cottonwood tree, sort of leaning, some fifty feet high. He took off his shoes and climbed that tree like a monkey. Stokely had powerful hands and could swing from limb to limb, easily.

We camped in Monument Park. He was quick to unpack, gather straw for our beds and get the meal going. I supposed it was time for retiring, but Stokely was not finished yet with his day's work. We went down the creek a quarter mile, set a trap for a fox. It was getting too dark for me to see what he was doing. We returned to camp and shortly we heard a fox howl so we went back for it. Stokely hit the fox a small blow on the nose, stunning it. He reset the trap in the dark; I holding the fox in my arms, perfectly docile. We took this fox to camp and set it by the campfire. It was there, looking into the fire for some time. Finally it started to run off, but Stokely caught it and placed it into one of the panniers. Then we heard another fox howl, so went and got it. Enough for one day.

Next day we went six miles west to the old Curtis place on Turkey Run, with the burros. I did not know what for until we arrived there. Stokely said Curtis had given him a combination folding bed springs. We packed it onto the burro and returned by noon to camp. Then we searched the north side of Lookout Mountain for a certain owl's nest, but could not find it. We returned to camp, packed up and made it to Chloride by dark. I kept the foxes for a while, but one got away from the dug out I put them in.

Ligon emerges from Schmidt's description as a quiet and confident man and kind instructor. The fact that he took the lad along suggests that he was willing to share his experience and knowledge. Ligon was clearly a master trapper—catching two foxes at a single set in a short evening. He also had developed considerable experience in handling animals, both alive and dead, and he had a good ear for bird calls. Finally, he was capable of rather amazing physical feats, without fanfare. Interestingly, Schmidt fails to mention Ligon's interest in photography, although Schmidt's father, Henry Schmidt, was a well-known photographer in Chloride.[19] Ligon never mentions Henry in his diary, although he mentions in his photographic journal paying him for prints.

Ligon's "strong hands" and comfort with heights may have come from his days as a windmiller. Only in later life did he admit that he had had close calls in some of his egg-hunting efforts. In the Blachly interviews (1952), regarding collecting raptor eggs, he says:

> I've collected several sets of them and gotten into some very close places trying to get them . . . fortunately I've never fallen but there have been ornithologists who have lost their lives. . . . When you get a falcon's egg you're risking your neck. . . . I've swung off many bluffs to get eggs of hawks and eagles and falcons. . . . You had to pull yourself up. . . . A fella wants to have good anchorage there if he's going to swing off a hundred to a hundred and fifty foot ledge on a rope . . . they try to defend their young. But I've never had one to strike me but one time and that was a horned owl.

When Ligon arrived in Chloride, it was still an active mining town. It had been settled in 1877 in the heart of Hot Springs Apache country, and Schmidt (1977) and Merle B. Brown (1967) tell of several residents who were killed by Apaches during the settlement era. Although southwestern New Mexico had been mined and prospected since the days of the Spaniards, it was perhaps the last state to experience the gold mania that had hit California, Colorado, and Nevada. Remoteness from settled areas and, more importantly, the presence of hostile Apaches and Navajos held the prospectors at bay until the late 1870s. Added to this was the disruptive influence of the Civil War, which removed military protection for settlers from the Southwest between 1863 and 1866. The near-simultaneous subduing of the Apaches and the arrival of the railroad along the Rio Grande in 1881 stimulated settlement. By 1882, Chloride had stagecoach service (M. Brown, 1967). By 1895, two stages ran to Chloride: one from Engle, the nearest railroad station, and the other from Cuchillo (Schmidt, 1977). The stage delivered mail daily. The first automobile delivery of mail occurred in 1916, so horse and foot travel were still the main forms of transportation when Ligon arrived. By 1916, Sierra County had a Ford dealer—businessman Frank Winston, for whom the town of Fairview was eventually renamed (Sullivan, 1994, 92).

Chloride had a population of more than one thousand people, including the miners and prospectors from the surrounding countryside, by 1886. At its peak, the town had three general merchandise stores, two feed and livery stables, a meat market, a hotel, a boot and harness shop, a drugstore, a confectioner and baker, a cabinet builder, a jeweler, a blacksmith, two dressmakers, two milliners, a justice of the peace, assayers, two photographers (one of whom was Henry Schmidt), general contractors, freighters, and two doctors. *The Black Range*, a weekly newspaper, was being published, and between two and five saloons were present. The town was never known to have prostitutes and was considered a good place for families to live (M. Brown, 1967, 7). A large oak tree stood in the center of town, and a short distance from the town well, a trough was kept full of water for horses, mules, and burros.

As late as 1890, two prospectors near Chloride were killed by Indians, and detachments of soldiers were still pursuing Apaches that left the San Carlos Reservation. In 1907, the year Ligon went to work on the Jornada, an Apache, by local legend the notorious Apache Kid, was killed by a posse of citizens in the San Mateo Mountains. Conflict with Navajo and Pueblo tribes regarding hunting and hunting regulations had been brewing since at least 1905 (Warren, 1997, 71). State and federal officers were trying to stop their annual hunting forays, which Anglo sportsmen from the Silver City area felt were depleting deer and pronghorn. This part of New Mexico had been traditional hunting territory for these tribes, and they depended upon the meat for their winter food. As late as 1913, volunteer game wardens, New Mexico Mounted Police, US Forest Service personnel, and armed sportsmen were still having uneasy encounters with armed Indian hunting parties, although without serious outbreaks of violence. Such a conflict became the subject of Frank Waters's book, *The Man Who Killed the Deer* (1942). In addition, skirmishes with scattered Apache and Yaqui bands continued along the Mexican border, and the Mexican Revolution was in full swing in 1913 (Truett, 2006). An element of risk still existed for a lone rider in southern New Mexico.

The first two decades of the twentieth century were a period of drastic change on the rangelands of this area. Forty years of heavy grazing, along with the drought of the 1890s, had depleted forage and stimulated growth of increasingly dense stands of trees and shrubs. In order to better control their cattle and protect their grazing rights, ranchers fenced more and more of the commons. It was during this volatile time that Ligon began to explore the area, alone and initially afoot, leading two burros.

CHAPTER THREE

The US Biological Survey

In 1913, the US Biological Survey (USBS) already had a convoluted history. From 1886–1896, it was known as the Division of Economic Ornithology and Mammalogy. In 1896, it became the Division of Biological Survey. In 1905, it became the Bureau of Biological Survey. In its earliest form, its job had been to "study the interrelationship of birds and agriculture," a task it had assumed as the stepchild of the Division of Entomology. Through this entire developmental period, it was funded under the US Department of Agriculture (USDA)(Cameron, 1929).

Birds had been an object of federal legislation since at least 1862, when agricultural matters were administered by the US Patent Office. Funding for 1862 included a provision for "the introduction and protection of insectivorous birds," acknowledging their value in protecting crops. That same year, the USDA was created, and an identical clause was written into its funding legislation.

In 1883, a group of leading naturalists founded the American Ornithologists' Union (AOU). This organization successfully petitioned Congress to create the Division of Economic Ornithology under the existing Division of Entomology. Until this time, most biological work of the federal government had been done by the US Army Topographical Engineers and, later, the US Geological Survey, in collaboration with the Smithsonian Institution. From Lewis and Clark on, one of the main functions of government explorations had been documentation and collection of plants and animals. The US Army surgeons accompanying the various survey teams were expected to serve also as naturalists. In some cases, full-time naturalists in addition to the surgeons traveled with the parties. The specimens collected by these explorers were identified and preserved by Smithsonian scientists. By the time the AOU, largely made up of Smithsonian scientists, asked Congress for dollars to protect and study birds, the boundaries among the Smithsonian, the AOU, the ongoing federal governmental surveys, and the newly formed Division of Economic Ornithology were blurred indeed. In 1885, Dr. C. Hart Merriam was appointed as chairman of the AOU Committee on Migration and Distribution, which took charge of funds allocated by Congress. Because of demands from agricultural interests, especially in the West, the bureau became increasingly involved in wildlife damage control. It first served in an advisory capacity for the US Forest Service, states, and private individuals, but in 1914 it received funds to experiment with wildlife control methods, including poisons. Ligon was involved in some of these experiments back, as it turns out, on the Jornada del Muerto where he had worked as a windmiller.[20]

In addition to its wildlife surveys and animal-control functions, the bureau was asked to provide technical support in the enforcement of the Lacey Act of 1900, which regulated interstate transportation of illegally taken wildlife. This led to an increasing involvement with migratory birds, which could not be properly managed within the bounds of single states, or for that matter within the United States. This led to passage of the 1913 Migratory Bird Treaty Act, an initial, albeit weak, effort at managing interstate and international migratory birds, which placed "wild geese, wild swans, brant, wild ducks, snipe, plover, woodcock, rail, wild pigeons, and all other migratory game and insectivorous birds" under the authority of the US government.

The 1913 act was not a permanent law, but rather an addition to the general funding bill for the USBS for the 1913–1914 fiscal year. It gave the USDA authority to establish closed seasons nationwide, while having due regard for "the zones of temperature, breeding habits, and times and line of migratory flight, thereby enabling the department to select and designate suitable districts for different portions of the country." This statement could be construed to justify gathering information regarding migratory bird flight patterns and breeding range, and was probably the force behind Ligon's 1913 survey (Cameron, 1929).

At the time the act was passed, Welles W. Cooke was working for the USBS and was well established as the North American authority on bird migration. He had developed a nationwide network of paid and volunteer observers, who sent him records of bird occurrences. He had joined the USBS in 1901 and spent the remaining fifteen years of his life accumulating and compiling bird migration records, while at the same time beginning the *Birds of New Mexico* book, which Florence Merriam Bailey (1928) later completed. In 1913, no single individual would have been more aware of gaps in knowledge about New Mexico migratory birds (Palmer, 1917). Cooke, perhaps in collaboration with Vernon and

Florence Merriam Bailey, undoubtedly set Ligon's 1913 survey in motion, very likely in anticipation of the 1913 act.

In an undated letter to Vernon Bailey, Ligon wrote: "I will appreciate yours and Dr. Cooke's opinion on my plans of work. And when it comes convenient, and satisfactory, I shall be glad to receive any aid in the way of field work, and I assure you, I shall do my best at all times to render satisfactory service."

Between the time the above letter was written and May 24, 1913, additional correspondence must have occurred and Ligon's breeding bird survey conceived. A letter from Vernon Bailey[21] to Ligon on this date states: "In your letter of May 16th to Prof. Cooke you say you will be able to start about the first of June to make a study of the breeding water birds of New Mexico. We have secured your appointment for the month of June."

This letter provides us with a surprising insight regarding the rapidity of mail delivery in 1913. On May 24, Bailey, in Washington, D.C., is responding to a letter that Ligon mailed in Chloride on May 16—eight days earlier.[22] Even if Bailey wrote and mailed his reply on the day Ligon's letter arrived, this seems to be rapid delivery of mail, which had to leave Chloride by stage, be sorted and placed upon the appropriate train (most likely at Engle), arrive in Washington, D.C., after an unknown number of transfers, and be delivered to the offices of the USBS in eight days or less. Modern first-class mail seldom works this well.

The USBS hired Ligon at a volatile point in its history. It needed more information on migratory birds to support implementation of the 1913 act, and it was being pressed to become involved in animal damage control. Ligon was hired because of his knowledge of southwestern birds and his ability to move and live in unsettled areas. Because of his trapping and hunting skills, as well as his knowledge of the country, he would later be moved into the animal damage control branch of the USBS.

I have been unable to determine how Ligon's correspondence with Bailey and Cooke began. His movements during 1912–1913 suggest that he anticipated being hired, because he left his job at Engle, returned briefly to Pecos, spent the fall with his father, uncle, and brothers hunting in the San Mateo Mountains, then began observing and collecting birds within the Gila Forest Reserve in early January 1913. However it happened, Bailey's above-noted letter of May 24 went on to spell out Ligon's first month of work:

> From Chloride you will make a trip of a few days to Beaver Lake (V + T Lake) to determine the species of water birds breeding there, unless you have already thoroughly covered that locality and can give us a report on it without making another trip. You will then return, strike the Rio Grande at Elephant Butte or some place where there may be

a chance of finding some water birds along the river or in neighboring sloughs or marshes, and spend a day or two there to identify any ducks, shorebirds, rails, wrens, blackbirds, or Maryland yellowthroats found breeding in that locality. You will then proceed to the great salt marshes and sloughs in the Tulerosa [*sic*] Valley and spend a few days there; then proceed to the Pecos Valley near Carlsbad. If you find plenty of water birds in the sloughs of the Tulerosa Valley it may be worth while to go southeast down the valley to the Salt Lakes on the Texas line to learn if there are any shorebirds breeding in that region, then over or around the south end of the range to Carlsbad. In the vicinity of Carlsbad we need to know what species of birds breed around the alkaline marshes and at the reservoir. As you are familiar with that country you will know the best localities at which the breeding birds can be found and it will probably be worth while to spend a week or ten days in that part of the valley. You will then go to Roswell and, after stopping for a few days at the reservoirs and marshes in that part of the valley, proceed northward to Santa Rosa. There you will find one of the best water bird localities in the State, but we have very little information as to the species remaining through the summer to breed. There are numerous spring-fed lakes around the edges of the valley and some large marsh areas in which shooting is prohibited and where the birds are said to remain to breed. You can spend a week or ten days in this locality to good advantage.

While the water birds are the species concerning which we are mostly in need of data as to the breeding habits, we need full reports on all birds encountered, not only at the various localities but along the way. It will not be necessary to collect a large series of specimens of any species, but whenever there is any doubt as to the species or subspecies a few specimens should always be collected, if possible. Full notes on habits, and especially nests, eggs and young, are important, but we do not care for eggs of any except very rare and little known species. Specimens of young birds are usually desirable.

Any interesting small mammals which you may be able to pick up along the way should be saved, but that region has been pretty thoroughly worked for mammals and we have a fairly complete collection of the birds except those necessary to represent the breeding season of certain species.

I assume that you have a saddle horse and pack horse or will be able to procure them for this trip, as it can be made much more economically and to better advantage this way than by train and wagon. You will have to plan carefully and work rapidly, however, to cover the itinerary indicated in one month, and if you find you can not do it in that time, you may leave out the less important localities, such as the

> salt lakes, and give more time to the Pecos Valley localities. By heading from the Tulerosa salt marshes across to Roswell, leaving your horses there and working south and north along the railroad, you would be able to economize time. Supplies will be sent to you at Chloride, and if there are things needed for the trip other than are indicated on the accompanying list, please let me know as soon as possible. You will have to advance money for expenses as in the Government Service payment for services cannot be made until after the time of service is completed. I should like very much to make this trip with you as I have been over most of the ground and know what interesting country it is, but unfortunately, I have not been over it during the breeding season and your work is intended to supplement that already done.

In 1912, Vernon Bailey wrote a ten-page, illustrated bulletin entitled *Directions for Field Work of Assistants of the Biological Survey* (V. Bailey, 1912). This bulletin details equipment needed, equipment furnished by the survey, equipment the assistants will furnish themselves, and handling and tagging of specimens and recording notes. It requests reports on life zones, physiography, mammals, birds, plants, reptiles, and crops and provides a standard outline for such reports. Bailey's referral to an enclosed equipment list suggests that he sent a copy of this bulletin with his letter.

Bailey's assumption that Ligon would do at least the first month's work by saddle horse and pack animals demonstrates that this was still a common mode of travel. While a ride of this length was perhaps decreasingly common by 1913, full conversion to motorized travel was certainly a decade or two in the future. Automobiles, while not yet common, were present. N. L. Dodson bought a steam driven "Locomobile" in Denver in 1897 and drove it to Albuquerque.[23] The first car arrived in Roswell in 1901—a 10-horsepower Oldsmobile. It was little more than a wagon bed mounted on bicycle-like wheels (Adams, 1986, 235). The Roswell Automobile Club was formed in 1909. Longer distances were increasingly traveled by rail, and most rural, especially poorer rural, people still traveled on horseback or by wagon.

Ligon was not the only naturalist taking long rides during this era. In 1908, Vernon Bailey made a whirlwind trip, alternating train and horseback, through central and western New Mexico. Starting in Albuquerque on July 28, he traveled southward to Belen, visited Mountainair and Manzano Peak, continued southward to San Marcial, and then went on to Rosedale in the foothills of the San Mateo Mountains. He stopped in Engle, then continued south to Mesilla Park, El Paso, Deming, the Animas Mountains, Playas Valley, and Silver City. He then rode northward to G O S Ranch, Diamond Creek, and V + T Lake. He continued northward across Elk Mountain through Reserve, Luna, the Zuni River, and the Chuska Mountains to Farmington. At Farmington, he caught the train once again, visiting Engle and Mesilla.[24]

In 1909, E. A. Goldman spent time near Engle.[25] Arriving in Socorro in late August, he explored the Magdalena, Socorro, and San Mateo mountains. He then traveled to Ojo Caliente, Alamosa Creek, Fairview, Chloride, and Cuchillo. Swinging through Las Palomas, he rode through the Salada Hills and visited Hillsboro and Kingston, riding to the top of Sawyer and Hillsboro peaks. He passed through Lake Valley, Rincon, and Garfield, and explored the Caballo Mountains. He ended his explorations at Rincon.

Also, to keep Ligon's ride in perspective, it is worth noting that on August 23, 1909, Louis and Temple Abernathy arrived in Roswell, having traveled on horseback from their home in Guthrie, Oklahoma (Abernathy, 2004). Louis was nine, Temple seven. They rode without adult supervision. After a three-day rest, they headed on to Santa Fe, then returned to Guthrie, passing through the high country in the Pecos Wilderness. What is significant about the trip these boys made is that they carried no camping equipment or food. With the exception of one night spent foodless and bedless in the Texas Panhandle, they were able to end each day either in a town, where they slept and ate in hotels, or at a farm or ranch house with friendly folk. In a few cases, motherly ranch women provided them with a lunch for their day's ride. This characterizes horseback travel in 1909—the country was settled to the point that travelers could traverse even the Texas Panhandle and the Llano Estacado with little preparation, given good horseflesh. An even more famous long ride was made by A. F. Tschiffely between 1925 and 1928, wherein he rode and packed his horses Mancha and Gato from Buenos Aires to New York City—some 10,000 miles (Tschiffely, 1933).

Ligon's ride, taken alone, was therefore not all that exceptional for the time. In 1913, he probably could have reached a place of lodging most nights, even when crossing the Jornada del Muerto or the Tularosa Basin. That he chose to use pack animals and to camp out speaks to his independence. Because he needed to view the various wetlands along the route, he necessarily stopped where the night found him. Water for his animals was his main constraint, and it might have been a problem for him in crossing the Jornada and the Tularosa Basin had he not known those landscapes from his years of employment on the Bar Cross Ranch.

All other areas he crossed were well settled, some perhaps more populated than today. Eastern New Mexico had been heavily homesteaded in the late 1800s, and small ranches were scattered over the land, although by 1913 some of these homesteads were failing and were being incorporated into larger ranch holdings. It would be extremely difficult now for anyone to move across these landscapes as Ligon did, because of myriad fences and busy highways. Were they to try, they would probably be arrested for trespassing. Present-day long riders are limited to highway easements or the few maintained trails that still exist on public lands.

His 1913 ride around the state surveying birds was actually a continuation of a lifestyle he had begun by 1907 and would continue to pursue for at least another five years. He lived comfortably in the woods, winter and summer, camping for the most part alone. While he worked on the Bar Cross Ranch, he undoubtedly camped much of the time. He took his pack animals on long forays into the San Mateo Mountains and the Black Range. From the time he and his brother Ed left Pecos in mid-1912, he lived continuously in camp, traveling from Pecos to the San Mateos to Chloride and making a circle through the Black Range and upper Gila River even before he started the formal bird survey. He continued this lifestyle after completing the survey, living with his pack outfit while he surveyed prairie dogs in western New Mexico and eastern Arizona. Hence, he lived in camp from at least 1907 to the end of 1914, perhaps 1915, moving frequently. His 1,200-mile breeding bird survey was only a small part of the miles he rode during those years. If he had any conflicts with other humans or any significant hardships, they were never mentioned in his diary or his photographic notebooks. The title "gentlest of the mountain men" aptly applies.

With his pack animals, Ligon was able to carry camp equipment and enough food for several days, and his survey route took him through a settlement every two or three days, so he could easily replenish his supplies. He turned his animals out at each campsite, allowing them to graze, hence he probably carried little more than a supply of oats or corn to supplement their feed and lure the animals to their halters. Considering the assignment, he chose a mode of travel with which he was comfortable. It was more direct and efficient than rail and allowed him to explore rougher terrain and cover more miles per day than he could by wagon.

Although Ligon was anticipating his appointment to the USBS by late 1912 or very early 1913, the official request in Washington, D.C., did not occur until May 24, 1913. On this request, directed to the acting secretary of agriculture, Chief of the Biological Survey H. W. Henshaw noted: "Mr. Ligon's appointment is desired because of his familiarity with the bird life of the region, and because he is the best equipped person for this temporary piece of work in that locality."[26]

The official notice of appointment was dated May 26, 1913, and signed by R. W. Roberts, appointment clerk, who provided Ligon with formal notification. The notification of appointment, along with Bailey's letter, reached Ligon on May 31, and he replied on June 1 from Chloride. In it, he thanks Bailey and Cooke for obtaining the appointment and asks for

Ligon's camp and equipment, 1912. This is the setup Ligon used during his 1913 breeding bird survey.

clarification regarding Bailey's mention of Beaver Lake (which was actually V + T Lake).[27] He notes:

> being that I have to go back to the head of the East Gila to get my horse, I shall re-visit this lake and also the marshy meadow at the V + T Ranch, and back here. I was at these places a while back and found quite a lot of water birds.
>
> Further, everything in the list of supplies is here except: arsenic, 2 rolls of cotton, catalogue of birds and mammals. I expect these in tomorrow. Is the tow[28] to be used in stuffing birds, and the absorbent cotton, what in particular is it for? I have never used either of these in preparing specimens and ask for instructions.
>
> In collecting specimens of young bird, shall I care for them as I do adults?
>
> I have written the Post Master at Engle to hold my mail. So you will likely have time to get me a letter there. Then, unless otherwise ordered by you, I shall get mail at Tula Rosa [*sic*].
>
> I think that our route, as selected, is about the best. I can make it, even if I have to fudge into July a little, about Santa Rosa. I can find

Ligon with his horse, Gila Red, and his burros, Albert and Smokey, packed up and on the trail, September 1913.

> out if there is water in the Lakes about Orange, near the State line. If there is, I shall try the entire round, unless otherwise ordered by you. I much prefer my pack outfit, to rail from Carlsbad Northward.
>
> I was at the lakes near Tularosa, above the "White Sands," last August, and found many ducks there. And the upper end of Salt Flat about Orange, when there is water, is another duck favorite. Do you want photographs of nests, young and nesting sights?

Ligon wrote a brief acknowledgement of receipt of his appointment to Henshaw on June 2, noting that the remainder of his supplies had arrived and that he had taken the oath of office. The oath of office amounted to a statement administered verbally and signed by Edwin F. Holmes, the presiding judge in Chloride in 1913.

CHAPTER FOUR

The Breeding Bird Survey

Once underway on the breeding bird survey, Ligon moved steadily, and his descriptions are brief. The trip lasted seventy-three days, not including his unrecorded return down the continental divide. Total distance covered, including the return ride, was some 1,200 miles. He rode that summer a distance longer than the Santa Fe Trail between St. Louis and Santa Fe—a trip that many travelers had found to be a major hardship up until about the time Stokley was born. A trip like his required an ability to assess terrain, determine availability of water, and gauge the endurance of his animals—skills that modern biologists, darting from location to location in air-conditioned pickups, staying in motels, and monitoring radio-marked animals via satellite, no longer need to consider. We do not know how much time he spent returning south or what his exact route might have been, although his photographs show that he visited Putnam in Chaco Canyon and passed through Thoreau and Ramah.

In making the survey, all of the skills acquired during his youth came together—his abilities with horses, his photographic talent, his knowledge of birds, his shooting skill, his simple self-sufficiency, and no doubt his genial manner that allowed him to move in and out of remote communities. This was still a time when strangers, especially those working for the government, might well be viewed with suspicion. Communication with his employer was limited, and he was on his own. Such a trip today would be an undertaking that few, if any, people are prepared to do. Yet Ligon moved through the country easily and accomplished the work he set out to do, all the while seeing to his own food, putting up specimens, taking photographs, and caring for his animals.

Among his equipment was his view camera with 5" × 7" glass plates, and a single-shot, break-action 16-gauge shotgun, which he used in collecting bird specimens. Sometime in 1912, he purchased a Savage Model 1899 rifle in 30–30 caliber, but he did not take it along on the survey. For collecting specimens, the shotgun was essential, but the rifle would have been dead weight. Insofar as I can determine, he never carried a handgun.

The Diary and Report

As already noted, Ligon's original diary and handwritten report for the 1913 breeding bird survey reside at the Smithsonian Institution Archives. His daily notes are in a US Department of Agriculture (USDA) standard field diary, probably maintained by all USDA field personnel.[29] The report is in a bound record book.

A few observations of interest regarding the field diary:

1. The line for the diarist's name is pre-labeled *Mr.*, showing that the possibility that a woman might do fieldwork for the organization was not a consideration, even though Florence Merriam Bailey had been assisting her husband, Vernon, presumably without pay, for twenty years or more by this time.
2. Ligon's title was field assistant, but his legal status with the agency seems uncertain. As noted in a letter from E. W. Nelson of the US Biological Survey (USBS), his appointment was for a month at a time ending July 30; hence he worked free for several days after his appointment expired. He advanced his own money for expenses, being paid only after the entire survey was complete. He returned to Chloride on his own time. By modern standards, he would have been considered a private contractor, but he started the job with an oath of office and, as we'll see, experienced tight constraints upon any specimens collected during the survey.
3. These government diaries were considered important enough that a provision was made for free postage to Washington, D.C., if found.

The fact that Ligon chose to use what is obviously a quality notebook for his breeding bird report shows that he was aware of its value and need for permanence. Perhaps the notebook had been provided by the USBS. At this time of his life, he was using just Stokley. By 1928, he was using J. Stokley Ligon.

On the inside cover page of this report, we perhaps get a glimpse of Ligon's self-image and goals at this time. Such self-revelations do not appear often in his writings, but here, pasted inside the cover, is what appears to be the cut-off top of a printed letterhead. At the top left of the

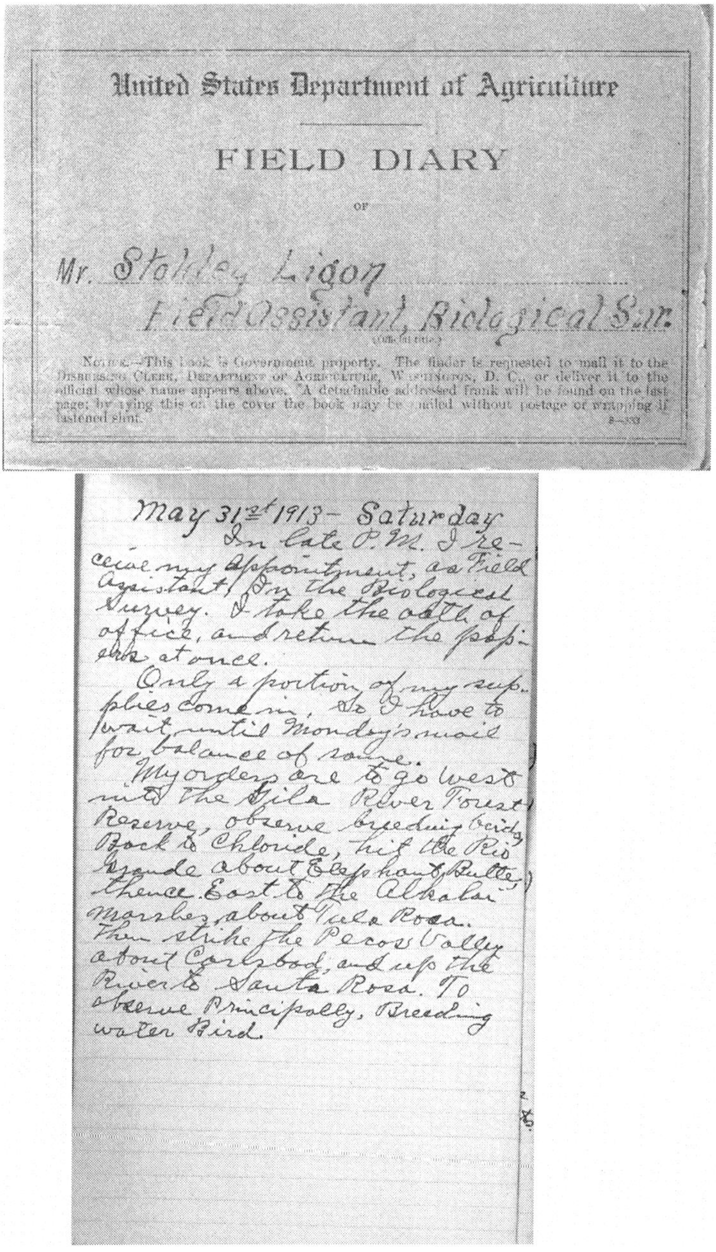
United States Department of Agriculture

FIELD DIARY

OF

Mr. Stokley Ligon
Field Assistant, Biological Sur.
(Official title.)

NOTICE.—This book is Government property. The finder is requested to mail it to the Disbursing Clerk, Department of Agriculture, Washington, D. C., or deliver it to the official whose name appears above. A detachable addressed frank will be found on the last page; by tying this on the cover the book may be mailed without postage or wrapping if fastened shut.

May 31st 1913 – Saturday
In late P.M. I receive my appointment, as Field Assistant, in the Biological Survey. I take the oath of office, and return the papers at once.
Only a portion of my supplies come in, so I have to wait until Monday's mail for balance of same.
My orders are to go west into the Gila River Forest Reserve, observe breeding birds, Back to Chloride, hit the Rio Grande about Elephant Butte, thence East to the Alkali Marshes, about Tula Rosa. Then strike the Pecos Valley about Carlsbad, and up the River to Santa Rosa. To observe principally, Breeding water Bird.

The cover and first page of Ligon's field diary. Smithsonian Institute. (Photo by Michael Campbell)

The cover of Ligon's report on the breeding birds of New Mexico. (Courtesy of the Smithsonian Institution; photo by Michael Campbell)

letterhead is MY MOTTO: TRUTH IS HONOR AND POWER, followed by his name printed in large type and NATURE STUDENT, PHOTOGRAPHER, AND WRITER. Below this, ARTICLES SUBMITTED FOR PUBLICATION, then, at present—Chloride N. Mex–permanent address, Pecos–Texas.

Perhaps the most curious statement is the motto. It seems ambiguous and pompous. Based upon what we know about Ligon, "Truth," insofar as he could determine it, was important to him. He depended much more upon his own observations than on the writings of others. I find it hard to equate truth with the sum of honor and power, especially the latter. Certainly in day-to-day politics, the world of political power, truth is always subjugated. Perhaps he was trying to say that Truth led to or resulted in Honor and Power. Considering his lifelong tendencies to work

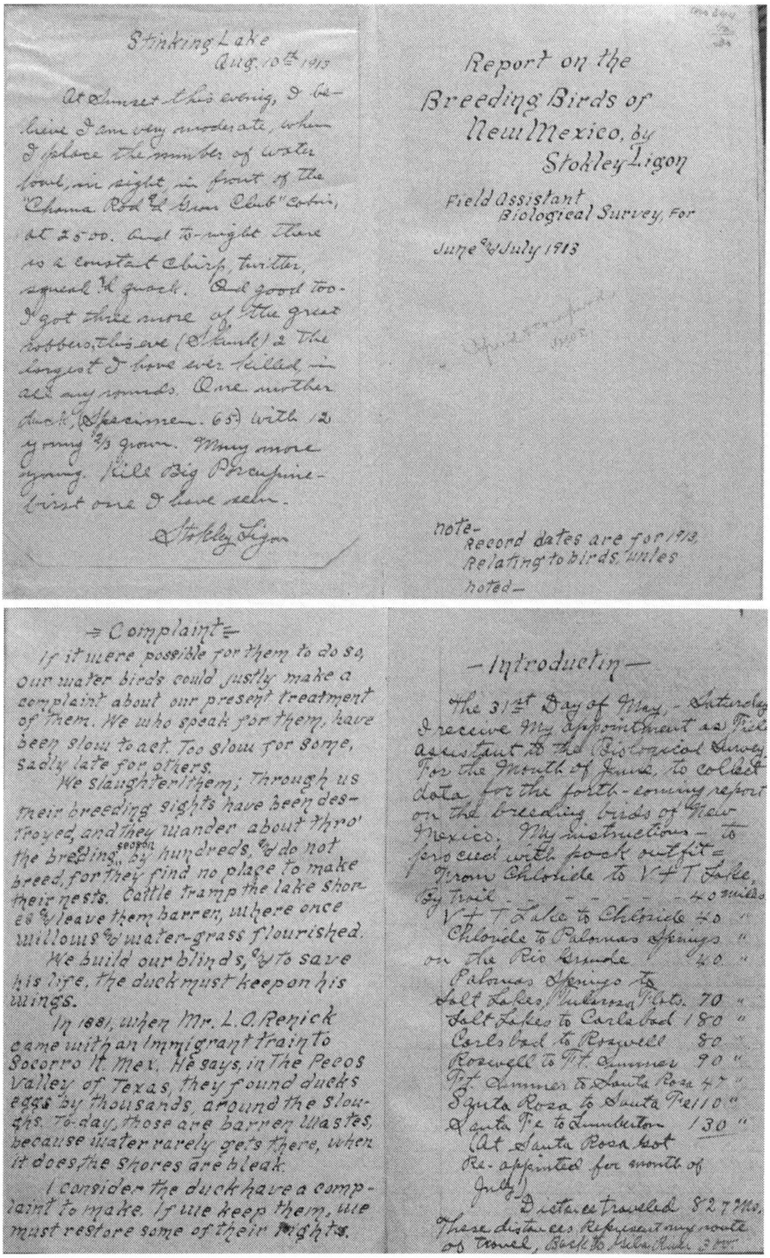

Stinking Lake
Aug. 10th 1913

At sunset this evening, I believe I am very moderate, when I place the number of water fowl, in sight in front of the "Chama Rod & Gun Club" cabin, at 2500. And to-night there is a constant chirp, twitter, squeal & quack. And good too. I got three more of the great robbers, this eve (Skunk) 2 the largest I have ever killed in all my rounds. One mother duck (Specimen 65) with 12 young 2/3 grown. Many more young. Kill Big Porcupine—first one I have seen.

Stokley Ligon

Report on the Breeding Birds of New Mexico, by Stokley Ligon

Field Assistant Biological Survey, For June & July 1913

note—
Record dates are for 1913, Relating to birds, unles noted—

=Complaint=

If it were possible for them to do so, our water birds could justly make a complaint about our present treatment of them. We who speak for them, have been slow to act. Too slow for some, sadly late for others.

We slaughter them; through us their breeding sights have been destroyed, and they wander about thro' the breeding season by hundreds, & do not breed, for they find no place to make their nests. Cattle tramp the lake shores & leave them barren, where once willows & water-grass flourished.

We build our blinds, & to save his life, the duck must keep on his wings.

In 1881, when Mr. L. O. Renick came with an Immigrant train to Socorro N. Mex. He says, in the Pecos Valley of Texas, they found ducks eggs by thousands, around the sloughs. To-day, those are barren wastes, because water rarely gets there, when it does, the shores are bleak.

I consider the duck have a complaint to make. If we keep them, we must restore some of their rights.

—Introduction—

The 31st Day of May,—Saturday I receive my appointment as Field assistant to the Biological Survey. For the month of June, to collect data for the forth-coming report on the breeding birds of New Mexico. My instructions—to proceed with pack outfit=

From Chloride to V+T Lake, By Trail — — — — 40 miles
V+T Lake to Chloride 40 "
Chloride to Palomas Springs on the Rio Grande 40 "
Palomas Springs to Salt Lakes, Mulberry Flats. 70 "
Salt Lakes to Carlsbad 180 "
Carlsbad to Roswell 80 "
Roswell to Ft. Sumner 90 "
Ft. Sumner to Santa Rosa 47 "
Santa Rosa to Santa Fe 110 "
Santa Fe to Lumberton 130 "
(At Santa Rosa Got Re-appointed for month of July)
Distance traveled 827 Mi.
These distances Represent my route of travel, Back to Hillsboro...

The title page and first three pages of the text of the breeding bird report. (Courtesy of the Smithsonian Institution; photo by Michael Campbell) relatively quietly behind the scenes, one wonders what significance the word "Power" had to him. However, in a sense, this motto carried him through life in that his reputation for knowledge and honesty gave him a certain power—which he seldom used—when he was drawn into conflicting issues.

One wonders if he ever looked back at this motto with embarrassment. Certainly, those receiving the report at the USBS office must have smiled, considering that they were dealing daily with all of the big names in natural history of the time as well as Washington politicians.

At the upper right corner of the title page is noted in pencil "No 344 ba/30," cataloging marks placed in the document by the Smithsonian archivists. The title is then given in Ligon's writing: "Report on the Breeding Birds of New Mexico by Stokley Ligon, Field Assistant for Biological Survey, For June and July, 1913." Below this, in pencil, is "Aprvd & compared W. W. C." W. W. C. was Wells W. Cooke. At the bottom of the title page, in Ligon's script, is "note-record dates are for 1913, Relating to birds, unless noted—."

On the reverse side of the title page is the following:

—COMPLAINT—

> If it were possible for them to do so, our water birds could justly make a complaint about our present treatment of them. We who speak for them, have been slow to act. Too slow for some, sadly late for others.
>
> We slaughter them; Through us their breeding sights [*sic*] have been destroyed, and they wander about thro' the breeding season by hundreds and do not breed, for they find no place to make their nests. Cattle tramp the lake shores and leave them barren, where once willows and water-grass flourished.
>
> We build our blinds, and to save his life, the duck must keep on his wings.
>
> In 1881, when Mr. L. A. Renick came with an immigrant train to Socorro N. Mex. He says in the Pecos Valley of Texas, they found ducks eggs by thousands, around the sloughs. To-day, those are barren Wastes, because water rarely gets there, when it does, the shores are bleak.
>
> I consider the duck have a complaint to make. If we keep them, we must restore some of their rights.

This entry feels like an introduction to an article, perhaps something Ligon had in mind. He is clearly concerned over the effects of habitat degradation on waterfowl nesting areas and gives overgrazing blame equal to overhunting for their decline. His comment on the change in the Pecos Valley reflects irrigation projects diverting waters away from historic wetlands. L. A. Renick was a half-brother to Seddie Ligon, Stokley's father. He owned a ranch in the north end of the San Andres Mountains in 1909, when Ligon was working in that area.[30] This ranch was near Sulphur Canyon, along the route Ligon took crossing the mountains. Renick also operated a well-drilling company on the Jornada del Muerto and lived at least part of the year near Cutter, New Mexico. The 1900 US census shows Renick and his family living at Aleman; in 1910, they are living at Cutter, and Stokley Ligon is listed as part of Renick's household. Ligon therefore lived with the Renicks at least part of the time he was working on the Bar Cross Ranch. Ligon may actually have been employed by Renick, contracting well and windmill installations on the Bar Cross, rather than directly employed by the ranch.

Amazingly, Ligon speaks in the above complaint of ducks' "rights," a concept that became common only in the 1960s and 1970s. I doubt that many people thought of animal rights in 1913.

Ligon follows the complaint with an introductory page for the report. He wrote most of the report while he was staying in the cabin at Stinking Lake on the Jicarilla Apache Indian Reservation. This would explain the rounded estimate for the trip home. Records from Ligon's report were incorporated by Wells W. Cooke and, ultimately, Florence Merriam Bailey into *Birds of New Mexico* (F. Bailey, 1928). As a result, the information he provided did not see print until 1928, and it was then scattered throughout Bailey's book. Ligon also referred to records from the report in his *New Mexico Birds* (1961), which he apparently wrote over an extended period. It was published posthumously.

For this book, I have dissected the breeding bird report, using dated entries and area descriptions where they fit chronologically with the diary entries. All of the bird species accounts are presented in the appendix. In quoting the diary and report, I have retained his spelling, punctuations, abbreviations, and sentence structure, all of which were poorly developed at this early stage in his career. I also attempted to explore certain word usages in 1913. For example, he obviously had hopes of becoming a freelance writer and photographer. The term naturalist would seem to have been more appropriate than "nature student," and the phrase "articles submitted for publication" seems amateurish. He came from a culture that might have viewed working for the government as failure. Perhaps he felt that by articulating his personal goals he might retain them.

[from the breeding bird report]

—INTRODUCTION—

The 31st Day of May,—Saturday. I receive my appointment as Field Assistant to the Biological Survey, for the Month of June, to collect data for the forth-coming report on the breeding birds of New Mexico. My instructions—to proceed with pack outfit

—From Chloride to V + T Lake,

By trail	40 miles
V + T Lake to Chloride	40 "
Chloride to Palomas Springs	"
on the Rio Grande	40 "
Palomas Springs to Salt Lakes, Tularosa Flats	70"
Salt Lakes to Carlsbad	180 "
Carlsbad to Roswell	80 "
Roswell to Ft. Sumner	90 "
Ft. Sumner to Santa Rosa	47 "
Santa Rosa to Santa Fe	110 "
Santa Fe to Lumberton	130 "

(At Santa Rosa Got Re-appointed for month of July)
Distance traveled 827 ms. These distances Represent my route of travel, Back to Gila River, 300.

I wonder how Ligon was determining his mileages. Considering that he used various spellings of some place names (e.g., Tularosa), he seemingly did not have maps of the entire route. Although the US General Land Office had been developing topographic maps for New Mexico since 1883, most of Ligon's route, especially in the southern part of the state, was not yet covered. An area that included V + T Ranch had been mapped in 1911. Once Ligon left that part of the state, however, no detailed coverage was available until he reached Santa Rosa. From there through Santa Fe, and on to the Jicarilla Apache Indian Reservation, some topographic coverage was available (Moffat, 1985). This portion of his route, however, was the one where he seemed to have the most uncertainty and depended upon information from local citizens. I cannot determine from his diaries if he used maps at all.

I've made a crude check of his estimated mileages against a present-day map, and if anything, they seem a bit low for ground travel. If we include side trips he made and the trips he made into Lumberton and Dulce on the Jicarilla Apache Indian Reservation, as well as Chaco Canyon, he had easily covered 1,200 miles by the time he returned to Chloride.

The Gila Forest Reserve

Once his materials arrived, Ligon quickly struck out over the assigned route, traveling initially on foot and driving his burros. Somewhere on the upper Gila River, probably at V + T Ranch, he picked up his horse. Its name was Gila Red, but he never referred to it or his burros by name in his diary or report. In his photograph list, he simply called the horse Red and the burros Smokey and Albert. He began his survey on June 1, 1913, but posted an entry for May 31.

[from the diary]
May 31st 1913—Saturday

In late P.M. I receive my appointment, as Field Assistant, in the Biological Survey. I take the oath of office, and return the papers at once.

Only a portion of my supplies come in, So I have to wait until Monday's mail for balance of same. My orders are to go west into the Gila River Forest Reserve, observe breeding birds, Back to Chloride, hit the Rio Grande about Elephant Butte, thence East to the Alkali Marshes about Tularosa. Then strike the Pecos Valley about Carlsbad, and up the River to Santa Rosa. To observe principally, Breeding water Bird.

Based upon correspondence during the survey period, Ligon was taking orders from Vernon Bailey and E. W. Nelson. Wells W. Cooke was providing guidance, and Bailey provided a list of the most important birds that Ligon was to collect.[31]

[from the diary]
June 1st—Sunday

I stay at my camp, 2 ms. West of Chloride this day. Write some letters, and take some records of birds. Many of the smaller birds have just begun making nests, while others are hatching.

—Birds Observed—

Western Robin, Nesting.
White Throat Swift "

Black Phoebe	(no. 88)
West. Wood Pewee.	(no. 89)
Curve-bill Thrasher.	(no. 90)
Vero-	(no. 91)

Woodhouse Jay.
Western Horned owl (with young)
Poorwill.
Mearns Quail.

—Mammals Observed—

Rock Squirrel in abundance here, feeding on the dwarf walnuts
Chipmonks every where.
Aberts Squirrel, begin with the pine 5 or 6 miles west of Chloride.

Current topographic maps would place Ligon's camp in the vicinity of the now-abandoned Wall Street and Nana mines and Lucky Well, probably just within the Gila National Forest boundary.

Taking the birds he observes in order, we can acknowledge that all of the species he recorded remain in the area. The robin is ubiquitous during spring and summer and can be seen at lower elevations throughout the winter. The presence of the white-throated swift bespeaks Ligon's nearness to the steep cliffs in the narrows of Chloride Creek. The Woodhouse jay refers to scrub jay. Because Ligon is noticing it in this riparian forested area, and because he later describes this habitat as typical of the Mexican jay in the Black Range, I have to wonder which bird he was seeing here and if, in 1913, he was aware of the difference. In *New Mexico Birds* (1961), he mentions the scrub jay nesting in the Cuchillo Hills. The vireo he notes could have been either a solitary (plumbeous) vireo or warbling vireo. The plumbeous vireo is most likely because in *New Mexico Birds* Ligon mentions this species nesting in early May near his cabin at Chloride. He does not give the year, but I suspect that this observation comes from his notes taken during his initial survey.

Ligon fails to mention the hermit thrush in his diary or report, a species that is common along riparian drainages such as Chloride Creek and, if difficult to see, should have been singing throughout the canyon. I find no reason to believe that it wasn't present in 1913 and wonder why he failed to mention such a remarkable songster. He noted it as common in the Black Range many years later in *New Mexico Birds*. The selectivity of his observations during the survey seems curious at times.

Ligon's misspelling of vireo (vero), as well as other common names, raises the question regarding what his source for identifying birds might have been. He also misspells chipmunk (chipmonk). In 1913, the most probable bird guidebook he might have used would have been Florence Merriam Bailey's *Handbook of Birds of the Western United States*, published in 1902 and in its third edition by 1913. The common bird names

Ligon uses generally match those in this handbook, and I suspect he used it for field identification of species he didn't recognize. Names misspelled were probably of species he recognized, so he felt no need to consult the handbook. The scientific binomials and trinomials at the tops of the pages in the report are spelled correctly and match the 1910 American Ornithologists' Union Check-List of North American Birds. However, these names are written with a different pen than that used for the report, and the more I look at them, the more I'm convinced that someone, most likely Cooke, entered them later.

His comment on the location of Abert's squirrel sightings suggests that he is reporting observations from memory for a stretch of Chloride Creek rather than merely listing species at his campsite. The chipmunks he saw were probably cliff chipmunks, which occur in the Black Range at the elevation Ligon was camped (Findley et al., 1975). The Colorado chipmunk also occurs in the Black Range, but mainly at higher elevations. Ligon fails to note the golden-mantled ground squirrel, which also occurs in this area, but he may have been including them in his generic "chipmonks." Rock squirrels are still common.

Human activity, especially in the winter, is probably lower along Chloride Creek now than it was in 1913, because mining has largely disappeared. Virtually all human use of the canyon is now camping, hiking, hunting, or herding livestock, activities that are largely seasonal.

The numbers accompanying the bird species names in Ligon's diary represent specimens collected on that day and recorded in his private catalog. They provide insight into the number of specimens he had previously collected, some of which came from other locations—the Jornada del Muerto and the San Mateo Mountains. Ligon was already building a private collection of study skins and selling specimens to other collectors or museums. According to John Hubbard, many of Ligon's earliest specimens ended up at Yale University, with others at the University of New Mexico and the USBS.[32] Marketing specimens to the USBS would explain their hiring him when the need arose for a local naturalist to make the breeding bird survey.

He had collected eighty-five specimens before his diary begins on May 31, 1913, and continued using his personal numbering system through June 1. On June 2, he began a new numbering system for specimens collected on his job, an acknowledgement that these were government property and not part of his private collection. He had a different cataloging system for eggs and apparently didn't bother to start a new list for any collected during the survey. Once he started numbering for the survey, he proceeded sequentially, collecting sixty-nine bird specimens during the survey period.

[from the diary]
June 2nd—Monday.

> I collect some specimens of birds. Many small birds nesting. I conclude after close observation, that the jays are responsible for the rarity of many of the smaller birds. Many of the birds fight for their nests and young, so the Fly catchers, and even the Humming birds, and those that nest in holes are less exposed, and are too-generally more common, but many small birds, those that build their nests in swinging and conspicuous places, suffer from these highway robbers, as the fragments of nests prove. I see many new nests torn and scattered, and the jays & woodhouse and Long Crested are continually prowling the canyon beds. These birds do not deserve protection. The fact that, the small birds are continually warning at the Jays, is evidence sufficient, that they are enemies.

Ligon's tendency to apply human ethical mores to nature appeared early and remained a common theme in his writings throughout his life (Ligon, 1927). For Ligon, at least early in his career, the natural world was viewed from a west Texas Judeo-Christian viewpoint (Wallace, 2007) wherein there was a clear distinction between good and evil. Those creatures that benefited humans were good; those that fed upon or competed with good species were enemies. Value to man was the measure of all things, and man stood outside nature as an agent of God attempting to eradicate nature's flaws. Ligon referred to jays as enemies of smaller, insect-eating birds that benefitted mankind, inferring that they therefore were also the enemies of humans and should be removed. Ligon had seemingly not factored Darwinism into his thinking, but saw nature as subordinate to and serving humans. He envisioned a sanitized planet wherein carnivores might be removed to protect beneficial creatures. While some may have changed their viewpoints over time, most of the people in the USBS at the time—Nelson, Bailey, E. A. Goldman, and Stanley Young—probably shared this point of view (Robinson, 2005).

Ligon's observation regarding the destructiveness of jays was accurate, and he still referred to the long-crested (Steller's) jay and the Mexican jays as thieves in *New Mexico Birds* (1961). In recent years, Steller's jays have been observed destroying nests of the endangered marbled murrelet in California (Ruth, 2005, 176). While modern ecologists may not moralize over the behavior of predators, they nonetheless sometimes face the same dilemmas that biologists of Ligon's era faced with regard to wildlife management goals.

[from the diary]
June 3rd—Tuesday

Pack up, and am traveling early. Thermometer Registers 50 degrees at Sun up. The canyon is alive with bird songs all the way up. 12 miles to Monument Pass, Summit of the Black Range, and Continental Divide. Elev. at Chloride about 6200. Monument Pass 8000. Little green vegetation on East side. From Summit west for 6 ms. everything green, where the Snow was deeper and lay longer. 62 degrees here at 12 M. Thunder Showers about, but do no good.

Many birds about the Summit, few have laid yet.

At my camp, where I stop to make some observ. Just West of pass, are downy Red Tail haw[k]s 60 feet up in dead Spruce. I also find nest of young Flicker.

Band Tail Pigeon rather numerous—breeding—

The lateness of the season, I believe accounts for lateness of nesting, here the oak and Qaking Asp, as well as Mt. Cottonwood, just getting into leaf. Wild Flags blooming. Abert's Squirrel common. Wind from N.W. in P.M.

Ligon traveled up Chloride Creek to the summit. His estimate of the distance to Monument Pass is high. Map measurement places it approximately eight miles on the ground from his campsite. The present road turns out of the canyon at its juncture with Blackhawk Gulch, passing through Monument Park. It crosses the continental divide and enters the Gila River watershed at the upper end of 74 Draw. With his pack animals, Ligon probably simply followed the trail up the creek to the pass. He photographed Silver Monument Mine, which the present road bypasses.

Ligon's observation regarding the limited green vegetation on the east slopes reflects the rain shadow effect of the Black Range and other mountains, a condition that still exists. Storms that pelt the Mimbres and Gila rivers often do not make it over the Black Range, or if they do, they drop much less moisture on the eastern slopes. This difference in moisture has affected land use of the area. The western slopes are used much more for recreation, having perennial streams, and hence game fish. The eastern slopes have only one drainage, Animas Creek, that harbors trout, and receive much less recreational use of any kind.

Chloride Canyon runs west to east passing from mixed white pine, Douglas fir, ponderosa pine, Gambel oak, and Rocky Mountain juniper downward through a ponderosa pine/alligator juniper association and ultimately emerging at Chloride at the upper edge of the shaggy bark juniper/pinyon pine association. The mountain cottonwood Ligon mentions is narrowleaf cottonwood, which grows at higher elevations in western mountain ranges. At lower elevations, the broad-leafed species, either Fremont or eastern cottonwood, is present. In many drainages, a hybrid between the narrowleaf and broadleaf cottonwoods exists at intermediate elevations (Witham and Maschinski, 1996). Upstream from Chloride perhaps four miles, the canyon narrows and passes between sheer rock cliffs—the cliffs Ligon descended to gather the eagle eggs as described by Raymond Schmidt in chapter 2.

> [from the diary]
> June 4th—Wednesday
>
> Cool morning at my Camp on "74" Canyon, Six miles West of Monument Pass. Thermom. Registr. down very near freezing. Elev. 7300 (about). From here West to head of East Gila River. Black-tail deer rather Abundant, also Merriam's Turkey, and Mearns Quail. Some fish from here down mostly a small, big Mouth Sucker, that it is said, destroy the trout spawning accounting for absence of trout here and In the East Gila where these, suckers are so very numerous.
>
> 15 miles down this side—.after entering Haut [Hoyt] creek, I collect specimen of Pygmy owl, the first I have observed in this region, with its 2 eggs. Strike breeding range of Swallows at mouth of Haut Creek, where they are buisly engaged in carrying mud and building houses. (nests). The first Cliff Dwelling ruins here, to be found, as one comes down.

On May 25, 2009, Patty and I camped in the Taylor Creek drainage, just north of 74 Draw. We thought we had reached 74 Draw, but our GPS reading, plotted on a topo sheet, told us we had stopped short. Trips like this bring home a sense of the magnitude of this landscape and the difference in the circumstances in which Ligon lived versus ours in the present. We traveled to the site in our SUV, pulling our camp gear in a small utility trailer, which also serves as a kitchen. After an early supper, accompanied by red wine, we hiked down the draw a couple of miles, watching birds and observing animal signs. A fairly large black bear had hiked the trail recently ahead of us. We saw one cow elk, a single creeper, western tanagers, Steller's jays, a house wren, and robins.

Our camp was in a stand of mid-sized narrowleaf cottonwood, the surrounding slopes covered with ponderosa pine and Douglas fir. On this particular trip, we chose to sleep in the Chevy Suburban due to threatening storm clouds. This turned out to be a good choice for two reasons: we had a lively thunderstorm sometime during the night that would have sent us to cover had we slept outside, and we awoke with a quarter-inch crust of ice on the surfaces of our trailer and vehicle.

Ligon lived outdoors full time, in all seasons. He was a young man in his prime and seemed to revel in his freedom and solitude. Much of the time, he was miles from other humans. Had illness or emergency occurred, no one would have known his whereabouts. He was truly on his own, covering long distances daily and setting up camp at night. He undoubtedly encountered serious storms at times and perhaps had to hole up in camp until they passed. I wonder if he read to pass the hours, and if so, what books he might have had along.

I have to compare Ligon's comfortable independence with current urbanite attitudes. On a recent evening trip Patty and I made from Hillsboro to Silver City, where we attended a "Westerners'" gathering and a program on local history, at least five different individuals expressed surprise and concern that Patty and I would consider driving back over the Black Range at night. I'm sure they would have been shocked to learn that we, at our advanced ages (me 74, Patty 69), deign to drive to remote canyons and sleep overnight in the woods. Such are modern "Westerners."

The mouth of Hoyt Creek is near the present-day site of Wall Lake, an artificial lake built by the State of New Mexico. This lake is on private property and now provides waterfowl habitat that was not present in 1913. We first visited the lake on October 14, 2007, and saw shovelers, gadwalls, ringnecks, and coots. We did not have time to develop a complete list. We visited Wall Lake again on May 26, 2009, recording two elk en route and mallards, coots, and green-winged teal on the lake. One of the mallard hens had a brood of young. We also saw a crow—a species Ligon did not record for the Gila vicinity in 1913. There is a good, all-season gravel road connecting Wall Lake with Beaverhead Ranger Station. The road also connects Wall Lake with the Mimbres River valley, although the road is rough and less traveled. A guest ranch now exists at Wall Lake.

Florence Merriam Bailey failed to acknowledge Ligon's record of the pygmy owl in *Birds of New Mexico* (1928), but the species had previously been collected by other naturalists from several sites in the general vicinity of the upper Gila River and the Black Range. The type specimen had been collected near Alma, New Mexico. Ligon's specimen did not expand the species' range. On January 22, 2009, we heard it calling a couple miles upstream from Chloride, so it remains in the area.

[from the diary]
June 5th—Thursday

The night and morning almost cold enough for frost I go down East Gila a few miles, come back and go up Beaver and make some observations. I notice walnut and cotton-wood trees, ragged and scorched looking, on examination, I find that they are infested, the Walnut by a web worm, the cotton-wood by a little black worm, that has sucked the life and green from the leaves of entire groves. I collect specimens of each, with infected branches to send to the Biological Survey.

See more evidence of Jay's raiding the small birds nest. Beaver is the most beautiful of any of the Gila tributaries, tho' it runs water only about 6 miles, the distance, especially, last three miles, is lined with springs.

Prevailing wind from S.W. day hot and dry. No grass to speak of in this district. Cattle poor.

At the time Ligon was doing his survey, the study of birds was still justified largely on the basis of pure economics—which birds were valuable as a result of their ability to control crop- or forest-damaging insects and rodents. Observing insect infestations was an implied mandate for his job. Ligon obviously had little knowledge of entomology, but observed and recorded as best he could.

Beaver Creek is still a beautiful stream and now hosts a population of smallmouth bass imported some time during the past century. By 1913, at least one homestead had been developed and abandoned, a fact Ligon fails to note (Kemp, 1968, 134).

[from the diary]
June 6th/—Friday

Cold morning, I go to the V + T Headquarter ranch to make some observations. Find a demonstration of a protected breeding ground. There is, above the ranch, in the wide canyon bed, a marshy meadow, that is fenced and protected from stock. In a portion of this is thick willow thickets and weeds, while a portion is a marshy meadow. Just out of the fence is barren rocks, on the hills and sand in the canyon, the thick willows line with the fence, but not one outside.

I found nests of two species of Black bird and one variety of duck with young. Altho' this is at the ranch, and a much traveled road near, and the ducks are constantly being persicuted, some manage to breed. Above 2 ms is a lake, that is usually a mile or more in length, and 200 yds. wide Here are found ducks during the warmer months, but its shores are barren of vegitation owing to the hundreds of head of cattle that constantly beat down its shores and bottom. At the meadow is also, Kildeer with young. And

Birds

Lesser Cliff Swallow?—Breeding In Abundance—
Western Robin
Violet Green Swallows feeding over the marsh.
Turtle Dove.
Black headed Grosbeak [Ligon initially records "tanager" here, then crosses it out and substitutes grosbeak.]
Blue Birds,
Mawkingbird, rare.
Mearns Quail

Kildeer Breeding in abundance at the lake above the ranch.

A mile below the ranch, In a cliff, was about 100 occupied nests, of Lesser Cliff Swallow. These were old nests. 60 in one wad, under projecting rock

Forest Fire raging to the South-west, beyond the Mogollon Mts. South-west wind.

[from the breeding bird report]

—V + T Lake—

The V + T Lake is in the North side of The Gila River Forest Reserve, in a dry prong of Beaver Creek, a tributary of the East Gila River.

The Lake, when full is about one mile long, and about, on average, 150 yds. wide. It is a resting and feeding place for many waterfowl during Spring and Fall migration, but is frozen over during winter. Elevation about 7000 feet.

Owing to the fact that the Lake is an important watering place for hundreds of range cattle, Its condition, in Summer is not fit for water birds to breed. The shores constantly being tramped and tracked over, Hence, there are few water bird there in Summer, and none except Killdeer, did I find breeding, these, breeding abundance.

Two miles below this Lake is the V + T Ranch. Here is a marshy, meadow, that is fenced, for the purpose of saving Hay. And in this meadow, which covers perhaps 50 acres. I find Duck and Blackbird nesting, although the duck are nesting sparingly, If they were let alone in early Spring, I am sure many would nest, as it is an ideal place. But from the fact that the ranch house is near and there is a

The V + T Ranch headquarters, May 26, 1913

The V + T Ranch headquarters, May 14, 2009. (Photo by Harley Shaw)

rather public road passes by, the duck are constantly being hunted.
I was at these Places June 6th Had visited them several times before, in April and May.

Ligon has applied a crude "natural" experiment here, discussing the difference in use by waterfowl between the trampled lake and the protected hay meadow. Note that V + T Lake lies just outside of the Gila National Forest boundary. If the boundary was fenced in 1913, this may explain the heavy use of the lake by cattle.

Ligon's comparison of waterfowl use on the lake with the meadow is only loosely valid. The lake lies about two miles up canyon (north) from the sub-irrigated wet meadow at the V + T Ranch (now Slash Ranch), at the junction of the Railroad and Mule canyons north. It is entirely dependent upon runoff from surrounding hillsides. If it was ever spring fed, the spring no longer exists. When I first visited it on October 16, 2007, after a relatively wet summer and fall, it was dry, with no sign that water had been there for some time. I would not have known it had ever been considered a "lake" without Ligon's notes and my US Forest Service map. The fact that it still shows on this 1997 map leads me to wonder if it has functionally disappeared since then. Or was it always ephemeral? One might interpret Ligon's comments as suggesting that grazing is the reason the lake lacks aquatic vegetation, but in reality, it was probably always different from the wet meadow, with or without grazing, having open banks compared with emergent vegetation downstream. In 1913, V + T Ranch was owned by the Red River Land and Cattle Company. Cole Railston was the foreman of V + T Ranch at the time Ligon visited there. He was canonized by Eugene Manlove Rhodes in several of his stories (Lee, 1960). The V + T was sold to the Means and Evans families in 1917 and renamed Slash Ranch. It was given some notability in Dub Evans's book, *Slash Ranch Hounds* (Evans, 1951).

The wet meadow begins immediately below the lake and goes all the way to the ranch headquarters. It is now fenced, and the vegetation on it is largely sedges. I don't think it any longer produces hay. It is probably still suitable for some duck nesting. It has a stream meandering through it that is apparently perennial, and at least one small, open pond lies within the sedges. I saw little sign of willows.

On later visits in 2009, Patty and I reshot the photographs of the ranch, V + T Lake, and the wet meadow. Ligon's photograph of the headquarters was taken on May 24, 1913; ours on May 26, 2009. The old log cabins, once the ranch headquarters, are long gone. A more modern ranch house occupies the site where they once stood. Log corrals have been replaced by barbwire fences, themselves now old. The number of ponderosa pines on the hill behind the house has decreased, and juniper

V + T Lake, May 24, 1913

V + T Lake, May 26, 2009. (Photo by Harley Shaw)

The wet meadow at the V + T Ranch headquarters, May 24, 1913

The wet meadow, June 5, 2009. (Photo by Harley Shaw)

has filled in the interstices. Ground cover in the foreground has greatly improved since 1913, and a line of cottonwoods has grown along the edge of the lake behind the house. The eroded ditch in the foreground has healed.

Ligon's photograph of V + T Lake was taken also on May 24, 1913, and we reshot the photograph on May 26, 2009. The heavy overgrazing described by Ligon in 1913 is apparent in his photograph, and the lake holds little, if any, water. A large corral is visible in the background. In 2009, groundcover was decidedly better, although we did not try to determine species composition. The heavy pole corral visible in 1913 is gone and has been replaced by another somewhat forward from the location of the original corral. Woody vegetation has increased moderately in the draw on the distant hill. A phone line now crosses the meadow.

We reshot the photograph of the wet meadow on June 5, 2009. Superficially, the meadow appears to have much less vegetation and to be less of a wet meadow in 2009 than in 1913. Willows have disappeared from the site, and emergent vegetation is much shorter. At the same time, the woodland and riparian vegetation along the far margin of the wet meadow has increased. When we took the photograph, a herd of yearling cattle had been grazing it. The wet meadow itself began from the point we took the photograph. When I first saw the meadow in 2007, the emergent vegetation was about as tall as it is in Ligon's photograph. The shortened condition in our 2009 photograph is probably a temporary situation, but the pasture is receiving heavier grazing than it did in 1913, not only by cattle but also by elk.

I had never encountered the use of the word "prong" to designate a tributary of a stream until I moved to New Mexico. However, in the Black Range, two or three branches of Animas Creek are named prongs, e.g., Holden Prong. Ligon's use of the word in 1913 suggests that it goes back in time and has a regional usage. According to the *Oxford English Dictionary*, the word is used in the southern United States to denote a branch of a creek or river.[33] The dictionary traces its usage back as early as 1725 and has George Washington using it in 1784. In using it, Ligon reaches back into his family's Virginia roots, no doubt.

According to Ligon (1927), elk had been exterminated from New Mexico by 1900. Reintroductions began in the northern part of the state in 1911, but elk were not returned to southwestern New Mexico until 1926, when twenty-five elk were brought to the G O S Ranch near the divide between the Mimbres and Gila rivers watersheds. This is approximately thirty miles airline directly south of Slash Ranch. There may have been other transplants of elk into the area since then as well.

They have succeeded beyond all expectations. In 2005, Tom Waddell, Patty, and I passed the Slash Ranch Meadows late one summer evening.

The meadows were full of grazing elk. We stopped counting at three hundred, and I'm sure there were half that many again. This, undoubtedly, has changed the composition of the meadow, because elk, unlike cattle, can jump the barbwire fence and graze at will.

Another native mammal that has extended its range into this area is the collared peccary, unknown here in 1913. Ligon (1927) stated that peccaries formerly occupied a narrow zone along the southern border of New Mexico, but that they had been nearly extirpated. By 1967, they had expanded into the Gila and San Francisco rivers drainages, and a single animal had been seen near Carlsbad (Findley et al., 1975). The species is now abundant enough to be legally hunted north of US Highway 60 on the west side of the state, as well as in the Mogollon Mountains and Black Range, and in the southeastern corner of the state (Albert et al., 2004).

Ligon's failure to provide species names for ducks in his daily diary is puzzling, but perhaps he felt that his collections and catalog provided adequate identifications. He summarizes species observations in the report, so was undoubtedly maintaining notes separate from the USBS diary. As noted earlier, these notes have apparently long since disappeared.

Ligon felt that human disturbance along the road passing the hay meadow limited nesting more than trampling by cattle. How much traffic could there have been in 1913? More than now? It would have had to be mainly horseback and wagon travel.

I believe that Ligon is ignorant of some important elements of waterfowl behavior at this stage of his career. He had visited V + T Ranch in late winter and early spring and observed quite a variety of waterfowl using the area. He therefore held high expectations for the lakes and meadow as a duck nesting area. What he failed to understand at that time, perhaps, is that many of the species he saw there in the winter migrated northward to nest.

Presently, the dry V + T Lake provides no waterfowl habitat, nesting or otherwise. Whether the meadow at the ranch is better or worse now for waterfowl than in 1913 is difficult to determine. It seems that the fenced portion of the meadow is greater, extending upstream all the way to a point just below the lake. It is possible that more potential nesting habitat exists now than in 1913. However, by 2009, the nearest open water of any consequence was at Wall Lake, some nine miles south of the ranch headquarters. In addition to Wall Lake, many earthen dams have been developed widely throughout the area. While dependent upon precipitation, these provide potential feeding and resting habitat for waterfowl, but probably little for nesting, even in wet years. Mallards nest throughout the area, along even very small permanent streams. On a visit on May 26, 2009, we saw no nesting swallows along the cliffs downstream from the headquarters, where Ligon had seen them in 1913.

Ligon's trip up Beaver Creek to V + T Ranch and V + T Lake was not the area's first visit by a naturalist. During the early fall of 1908, Vernon Bailey packed through this area during his ongoing studies of mammals in the state, and Bailey's awareness of this shallow lake explains why it was included in Ligon's instructions as a place to survey. Bailey had, in fact, visited almost all the places Ligon surveyed. He was aware of the limited wetlands in New Mexico and that his visits had been either too cursory or poorly timed to evaluate them as nesting habitat. Loeffler (2008) notes that, even with the artificial reservoirs now present, New Mexico has the least surface water of any state in the United States. Considering that Chihuahua in Mexico probably has even less surface water per unit area than New Mexico, the scattered lakes and wetlands in New Mexico are certainly important to migrating waterfowl as resting areas.

[from the diary]
June 7th—Saturday.

I head for Chloride, In P.M. Showers some.

Nothing of particular interest noted.

Cliff Swallows at mouth of Haut Creek breeding in abundance. They, with the Violet Green Swallows, feed in the wide canyon beds, over the running water and near.

All nests of the Cliff Species are old, many partly wrecked, yet they too contain eggs. The compliments, are two, three, and 4, well incubated.

June 8th—Sunday

I am reminded of the abundance of mice in this region, They having cut into my flour last night thro the sack. They and rats often cut my saddle strings, and in the dusty trails of mornings, their tracks look as if there had been a sprinkle of rain. and what seems a little queer too, near the Summit of the Black Range, Green flies are a great pest. during warm weather they blow saddle blankets, they are a pest all over the Gila River Reserve. See, on Chloride Creek, the presence of a green, soft worm, about an inch long that is stripping the Box Elder of their leaves. Leaving nothing but the frame of the leaf.

Hear Mearn's Quail chiming at Camp early.

He makes it back to Chloride this day, so he spent two days en route from V + T Ranch, as compared with three on his outgoing trip. He is now on horseback, having picked up Gila Red at V + T Ranch, where he was on pasture, hence making better time. He notes passing Monument Pass, confirming that he camped the previous night on the west slope of the Black Range.

Chloride to the Rio Grande

[from the diary]
June 9th—Monday

Leaving Chloride coming East, one Suddenly encounters new conditions, in the Nature world. From the Cuchillo Mts. the country slopes away toward the Rio-Grande, forming a plateau, or mesa land, between the deep canyons. Here I see the first creosote, greasewood and mesquite brush, and with this change, comes new birds.

1 pr. Scaled Quail at Willow Spring, East edge Cuchillo Mts.
Horned Lark
White Neck Raven.

I leave the Pinion Jays with the Pinion and Juniper Timber.

Ligon is apparently following the stage road, now more or less the route of present-day New Mexico State Highway 52, rather than going down Chloride Creek. Somewhere near Cuchillo, Ligon notes scaled quail and horned larks, as he moves from forest and woodland into the desert grassland. He distinguishes between creosote and greasewood, although greasewood is now a common synonym for creosote bush. I'm not sure what he was calling greasewood. Possibly tarbush? Or fourwing salt bush? He fails to place names on these changing vegetation associations, although Bailey and Goldman had religiously been using C. Hart Merriam's life zones in their field notes and reports since the 1890s. In a sense, Ligon's simple descriptions provide a better image of the gradual change of the landscape than the older naturalists' rigid life-zone categories. More and more, we get an image of an individual who is largely "self-taught" and out of the mainstream of biological knowledge.

For the first time, here Ligon mentions pinyon jays. His failure to mention them earlier is curious, given his diatribes on the destructiveness of Steller's and scrub jays. In *New Mexico Birds* (1961), however, he states that this species does not have the predatory behavior of other corvids. Pinyon jays are still common around Chloride and Beaverhead. Curiously, until the summer of 2009, I had not seen or heard them near Kingston, farther south in the Black Range. Ligon's discussion of the distribution of this species in *New Mexico Birds* is rather vague and, although mentioning the occasional presence of the species near the Mexican border, does not provide details of its normal range, other than to say it coincides with the pinyon pine–juniper vegetation zone. Pinyon jays are associated more with the Colorado pinyon–Utah juniper vegetation type rather than the Madrean pine-oak woodland.

As he moves into the desert, Ligon notes the white-necked raven, seeming sure of his identification of this species. He has so far failed to mention seeing the American raven in the higher country, although it was present because he notes collecting American raven eggs four miles above V + T Ranch in his report. Ligon's awareness of the distinction between the white-necked raven and the American or common raven demonstrates an apparent astuteness of observation. I have lived and worked in the range of the white-necked raven off and on over the past fifty years, yet I'm still hard-pressed to identify it with certainty. Alan Phillips et al. (1964, 106) note that "the White-necked Raven is impossible to identify in life unless seen right beside the Common Raven, when its smaller size can be discerned." Ligon, of course, was not constrained by the regulations protecting the species that are now in place. He carried a 16 gauge shotgun and probably felt entirely justified in shooting a bird to confirm identification. Perhaps his assurance was, therefore, well founded, although he says nothing of collecting a specimen.

I remember white-necked ravens as an element of my own budding awareness as a naturalist. I do not remember noticing ravens or crows in the deserts surrounding Phoenix when I was growing up (late 1940s to late 1950s). I can't say they weren't present, and I admit to being oblivious to many birds, but I recollect red-tailed hawks and turkey vultures, so find it hard to believe that I failed to notice something as conspicuous as ravens, had they been abundant. Alan Phillips et al. (1964, 107) considered them "rare as a summer resident near Phoenix."

When I moved to Oracle, Arizona, in 1957 and began banding quail for the Arizona Game and Fish Department, I immediately noticed ravens as something new. I knew such birds existed, of course, but here they were for the first time conspicuous, and they became symbolic (as were other species such as scaled quail and Mojave rattlers) of the fact that I was in a new habitat. My awareness, always perhaps myopic on a daily basis, was expanding, and it was the attention-demanding presence of ravens that helped me revel in my new surroundings.

Being armed with a brand-new Peterson's *Field Guide to Western Birds*, I looked them up. Based upon their distribution rather than on any ability on my part to distinguish the physical traits or calls, I concluded that I saw the white-necked species in the desert grasslands of southern Arizona. I honestly do not know, now, if such was the case, but by drawing this conclusion I increased my awareness of my new landscape. These were birds of the wilder desert! Of Mexico! The name, the knowledge they existed expanded my horizons. Literally, and I bemoan my ignorance even now, I realized that some black birds of sizes greater than pigeons had names other than crow. And I began to realize the immensity of the knowledge available to me, just by being aware. Ravens, maybe even white-necked ravens if that is truly what they were, helped set that process of growth in motion.

Now, living where three species of large corvids are present, I'm again confronted by my ignorance. Fifty years later, I still cannot glance at a large black bird and say with certainty "crow," or "common raven," or "white-necked," so I wonder how Ligon did it. By voice perhaps? Alan Phillips et al. (1964, 106) note: "The call [of the white-necked raven] is somewhat like a prolonged loud caw of a crow, but the voice of the Common Raven varies considerably and would have to be studied intensively before a means of distinguishing its relative by sound could be worked out. A raven nest in a yucca or low mesquite would almost certainly be a White-necked." On the Jornada del Muerto, Ligon saw white-necked ravens, but how or if he knew for sure what species he saw west of the Rio Grande or in higher elevations remains a mystery.

The white-necked raven has been, throughout gringo expansion, a bird that was inappropriately named. The common name (now obsolete among modern ornithologists) was derived from (or was the source of?) the scientific name *Corvus cryptoleucus*, which indicates that it is a crow with white somewhere that can't be seen. It refers to the white bases of the neck and upper breast feathers that are, in fact, white or gray. Unless you have the bird in hand, however, and can ruffle the plumage, the black ends of the overlapping feathers hide the lighter bases completely. On some occasions a wind will ruffle the feathers of a perched bird, disclosing the white, but such glimpses are rare and leave the observer uncertain over whether he has seen reflected light from feather sheen, or white bases of feathers. If one goes afield as an uninformed bird-watcher, searching for a raven with a conspicuous white neck, as the common name suggests, disappointment is assured. Seen sitting in trees or soaring above, all ravens and crows in the Southwest appear solidly black.

Modern ornithologists have acknowledged this, and the accepted common name has been changed to Chihuahuan raven, which, based upon present knowledge of the species, is also rather a misnomer. Historically, the bird was not limited to the Chihuahuan desert or to the Mexican state of Chihuahua. Its range included portions of the Sonoran Desert in Arizona, the Great Plains, the Great Basin, and even some montane habitats. It ranged as far north as Kansas and southern Colorado. So, while it is associated with the Chihuahuan desert, it is not limited to it. Nor are

American ravens or crows excluded from Chihuahuan desert habitats. One might question, for that matter, why the white-necked is called a raven at all. In size, it is hardly larger than the American crow and gathers in flocks more like that species. It forms large communal roosts. Why could we not call it the desert crow?

The area where Ligon grew up, near Pecos, Texas, is within the historic range of the white-necked raven, as is the Jornada del Muerto, where he had been working, so it is probably the raven with which he was most familiar. His first collected specimens of record on the Jornada were white-necked raven eggs.[34] Only when he began to explore the San Mateo and Mogollon mountains did he move into the habitat of the common raven, and perhaps the difference, either in physical appearance or behavior, was actually striking to him.

In his report, Ligon presents both raven species as beneficial consumers of carrion, failing to indict them as "bandits" as he did the jays. Since Ligon's time, the common raven has increased in numbers, becoming a problem in the conservation of such threatened species as the desert tortoise, whose young it eats, and the marbled murrelet, whose eggs and young it destroys.

[from the diary]
June 10th—Tuesday

At Cotton-wood Spring, on Cuchillo Creek, eight miles west of its mouth.

Here is a spring, and the only water for several miles around, and there is several big Cotton-wood trees, the only trees in that locality, here gather many birds. I think Gambel quail are more abundant here than any place that I have ever visited. I believe this is about the limit too, of the Texas Night hawk range. I observed one pair of these birds here. Mawking bird in abundance.

Turtle Doves very abundant.

Kildeer with young.

Very strong S.E. wind in late P.M.

Ligon is now following Cuchillo Negro Creek and has camped within a mile of the town of Cuchillo, although he does not mention it. In fact, his comment that the spring is "the only water for miles around" is puzzling, considering that Cuchillo was an established stage stop by 1913. I do not find Cottonwood Spring on any current maps, and I have asked three long-time residents of Cuchillo about the spring. They remember none by that name. At present, a flood control dam exists near the site where Cottonwood Spring most likely existed. This dam was built where

Ligon's camp at Cottonwood Spring, 1913

the canyon narrows and has rocky substrate that would have undoubtedly brought groundwater to the surface, even during droughts. A stand of scraggly saltcedar now indicates the presence of a shallow water table upstream from the dam.

Ligon's one photograph of Cottonwood Spring, taken on June 10, shows only two old cottonwoods surrounded by a rather barren landscape. Locating the exact place this photograph was taken is impossible for lack of identifiable landscape features, but it apparently represents a view to the north within a broad flat in the creek just downstream from Cuchillo. A well with a metal stock tank is on the south side of the creek directly across from where I suspect the photograph was taken. No cottonwoods are present, but a lone Arizona walnut and a large thicket of fruit-laden hackberry trees are present, and I wonder at Ligon's failure to note this species—an important source of food for birds and many mammals. Ligon seemed taken with the place, but his bird list for the site is spare. In early June, one would have expected orioles, tanagers, and an assortment of colorful and noisy warblers in a well-watered site with large cottonwoods. Presently, a road named "Willow Springs Road" heads down Cuchillo Negro Creek from Cuchillo, suggesting that the name of the spring changed over time.

Ligon's spelling of "mawking bird" seems strange. This spelling also is used in the breeding bird report, where one would expect it to have been corrected, if he had any kind of reference handy. I have looked in dictionaries, including the *Oxford English Dictionary* (OED), to see if this might have been an antiquated spelling of the word, but find no such usage. To mawk, according to the OED, is to infest with grubs or fly larvae. By the time he wrote *New Mexico Birds* (1961), he had adopted the correct spelling.

Turtle dove, used by Ligon, refers to the mourning dove, and is so-acknowledged in *New Mexico Birds*. Florence Merriam Bailey in her 1902 field guide called it mourning dove and does not acknowledge the name turtle dove. This common name, however, is still used in the southern United States for the species. Ligon reverts to the name "mourning dove" in his report for the survey. Herein lies an example of how confusing common names of animals (and plants) can be. Without knowledge of Ligon's roots, one could interpret his use of turtle dove in a variety of ways. The turtle dove is referred to regularly in interpretations of the Old Testament, and the name is still applied to several species of mid-sized doves of the genus *Streptopalea* that occur in Europe and the Middle East. Similarity of our mourning dove to these species undoubtedly resulted in transferral of the name by European immigrants to the American bird.

In the Southwest, however, the name becomes ambiguous. At times it is used to refer to the Inca dove, which in Sonora is called *tortola cola larga* (Russell and Monson, 1998, 124). The common ground dove is *tortola coquita*, and the ruddy ground dove is *tortola rojiza*. Although *tortola* actually translates as dove rather than turtle, which would be *tortuga*, one can see how Anglos already using the appellation "turtle" for one dove might have easily misinterpreted *tortola* or *tortolita*. Al Medina of the Rocky Mountain Research Station informed me that a name for the mourning dove in central and southern Mexico is tortolita. It would take a professional linguist to untangle the roots and variances of the term, especially when it apparently has been applied in Hebrew, Latin, and English versions. Here, however, because Ligon did not include Inca doves or ground doves in his breeding bird report, we can safely assume he was referring to the mourning dove.

Ligon's conclusion regarding the range of the Texas nighthawk is in error and betrays his limited experience at the time. According to Florence Merriam Bailey's 1902 field guide, the Texas nighthawk extended through the deserts of Texas, New Mexico, Arizona, and into southern California. Ligon's contention that Cottonwood Spring lay at the western limit for the species, an error he repeats in the report, suggests strongly that he did not have, or at least was not checking his observations against, this field guide.

[from the diary]
June 11th—Wednesday

At Palomas Springs on The Rio Grande.

Altho' there is now quite a town at these Springs, and much shooting, there are still some water bird breeding.

I observed a few duck, but I hardly think they are nesting this year, as they are constantly being hunted.

In the Bosques near are many smaller bird.

I found Young Robin, out of the nest.

[from the breeding bird report]

—PALOMAS SPRINGS—on the Rio Grande

The Palomas Springs, five miles below Elephant Butte, in the Rio Grande Bottom, is an other very favorable place for the nesting of water and marsh birds. But here too, the duck especially, are constantly being hunted.

The water here, comes from hot springs, runs out and forms a marshy lake, then runs through a ditch for some distance, to the South West, and forms a long Slough. I find quite a lot of duck here, but no hope, under the prevailing circumstances, for them to nest. Coot, Red-Wing, Yellowthroat, and Rail nest here, without being molested seriously.

If the State Game Law was only observed here, there would be a difference. But there is no regard given to the law, relating to the ducks.

Palomas Springs June 11th and 12th.

Palomas Springs, or Palomas Hot Springs, was near the site of present-day Truth or Consequences, although a marshy area existed roughly from the mouth of Cuchillo Negro Wash downstream to Truth or Consequences (Sullivan, 1994, 79). This area, especially around Mims Lake, is still marshy. According to Julyan (1998), the town of Hot Springs, now Truth or Consequences, was not so-named until 1914. The general area of growth was known as Palomas Springs up until that time.

According to historian James Sullivan: "In a very real sense, the mid-nineteenth century settlements at San Ignacio de la Alamosa and its trans-river sister Alamocita were the pioneer precursors for Palomas Hot Springs. Increasingly it was called simply Hot Springs after 1914 when the name of the post office was officially changed. . . . The ruins of those

Palomas Hot Springs, ca. 1912. (Courtesy of the Harry Ransom Center, The University of Texas)

first communities now lay engulfed by the waters of the new Elephant Butte Dam" (1994, 92).

Ligon apparently followed Cuchillo Creek to the Rio Grande. Construction of Elephant Butte Dam was in full swing by the time he passed the area, having begun in 1911. His comment on there being "quite a town" reflects, no doubt, the dam construction, and the year-round shooting of ducks may have been a recent phenomenon resulting from the increased numbers of people working at the dam site. By 1914, the construction community with workers and support population amounted to 3,500 people (D. Phillips et al., 1994). This does not include the resident population of Palomas Hot Springs. Thus, Ligon's failure to specifically mention the dam, probably the most newsworthy event in the entire Southwest, if not the nation, at the time, is remarkable and provides insight into the man's interests and focus. The "prevailing circumstances" undoubtedly refers to the dam construction and people it attracted, and his silence otherwise almost smacks of denial. His photographs show that he not only passed near the dam but also went out of his way to photograph it. Also, he took one picture from the so-called "pony bridge" just downstream from the dam site, confirming that he crossed the

The construction of Elephant Butte Dam, 1913

Elephant Butte Dam, 2009. (Photo by Harley Shaw)

The old Engle Ferry was used for crossing the Rio Grande near Palomas Hot Springs prior to the construction of the Elephant Butte Dam. (Courtesy of the Harry Ransom Center, The University of Texas)

river at this point en route to Engle. The old Engle Ferry was by then defunct.

Ligon does not mention a large number of cottonwoods in this vicinity, nor does he mention large numbers of doves, from which the name Palomas Springs derives. The word *palomas* applies to all members of the family Columbidae and requires a modifier to identify the species. In Sonora, another common name for mourning dove is *paloma huilota*, often simply *paloma* (Russell and Monson, 1998, 123). As best I can tell, *huilota* translates to ragged or dirty, an adjective I find difficult to apply to the mourning dove. This, of course, combined with the discussion about turtle doves, adds further confusion regarding the accepted common name of this wide-ranging bird. Ligon mentions smaller birds in the bosques, presumably mesquite bosques. Saltcedar had not seriously encroached on the Rio Grande in 1913.

In all of Ligon's writing at this time, he curiously uses the singular to denote plurals of wildlife—duck for ducks, robin for robins. He consistently uses birds as a plural, rather than bird. I see this vernacular still occasionally used—bear for bears, cougar for cougars. I wonder if this can be traced to some particular Old World language trait, of Scots, perhaps.

The Jornada del Muerto, Sulphur Canyon, and Tularosa Basin

[from the diary]
June 12th—Thursday

Jornada Valley.

The most important bird to be found here, and most abundant, is the Horned Lark. very abundant about Cutter. young birds following the old ones now.

White Neck Raven abundant, nesting in the tall soap-weed, Constantly stiring for food. Great scavengers they are, and do no harm in the ranch country.

Dry, windy and dusty. S. wind

Ligon does not describe his route after leaving Palomas Springs. His notes leave the impression that he went to Cutter, but this is subject to interpretation. It seems likely that he stopped at Engle, because he was expecting mail there, but Bailey's package to him apparently had not yet arrived. It is possible that he checked by phone or telegraph to see if mail was awaiting him at Engle and, if not, may have bypassed the settlement. What he fails to mention seems significant. By the time he passed this way, a railroad spur had been built from Jornada, a landing about seven miles south of Engle, and trains were hauling supplies to the dam. A wagon road between Palomas Creek and Engle had long existed, and it was undoubtedly being used for dam business, including considerable automobile traffic. Ligon's failure to remark on any of this activity seems almost disdainful. The photographs and associated notes are no help here. Apparently Ligon did not set up his camera again until he reached Santa Rosa, nearly three weeks later. He was covering a lot of ground and, I suspect, feeling a need to move on to the lakes in the Tularosa Basin and on the Pecos River valley. He had taken several photographs on the Sacramento Mountains the year before and probably felt no need to repeat them. Also, he had photographs across the Tularosa Basin and the San Andres Mountains from that earlier trip. Unfortunately, he took nothing going down the Peñasco River and across the prairie to Artesia.

Horned larks are normally associated with heavily grazed grasslands, so Ligon's comment on their numbers reflects the history of grazing on the Jornada (Desmond, 2004).

A question arises here regarding Ligon's communication with Bailey. In an earlier letter, he had told Bailey to write him at Engle. The letter dated June 7 from Bailey to Ligon, mailed to Engle, notes:

> You are right in supposing Beaver Lake to be the same as the lake near the V + T Headquarters.
>
> I am enclosing a letter from Professor Cooke in regard to the most important birds to be collected on your trip. I am also enclosing a circular of general directions for field work. . . . You will see by it that the cotton is for small specimens and the tow for larger ones. We are always glad to have photographs of birds' nests, nesting sites or other interesting objects.
>
> You had better write from Engel and again from Tulerosa so we will be able to keep track of your progress.

Nothing in future correspondence from the USBS suggests that Ligon mailed a letter to them from Engle. If Bailey's letter was written on the seventh, which was a Saturday, it may have not gone out until the ninth. If so, it seems very likely that it had not arrived in Engle by the twelfth and that Ligon did not receive this correspondence. No letter of reply exists in the files. Seemingly, therefore, he failed to receive Cooke's list of important birds and the published instructions to assistants until it caught up with him at Carlsbad on June 23. For Ligon to have stopped in Cutter to visit the Renick family seems likely, and he may well have depended upon them to pick up and forward mail at Engle.

> [from the diary]
> June 13th—Friday
>
> Weather characterized by cold nights and dry hot days. In early A.M. cool wind from North, shifts to west—See Antelope East of Cutter, as I come on my way,—Cutter and Tularosa road. West slope of San Andrea Mts. is a dry district, no wells or Springs, above Gilmore's ranch. Fine Tabosa and Gramma grass.
>
> Botany—Spanish Dagger. Soap weed, mesquite creosote, and grease-wood brush, after reaching Mts, that have long Western slope and short, abrupt Eastern, I strike, Shingle grass Sotol, jointed and Candle Cactus in abundance, some "Mescal". —green century—blooming now. In canyons, East side some ash trees. A few prairie dogs near Summit.
>
> Clear day, bright moon, many crickets—Sulphur Can.

Ligon's route from Cutter to the top of the San Andres Mountains is difficult to follow. A good gravel road now runs between Cutter and Woolf

Ranch in the San Andres foothills. This undoubtedly was the approximate route that Ligon followed. I've been unable to determine the location of Gilmore Ranch. It was located in the San Andres Mountains east of Cutter and may be the property that is now Woolf Ranch. Ligon's comment that the area is dry and that grass forage is good demonstrates that he was aware that livestock could overgraze a range only if water was present.

L. A. Renick owned a ranch near Sulphur Canyon, and Renick Spring shows on the topographical map for the area. The ruins of Renick's ranch are still present near the spring, which is up El Paso Canyon, the northern tributary of Sulphur Canyon. Ligon may have visited the Renick ranch site on his trip across the mountain. Its presence might explain, in fact, why Ligon crossed the mountain through Sulphur Canyon rather than taking the wagon road across Rhodes Pass. However, Ligon had been instructed to inspect the salt lakes in the Tularosa Basin, including Lake Lucero. Going through Sulphur Canyon provided a more direct route to the Salt Lakes lying at the north edge of the White Sands. Ligon was traveling horseback with pack animals, so was not restricted to the established roads.

Horned larks, white-necked ravens, and pronghorn are still relatively common on the Jornada del Muerto. The prairie dogs Ligon noted were probably on the gentler terrain near the head of Sulphur Canyon. Several of the valleys in this vicinity have deep alluvial soils and would be suitable as prairie dog habitat. On November 19, 2007, a group of us drove to the head of Sulphur Canyon, partly in search of evidence of past prairie dog colonies.[35] We were unable to detect signs of old eroded burrows or mounds. In 1892, Gaut reported them on both slopes of the mountains and at Rhodes Pass, but did not mention a colony near Sulphur Canyon (V. Bailey, 1931, 123). Bailey failed to acknowledge Ligon's observation in his 1931 publication, and Oakes et al. (2004), reviewing the history of the prairie dogs on White Sands Missile Range, also failed to note Ligon's Sulphur Canyon record. Based upon historic records and evidence of old mounds and erosion channels, Oakes et al. concluded that a large complex of prairie dogs once existed on the Jornada del Muerto and the Tularosa Basin, but Ligon did not mention them in either basin.

His failure to mention them for the Jornada is perhaps not surprising. Oakes (2000) and Oakes et al. (2004) found a historic record of only one village near Ligon's route. As reported by Mearns, Major Jack Martin of the California Volunteers sunk a well in a prairie dog town on the Jornada (Mearns, 1907, 344). Martin's well, dug shortly after the Civil War, was located south of Cutter and later became known as Aleman. By the time of Ligon's trip, this prairie dog colony was probably long gone. Decades of heavy grazing and the severe drought of the 1890s had occurred, and ranchers were beginning to poison the colonies. Oakes et al. note that poisoning of prairie dogs by the USBS began about 1915 and increased after

1918, but prairie dog poisoning had probably been carried out prior to 1913 by individual ranchers. Aleman lies south of Ligon's route, so, even if the colony did still exist, he could have easily passed it without seeing it.

Oakes et al. (2004) place the year 1913 near the end of the Early Settlement Period (1849–1919) and at the beginning of the Ranching Period (1913–1945). However, ranching had existed on the flatlands surrounding the mountain, including the Jornada and the Tularosa Basin, for at least thirty years prior to Ligon's ride, and as already noted, at least one ranch, owned by Renick, existed in El Paso Canyon, a tributary of Sulphur Canyon. On our first visit to Sulphur Canyon, we passed several abandoned ranches, all postdating Ligon's crossing of the mountain.[36] In 2009, we returned and found the remains of Renick's ranch.

Oakes et al. note that that livestock probably heavily impacted areas within grazing range of reliable water sources, and that the development of deep-cased wells and windmills had allowed cattle to expand across the rangeland. Ligon came to New Mexico as a windmill repairman in 1907, thereby contributing to this expansion. His photographs show steam and gas pumps being used on the Jornada by at least 1910.

Grazing has been much restricted on the San Andres Mountains since the 1950s, and when we visited Sulphur Pass in 2007, groundcover was so dense that we could see little of the ground surface. All of the ranches on the San Andres Mountains ultimately ceased to operate when they were taken by the US government during and after World War II. The first atom bomb was exploded on the Jornada in 1945, and the area has been retained for military research ever since. The area is covered by Chihuahuan grassland vegetation, with a wide diversity of woody and herbaceous plants. A few cattle still wander onto the range, but it is mostly ungrazed.

During the 1910s, 1920s, and into the 1930s, several of the ranches in this region ran angora goats, selling mohair mainly to Germany. The advent of World War II closed the German markets, thereby eliminating the goat ranches. They never returned, but the older junipers in the area retain the signs of goat presence.[37] One-seed juniper, when not browsed, will mature as a multi-stemmed tree with canopies going nearly to the ground. However, if the trees are browsed when young, they may develop single-trunks with a spreading canopy, more in the shape of an apple tree. Trees such as this could be seen on the slopes surrounding the Crockett Ranch ruins near Sulphur Canyon.

In crossing the Jornada, Ligon rode from Cutter to Sulphur Spring in one day, a direct line of some twenty-five miles, apparently without water for his animals, until he hit the head of Sulphur Canyon. His actual number of ground miles was undoubtedly more. With the exception, perhaps, of a few packers in wilderness areas and the rare horsemen who take long rides as an adventure, we have lost the knowledge and skills required for such long-distance horseback travel. We now climb in a car and travel seven hundred miles per day in daylight hours, worrying little about where we will sleep or eat. Motels, restaurants, mini-marts, and grocery stores service our needs. Travel by horseback required detailed knowledge of the landscape because men and horses alike could die on routes without water. Yet people used horses to travel known routes then much like we use motorized vehicles today, with distances scaled down accordingly. For someone to ride forty miles in a day on an established road or trail required little preparation, because an infrastructure existed that supported equine travel, which included ranches with friendly folk offering pastures or hay, liveries, and dispersed watering places.

> [from the diary]
> June 14th—Saturday
>
> I drop down Sulphur Canyon in to the great Salt and Gyp valley that lies between the San Andrea and Sacramento Mts. Not very much bird or animal life stiring here. The dry stretch, when there has been no rain for months is about 50 miles—from Springs in Sulphur Canyon to, or to, Tularosa. Rabbits are noticed pretty well over the district-cotton-tail and jack, some White-Neck Raven. A great lizard country, and many insects. Horned Lark rather rare. Some coyote.
>
> This flat is about level after one reaches the bottom of the Mt. Slopes. To the North is the Mal Pai Flow, at the South the White Sands, about 25 miles apart.
>
> June 15th—Sunday
>
> I go to north of road and Stop at Pickards Well, where I get water for my animals,— and self from cystern.
>
> Collect Specimens of small bug that is devastating the sage brush.
>
> In P.M. Visit Mal Pais Spring to North West, find some water Fowl. Bad water, especially where the water has formed cokes, they being too salty for water fowl. The spring comes from under south end of the Mal Pais.— Lava flow, and forms a channel that, during dry times runs about 2 ms., wet times further. The Mal Pai flow is noted for Scaled Quail, Cotton-tail Rabbit and Rattle Snake. Hot dry weather. The country, white and glaring, is death on one's eyes, and water, if not from the cystern, very bad and effective to drink.

Ligon continues to display a basic ignorance of botany in noting sagebrush in the area. Oakes et al. (2004) sampled vegetation throughout the Tularosa Basin and reported no species of Artemesia.[38]

Principal shrub species include tarbush, creosote bush, fourwing salt bush, honey mesquite, and Berlandier's wolfberry. Most likely, Ligon was referring to fourwing salt bush, which can take on a sagebrush-like appearance when present in extensive stands.

I can't find a definition for the word *cokes* as it is used here. However, Ligon must be referring to the mound springs in the basin. Perhaps it is a term that local cowboys mutually decided to apply to the springs.

In terms of wildlife, one of the major changes that has occurred in this area since Ligon passed through is the presence of gemsbok, or oryx. These were introduced by the New Mexico Department of Game and Fish and have thrived on the dry creosote and salt bush flats of the Jornada del Muerto and the Tularosa Basin. They now occupy much of the San Andres Mountains, as well as the Fra Cristobal Mountains. White Sands National Monument, being a National Parks installation, attempts to restrict them from expanding their range, and the White Sands Missile Range and San Andres National Wildlife Refuge allocate permits to hunt them. Their impact on the ranges they occupy and competitive effects on native ungulates remain a matter of speculation and concern among Chihuahuan Desert biologists.

[from the breeding bird report]

SALT LAKES AND MAL PAI SPRING

June 15th and 16th Tulorosa Flats

Before I reached these Gyp and Salt Lakes, that lie north of the "White Sands" and South of the Mal Pais Flow, I was told that there was many Ducks and snipe at them. On investigating, I find that there had been many water birds, but the lakes are very low now, and the water is so heavily impregnated with mineral that nothing can drink it. I see but one bird about these lakes,— a snipe. See quite a lot of duck carcasses,— dried,— perhaps wounded by hunters, as the empty shells about suggest.

The ranchers about, tell me that ducks do breed here some seasons, that they have seen the young duck, such is very likely during a rainy spring; but this has been a very dry one. And as the water is so very heavily charged with the mineral, the shores are barren, with a white crust for a distance out, even the salt grass near, is stiff and crumbly.

At the South-east corner is a crytalized formation. Looks at a distance, like rock, on the chunks and ledges of this, shows to have been a resting place for water fowl.

The white and glowing country Ligon traverses is the dry salt lakes. He is north of White Sands proper. I cannot find Pickard's Well on modern maps and am at a loss to delineate his exact route between Sulphur Spring and Malpais Spring. He spends a day descending Sulphur Canyon and moving down its bajada to the flats. Apparently, he made a dry camp near the salt lakes the night of June 14, then rode northward to Pickard's Well the next morning. Perhaps he was able to water his animals before leaving lower Sulphur Canyon, but he does not mention this. His comment of diverting north of the road suggests that he crossed the wagon road through Rhodes Pass. If so, Middle Well, still on US Bureau of Land Management maps, might be a candidate for Pickard's Well. This would place him in striking distance of Malpais Spring in the evening, where he apparently camped, even though the water was bad.

I would like to know more about Ligon's interactions with ranchers and who they might have been. He obviously is gathering information as he goes along, and it sounds as if he encounters more people in this area than one might meet today. Perhaps there was a Pickard living at Pickard's Well.

[from the breeding bird report]

MAL PAI SPRING

About 15 miles North from the Salt Lakes, is the Mal Pai Spring. The Spring flows from under the South West corner of the Mal Pai's, and forms quite a creek for a distance, when it spreads forming some small lakes and sinks. The water, where it comes out is cold and has no disagreeable taste, but is heavily charged with mineral, and is bad for person to drink, and stock, after the water passes through the Gyp beds, for a distance, refuse to drink it, especially in warm weather.

The channel of this creek, is elevated above the surrounding flat, caused, I judge, by flying dust and dirt, during windy weather being caught by the damp ground and settled. Hence now, there are lakes and marshes, to the sides, kept supplied by water that seeps through, or that comes out at cow-trails.

During dry times this water only goes about a mile and a half, where it forms a small lake, in rainy seasons it goes much further.

Redwing Blackbird
Meadow Lark and
Kildeer abundant with young.
Note two Blue Wing Teal that act as if they were nesting.
One coot.

The water every place, even out in the rank thick Salt Grass, is full of small fish, resembling perch. None over an inch in length. These are very abundant.

In the Mal Pai rock, or slag, near, Scaled Quail are very abundant.

The Salt Lakes lie directly West of Tularosa, about 25 miles.

In his June 1 letter to Vernon Bailey, Ligon had written, "I was at the lakes near Tularosa, above the 'White Sands,' last August [1912], and found many ducks there. And the upper end of Salt Flat, about Orange, when there is water is another duck favorite." In August 1912, Ligon was traveling by wagon across the Tularosa Basin with his brother, headed ultimately for the San Mateo Mountains.

For the first time here, Ligon remarks upon the presence and effects of livestock on the area. The springs, with live, fresh water, support much more life than the Salt Lakes, so he undoubtedly was able to water his animals here, although he felt the water was not suitable for humans. The fish were White Sands pupfish, a species indigenous to these springs, and now considered threatened by the State of New Mexico. They are managed under the White Sands Pupfish Conservation Plan by joint state and federal agencies and the military. Ligon was not the first to document the presence of these fish (Pittenger and Springer, 1999). Herrick (1900) and Meinzer and Hare (1915) had both noted them before Ligon passed through the area, and their reports provide evidence that considerable scientific interest in the Tularosa Basin and White Sands area existed prior to 1913.

The White Sands pupfish was not recognized as a distinct species until 1975 (Miller and Echelle, 1975). When Ligon saw these fish, they were limited to Salt Creek and Malpais Spring. New populations have since been established in Lost River and Mound Spring as a result of transplants. The original populations were isolated in the Tularosa Basin at the end of the Pleistocene. They were originally part of the fauna of prehistoric Lake Otero, which disappeared with Holocene warming and drying.

[from the diary]
June 16th—Monday

Dry, hot and dusty in to Tularosa, 20 miles. Sage brush, salt grass and soap-weed thrive over the gyp flats. See Golden Eagle in chase after Jack Rabbit. Rabbit dodges him in brush. Ravens and hawk follow Eagle out of sight

I name Tularosa the "Game Town," As Birds sing over its sidewalks.— Meadow Lark singing by the streets at the alfalfa's edge, and

> quail-Scaled Quail making their nesting calls on the principal dwelling street, Cotton Tail's feeding in the alfalfa patches with hogs. Tula rosa is a town of trees and shades, houses mostly made of mud. Many Jack Rabbit just west.

Ligon was seemingly taken with Tularosa, and this entry is one of the few places he embellishes with description. No doubt his long, hot ride across the Jornada del Muerto and Tularosa Basin rendered the irrigated settlement particularly appealing. After reaching the Pecos Valley, he was compelled to write further about Tularosa.

[from the breeding bird report]

—Tularosa—

> Tularosa, west of the Sacramento Mountains, a city of trees and alfalfa and truck patches, is another bird town,—a place that is a credit to the Inhabitants along the line of bird protection—
>
> The trees are swarmed with songsters, and Scaled Quail even, are to be seen on the main residence streets, tame and seemingly, unconcerned about the rush of vehicles near, often sitting on the fences, never stopping their nesting calls as one passes very near. Here too I noticed the Cotton-tail Rabbits abundant in the streets and with the hogs, they feed in the Alfalfa.

Ligon was not the first to be charmed with the town. May Davison Rhodes (1938, 13–14), wife of Eugene Manlove Rhodes, described it during the summer of 1900. "Tularosa—what magic the name holds! Dreamy, quiet, save for the thud of galloping horses' hoofs. Thick-walled adobe houses with majestic cottonwood trees shadowing deep doorways from the blistering sun. Mexicans wearing straw hats with high, pointed crowns, and brilliant sashes of purple or scarlet knotted around blue overalls. . . A pack of playing cards flung down in the dusty street. . . Pretty Mexican girls tripping up and down in high-heeled slippers, and over all the matchless New Mexico sun."

Ligon, a reserved and somewhat religious man, never mentioned the girls. Single at age thirty-three, he must have noticed them.

Tularosa was settled in 1862 by Hispanic families displaced from the Rio Grande Valley. It was apparently named for the large number of reeds in the marsh formed where Tularosa Creek fanned out into the flat valley, the suffix –osa signifying "in the extreme." I do not find *tula* in my Spanish dictionary and suspect a more correct form would be Tulerosa, as used by Vernon Bailey or, better yet, Tulosa, as suggested by Julyan

(1998). But the town is Tularosa on maps old and new, an apparent anglicization of the word.

The town's original settlers fought Apaches in order to stay in the area, and in spite of the idyllic picture painted both by Ligon and May Rhodes, a legacy of violence followed it into the twentieth century. It played a role in the Lincoln County War and the murders of Albert Fountain and his son and of Pat Garrett, events that were still fresh in the memories of locals in 1913 (Sonnichsen, 1960).

Tularosa has now grown to a much larger and more modern town than it was in 1913. While some of the early mud huts remain, newer structures have spread through the area, and like most Western towns, Tularosa is suffering from sprawl. It and the older settlement of La Luz are hardly distinct from Alamogordo, and they undoubtedly serve as bedroom communities for that small city with its military-based economy.

Ligon's knowledge of plants is again lacking. Sagebrush apparently does not occur in the area, at least not in amounts to be reported as a dominant plant. True salt grass is limited to marshy areas and is not a species of the "gyp flats." If by soapweed he refers to yucca, then he is correct in this identification. As Ligon notes, scaled quail was the only species of quail present in 1913. Sometime later, Gambel's quail were transplanted to the area (Ligon, 1927), and they are now abundant.

I find no correspondence between Ligon and the USBS at Tularosa, nor, from all appearances, did he receive communications from the survey from the time he left Chloride until he arrived in Carlsbad, having apparently missed Bailey's package mailed to Engle. Ligon sent a report of his activities and a box of bird skins from Tularosa. A letter from E. W. Nelson, dated June 17 and picked up by Ligon at Carlsbad, informs Ligon that his specimens were not correctly labeled and provides detailed instructions on how this should be done. This letter provides additional evidence that Ligon did not receive Bailey's package at Engle, because it included the manual for field technicians that would have provided the labeling instructions.

Nelson notes that Ligon's appointment is to be extended for another month, allowing him to go all the way to the Jicarilla Apache Indian Reservation. His letter has a slight edge to it, qualifying this extension with, "If your work continues to be satisfactory." He also says, "Do not fail to keep me posted in advance concerning your address so that we can reach you with certainty," perhaps suggesting that Ligon's communication has been something less than ideal. Nelson informs Ligon that Bailey is leaving for the field and that he will be taking over correspondence and supervision.

The Sacramento Mountains

June 17th—Tuesday

> Many Western Night Hawk on Tularosa and La Luz road. La Luz a town of very ancient Build. Big Cotton wood and many small orchards. Some complaint about the birds ruining so many fruit. I believe much of the damage caused by English Sparrows, as they are very abundant.
>
> I see some people who condemn all the birds for the damage done by a few, and never admit figures to estimate the damage they prevent in their constant destruction of insects. It is doubtless, rather alarming to the Foresters to see the great amt. of dead timber on the west side of the Sacramento Mts. to the summit, but gratifying to see the abundance of young growth coming with such thrift. Many birds in the Sacramento Mts. Steep and rough, West side.

La Luz predated Tularosa. According to Julyan (1998), Franciscan missionaries built a chapel at this site in 1719, but actual permanent settlement began in 1860. La Luz is now a sprawling suburb of Alamogordo, with ranchettes scattered up La Luz Canyon east of town for perhaps twenty miles. Ligon undoubtedly ascended the Sacramento Mountains via Fresnal Canyon, a route that he and his brother had traveled by wagon a year before. In his photographic journal, he calls it Ash Canyon, but the Spanish version of the name prevails on current maps.

Two months before Ligon passed through Tularosa and La Luz, a body of Chiricahua Apaches had been allowed to return from Fort Sill, Oklahoma, to the Mescalero Apache Reservation, northeast of La Luz. Only five years earlier, a young cowboy had been killed by a Mescalero Apache he found illegally butchering a beef cow. Apache tribal police had trailed the killer and shot him (Ball, 1988). Although the Apache wars were over, members of the Chiricahua and Mescalero tribes who had participated in those wars wandered the area, and memories of their treatment by the Americans were still vivid. Seemingly, a lone rider would want to be cautious even at this late date.

According to Cameron (1929), the English sparrow was introduced in Boston in 1850 and 1853. The fact that it was considered a pest in New Mexico by 1913, merely sixty-three years later, discloses the rate at which it had spread over the continent, often with additional help from humans who shipped small crates of sparrows westward for release. Ligon was already becoming a traveling evangelist for songbirds as controllers of insects, as well an early skeptic regarding the value of introduced nonnatives. In this, he was perhaps prescient. By 1916, apple orchards in the

Pecos Valley had been infested with codling moth, and farmers were rapidly switching to alfalfa or cotton as their major crops (Sheridan, 1975).

The dead timber he mentions on the western face of the Sacramento Mountains seems a mystery. By 1913, much of the forest on the Sacramentos had been heavily logged, initially to build the railroad up the mountain from Alamogordo and later to serve demands for lumber in Alamogordo, El Paso, and other settlements. Any dead timber was probably left over from these logging operations.

Although Ligon did not take photographs during his hurried trip across the Sacramento Mountains, those he took the preceding summer when traveling by wagon with his brother depict the route. Coming up Fresnal (Ash) Canyon, he shot a photograph of a beautifully situated farm with an orchard between Mountain Park and Cloudcroft. The hillside behind the farm shows the impact of logging that had occurred during the previous twenty years. The railroad is in the foreground. The point from which Ligon shot this photograph is alongside the present highway into Cloudcroft. The paved highway in the foreground has replaced the railroad, and a power and phone line traverses the frame. The farmhouse and other buildings are no longer present, and the fields and hillsides have returned to shrubland and forest. The day I repeated the picture, the paved highway was abuzz with traffic, and I had to time my shot between passing cars. The areas uphill and downhill from this point are highly developed with houses, small pastures, and various businesses catering to tourist trade along the highway. The photograph point itself is in the driveway of a hostel.

Somewhere near Cloudcroft, Ligon shot a picture of his horses feeding in an open, forested valley. Their wagon sits in an opening in the forest surrounded by young aspen. More mature mixed conifers exist beyond the aspen. Ligon entitles the photograph "Camp scene on way to Cloudcroft." I was unable to relocate this photograph, but the site undoubtedly lies within the residences or businesses in developments between Mountain Park and Cloudcroft.

Ligon also stopped to photograph the "S" trestle, just outside of Cloudcroft. This photograph shows a surrounding landscape that has been heavily logged and is in early successional regrowth stages. The railroad between Alamogordo and Cloudcroft had been completed in 1900, and much of the initial logging was done to supply ties and timbers for the trestles. However, the main purpose of the railroad was to haul lumber from the mountain, so by 1912, when Ligon took his photographs, spurs of the railroad ran in many directions through the forest, and the entire area had been logged. The railroad also hauled travelers and tourists to the top of the mountain, serving the tourist and logging industries until 1942.

A house above Mountain Park in the Sacramento Mountains, August 8, 1912

The site of the house in the Sacramento Mountains, July 8, 2009.
(Photo by Harley Shaw)

The S-trestle just southwest of Cloudcroft from its uphill end, August 21, 1912

The site of the S-trestle from its uphill end, July 8, 2009. The trestle has fallen down, with debris scattered on hillside below; forest encroachment obscures the old railroad grade. The site is now alongside a hiking trail maintained by the town of Cloudcroft. (Photo by Harley Shaw)

The developed trail, bench, and kiosk at the uphill end of the S-trestle, July 8, 2009. (Photo by Harley Shaw)

At its lower reaches, the railroad has now been replaced by the paved highway, but in the immediate vicinity of Cloudcroft, the railroad bed and trestles have been incorporated into a rails-to-trails program that provides hiking and running trails for residents and visitors. A faux depot has been built at a parking lot and picnic area associated with these trails, and interpretive kiosks occur at various points trailside, providing information on the scenery, history, and natural history of the area. A repeat of Ligon's 1912 "S"-trestle photograph is almost impossible due to dense forest regrowth. He took the original from the top of a cut at the lower end of the trestle. The cut visible in the original photograph can barely be seen in the recent photograph, and the railroad bed is visible but cannot be identified through the foliage at the lower left of the photograph.

An interpretive kiosk describing the original trestle, along with a bench for hikers to rest on, is present at the beginning of the trestle. The trestle itself is now only a pile of rubble in the canyon bottom below the kiosk.

Somehow, the dense forests now present in the photograph of the house at Mountain Park and at the site of the trestle seem less healthy than the recovering forest in early successional stages present in 1912.

Like many forested areas in the western United States, the Sacramento Mountain forests are suffering from a century of over-protection from fires and perhaps poorly managed logging. Logging still occurs on the Sacramentos, with lumber hauled to distant mills on logging trucks. For tourists, the thrill of riding the train across the various trestles along the railroad to the clouds has been replaced by the terrifying experience of meeting a log-laden semi descending the steep highway toward Alamogordo.

Ligon would certainly find it impossible to plod alongside the railway with horse and burro under present conditions, although he might be able to thread his way to the top of the mountain via other forest roads or trails that still exist. The route would be longer and most likely steeper.

[from the diary]
June 18th—Wednesday

Cool and damp at this Elev.—8500 near Cloud Croft.

Gentle slope of the Mts. and dense growth of timber noticeable as I come down James Canyon. East from Cloud Croft, for some distance the timber consists almost entirely of Spruce, with moss hanging from limbs. Sleepy-grass is conspicuous in the canyons, and further down, a tremendous growth of young pine, especially on the North side of canyons.

The young pine is making a rapid growth. first mud, since rain has just fallen. Oats 2 to 4 inches high. No other crop in evidence for miles. I see about the same birds as in the Black Ranges, 150 miles west.

Sleepygrass is *Stipa robusta*. Its common name is derived from the fact that it has a narcotic effect on livestock, especially horses. Kingsberry (1964) noted that in US Department of Agriculture (USDA) studies, feeding 0.6 percent of a horse's body weight (six pounds for a thousand-pound horse) of this grass would produce depression and drowsiness. Mild doses caused animals to be dejected, inactive, and withdrawn. Larger doses would put them to sleep. Cattle did not seem to be equally affected, but a 2 percent dosage in sheep created depression and an elevated temperature. These tests were published in 1929, but use of the common name by Ligon as early as 1913 indicates that its effects on animals were already known. There is now a Sleepy Grass Campground east of Cloudcroft on the Lincoln National Forest.

The USDA gives the distribution of sleepygrass as southern North America from Colorado to western Texas, Arizona, and northwestern Mexico. Herbalists sell the seeds. It is apparently unregulated, although some web pages require a disclaimer that it is being used for "research only." The active alkaloid is LSA (lysergic acid amide), a hallucinogen similar to but apparently milder than LSD. It also occurs in morning glory seeds.

Ligon's comment on oats and calling them a crop confirms that small farms existed along his route, even at higher elevations. Many small homesteads existed in New Mexico at this time, but few succeeded.

[from the diary]
June 19th—Thursday

I hit trail of flood and hail storm at Mayhill, 20 ms. East of Cloudcroft. Everything looks sick. Roads a wreck, Slow traveling. See first prairie dogs above Elk. Also first Scaled Quail to see on this side, Elev. about [75 crossed out] 6500. No more Pine below Elk, 35 ms. East of Cloudcroft. Good turf of grass, hills dwindling down gradually, and pretty country. River swollen some and thick so muddy. Find Cliff Swallows nesting in great abundance, under lime-stone cliff, of river (Penasco). I kill three with rocks, Some hatching, others building new nests.

Ligon did not take photographs along this route, and he and Ed did not travel this far east in 1912. He was trying to make time on this trip and left his camera packed, although he stopped to take a photograph of "desert roses" near Hope. In the photo, these are prickly pear flowers, with Ligon using a common name tongue-in-cheek.

I drove down the Peñasco River on March 6, 2008, in a spring snowstorm. I saw at least six flocks of wild turkeys feeding in the pastures along the river, in spite of the snow. Ligon did not mention turkeys in his diaries, but in the breeding bird report notes that he saw them as rather abundant on June 19, 1913, along the Peñasco. Wapiti had already been extirpated in southern New Mexico, but a settlement by the name of Elk, as well as an Elk Creek, remained. By 1927, Ligon was recommending reintroduction of elk into the Sacramento Mountains, where they have since thrived (Ligon, 1927).

[from the diary]
Diary. June 20th—Friday

The road cuts across the green hills below lower Penasco. Evidence of the hail and rain. See many birds building new nests, as a consequence of hail—see many broke up.—shells, and dead young in nests. See last trees,—except walnut and Hackberry along river—a few miles east of lower Penasco. Very few stock. Quite a lot of cotton-tail and jack rabbit.

Scaled Quail abundant Turkey Vulture abundant, No. Raven.

Mescal in abundance,—blooming, also cigar or jointed cactus in great patches West of YO crossing. Roads torn to pieces. Every where big rain has fallen, erosion is very noticeable, rocks piled at mouths of canyons and hills bleaching with them. Camped tonight 12 ms W. of Hope. Rains some.

I have searched for precipitation records near Ligon's route, but so far without luck. The storm apparently was widespread, because he notes its effects again on the plains north of Artesia. It sounds almost tornado-like. It is interesting that he mentions it at least three times in the diary but apparently failed to photograph the damage. A USDA report on a grasshopper outbreak in 1913 notes, "Throughout the month of June, 1913, the amount of precipitation in New Mexico was greatly in excess of normal" (Smith, 1915). Also, an extreme precipitation event has been recorded for Fort Union, New Mexico, on June 6, 1913. Fort Union is 100–150 miles north of the area where Ligon reported storm damage, but cyclonic extreme precipitation events such as the one reported can cover relatively large areas. Based upon the Fort Union record, Ligon was observing damage that had occurred two weeks earlier.[39]

The present-day highway leaves the Peñasco River and climbs onto the upland to the north where New Mexico State Highway 130 from Dunken comes in. This is probably the route followed by Ligon. Twelve miles west of Hope places his camp near the junction of US Highway 82 and New Mexico State Highway 13. In his travels from Cloudcroft to Hope, Ligon says nothing of ranches along the Peñasco River and its tributaries, but by 1913, as noted by pioneer Will Parker (2001), the area was widely settled. Goats were a major form of livestock at the time, along with cattle. Parker notes that around 1900, the Peñasco River was settled from the road to Piñion to the head of the river. Ranches were diversified with sheep, goats, and cattle. Potatoes were grown on farms at higher elevations. Lumber was hauled from Weed to Roswell, and produce to El Paso, Roswell, and Eddie (now Carlsbad). Parker notes that the Sacramento Mountains were heavily settled at high elevations. Potatoes and apples were common crops. He writes of wolves, trappers, and houndsmen in this area and notes that a $25 bounty was paid by the state on wolves. Parker writes of a large flood in July 1910 that destroyed their farm near Mayhill, but does not mention the 1913 storm. He says little of the years 1912–1913 and does not mention statehood.

[from the diary]
June 21st—Saturday

Coming east from the Summit of the Sacramento Mts. the country, from Mayhill, where the Mts. are rather high and rough, gradually levels until, at the YO Crossing on the Penasco, it has reached the stage of a rolling country, and at Hope, 15 ms. East, is level prairie, and extends on to Artesia, 21 ms. East. This prairie country contains some grease wood, "soap-weeds", and Tabosa and Gramma grass. I am surprised to find no White Neck Raven, It being rare that I note them (three since I crossed to the East side of the Sacramento Mts.)

Horned Lark very abundant from Hope to Artesia. Meadow Lark rather abundant in the same district. Prairie Dogs in very scattered towns.

In a report written for the USBS in 1918, when Ligon was supervising federal hunters and trappers, he noted, "Such reports as I received indicate that there are no antelopes in the Pecos Valley proper, but that there are some south and southwest of Dunlap, twenty five or thirty miles west of the river. Much of the country has been 'homesteaded'—but is now deserted. The homesteader could not withstand the repeated drouths; but he stayed long enough to kill out the antelopes."

In *Wildlife of New Mexico* (1927), Ligon shows pronghorns present north of Hope by 1929. This prairie is now sparsely settled and has a scattering of oil wells, which increase in density eastward from Artesia. Ligon's observations documented the failure of homesteading.

Pecos Valley–Artesia to Carlsbad

[from the diary]
June 22nd—Sunday

I come in near Artesia, get pasture to put my pack animals in, and in P.M. Start down River to look over Resivoirs. go horse back. Lay out on saddle blanket near Lakewood.

Scaled Quail, Red wing, Meadow lark, Burrowing Owl, Western Night hawk, and Horned Lark common.

Cotton-tail and Jack Rabbit common. some Prairie Dog. No Raven to be seen

June 23rd—Monday

I stop see game Warden, and other game observers at at [*sic*] Lake wood Station, which is West of the principal Resivoir of the Carlsbad Irrigation project. I learn from the Gentlemen here that, at present there are no Bob White near, Altho' before the heavy snows of six years ago, there was several bunches near the town. I am told few survived that winter, when the snow lay so long here. I also visit the Resivoir. See but three ducks, and they are wanderers. See one Great Blue Heron, also at upper Lake. At lower lake, nothing but a few Coot Kildeer and some Red wing. Western night hawk abundant. go in to Carlsbad get my mail, and start back on west side of river lay out on saddle blanket. Hot days.

[from the breeding bird report]

—Carlsbad a bird town—

It is surprising to see the great abundance of birds in the city of Carlsbad. Drawn here by the vast number of trees. The trees are alive with birds as well as the Alfalfa and Truck-patches in and near the town. Here is a fair example of Cultivation and Civilization aiding and attracting birds.—

I wonder if prairie dogs can be found along this route today. This area is now heavily settled and farmed until one reaches the Brantley Lake Wildlife Area and State Park. Ravens are common, although I'm not sure which species is present. Perhaps both.

As noted, Ligon received a letter dated June 17 from E. W. Nelson of the USBS in Carlsbad, which criticized his labeling of specimens. In it, Nelson also notes, "There are no topographical maps available for the country you were working in recently," suggesting that the USBS was providing Ligon with maps where they were available.

The office of the game and fish warden for New Mexico was established by a legislative act in 1903. In 1912, the Game and Fish Department was created, and the state game warden was appointed its head.[40] Federal game wardens were first paid by the USBS in 1909. Prior to that, volunteer wardens had existed. By 1913, state wardens were commissioned as federal wardens as well. Ligon does not say who the game warden was at Lakewood Station, nor does he disclose who the other "game observers" were, although this suggests that they were known and were corresponding with the Smithsonian or USBS, if not with Ligon.

According to Julyan (1998), Lakewood was initially named McMillan

Siding after Lake McMillan. It was also called White Town. In 1904, it became Lakewood. McMillan and Avalon dams were built in 1893 for irrigation and flood control. McMillan reservoir was named for W. H. McMillan, who helped organize the Pecos Valley Land and Ditch Company. Ninety years later, Brantley Dam was constructed and McMillan Dam breached. The new dam and lake were named for Draper Brantley, a farmer in the Carlsbad area. The lower end of Brantley Lake is now a popular recreational area administered by New Mexico State Parks, and the upper end is a wildlife management area managed by the New Mexico Department of Game and Fish. Hunting is allowed in the latter area.

Most of the lakes in southeastern New Mexico are wintering areas for waterfowl, and Ligon was visiting them at a time when most of the waterfowl were farther north. A brochure provided by Brantley Lake State Park lists 104 bird species for the area, but does not show season of use or breeding status. The list shows bobwhite quail present, so they have apparently returned. It also shows white-winged doves, unmentioned by Ligon in 1913 or 1927. He mentioned them only as occasional in Carlsbad by 1961. They have since expanded their range northward along most of the rivers of the state. An even newer arrival to the area is the non-native collared dove.

Ligon does not mention mammals in this area, but the state park's 2008 brochure listed twenty-six wild mammalian species, including pronghorn, mule deer, white-tailed jackrabbit (an error—only black-tailed jacks exist here), and six species of bats. It also shows thirteen snakes, including four rattlesnake species, ten lizard species, six toads, and one salamander.

Other than humans, the most conspicuous newcomer to the Pecos River valley, as well as to all other Southwestern river valleys, since 1913 is saltcedar. All land management agencies administering lands along the river include saltcedar control in their management plans, but they seem to be losing the battle. Saltcedar transpires enough water to lower water tables, and dense thickets of saltcedar will burn explosively, killing cottonwoods and willows and eliminating the native deciduous riparian communities. Saltcedar grows back quickly after a fire.

Saltcedar does not show up in any of Ligon's 1900 photographs taken during his float trip on the lower Pecos River, and he does not mention it on the Rio Grande or the Pecos in 1913. According to de Gouvenain (1996), saltcedar was introduced into the United States during the early 1800s. It was well established along the Colorado, Gila, Rio Grande, and Pecos rivers by the 1940s. In 1996, saltcedar covered 28,000 acres along the Pecos in New Mexico, reducing cottonwood germination and displacing native plants, reducing numbers of native birds and reptiles, and increasing frequency of fires in riparian areas (Lovich, 1996).

Suitability of saltcedar as wildlife habitat has been a subject of debate (Hildebrandt and Ohmart, 1982; Glinski and Ohmart, 1983; B. Brown and Trosset, 1989; Rosenberg et al., 1991). According to Livingston and Schemnitz (1996), the middle Pecos lacked a substantial woodland community prior to saltcedar invasion. Cottonwood galleries were historically narrow and localized stands adjacent to the river, with surrounding native vegetation primarily Chihuahuan grassland and shrub. Mourning and white-winged doves, Mississippi kites, and several passerine birds now use saltcedar for nesting, roosting, and protective cover on the middle Pecos River (Hunter et al., 1988). Livingston found forty-nine bird species using saltcedar along the Pecos. Positively associated with saltcedar were yellow-billed cuckoo, yellow-breasted chats, and spotted towhees. Birds that avoided it included Cassin's sparrows, lark sparrows, and meadowlarks. The endangered southwestern willow flycatcher uses it for nesting habitat at younger growth stages. Honeybees gather the nectar, which yields honey that, while tasty, is dark and viscous, resembling crankcase oil (Hunter et al., 1988). Mature saltcedar makes excellent firewood.

In general, dense stands of saltcedar are not used by small mammals. I became aware of this as a student working summers for the Arizona Game and Fish Department. I and another student spent portions of July and August from 1957–1959 crawling through mature saltcedar stands along the Gila River between Phoenix and Buckeye. Our task was to estimate the density of dove nests in saltcedar stands. We did this by following compass lines (as best we could), locating active nests, mostly white-winged doves, and recording them in a way that allowed us to estimate the number of nests per acre and the numbers of young produced. Much of the time we were on our hands and knees, sweating in the 100^{+}-degree heat and accumulating dust and needles from the trees, as well as copious cicada excrement emitted in tiny bursts from the tree canopies. We cooled and rinsed ourselves any time we passed a farmer's irrigation pump, and fortunately, we were lodged at a bunkhouse where we could shower at the end of the day. The water in the area, however, carried a generous solution of alkali, so as we dried, we were covered with a white crust.

We were extremely wary early in our work, knowing that desert diamondbacks and sidewinders were abundant in this part of Arizona, but we soon realized that few snakes hung out in the saltcedar thickets. Nothing was on the ground to feed them. We often found tree-climbing western king snakes coiled up around the dove nests, with the tiny bulges of baby doves along their bodies. But these were the only snakes we encountered. We later surveyed dove nests in the bosques of large, old-growth mesquite near the confluence of the Salt and Gila rivers, where we quickly realized that circumstances were different. The mesquites provided beans, and their more open canopies allowed a grass and forb understory which attracted small mammals. Here, our surveys would occasionally be interrupted by the loud buzz of a rattler, some of them coiled diamondbacks that looked like they would fill a washtub. Usually we had to freeze until we could locate the alarmed snake, because their warnings so filled the air under the mesquite canopy that we could not get a directional fix on them. Our greatest fear on those days was that we might find ourselves face to face with one of these behemoths entwined in the crotch of a large mesquite. However, they were invariably kind enough to buzz when we were still eight or ten feet from them, allowing us to circumnavigate.

Although lacking rodents, the saltcedar held high densities of dove nests. Mourning doves tended to use the younger stands along the edge of the thickets, while white-winged doves preferred the larger and older trees near the river channel. These larger trees had advanced to the stage that they were forming a single, central trunk, perhaps eight to ten inches in diameter, along with large limbs branching from it. Such tree forms provided nesting sites that white-winged doves found more acceptable (Shaw, 1961).

[from the diary]
June 24th—Tuesday

I inspect the river and Valley above the Flume. See several Texas night hawk, hear them flooting.

See three bunches of young Scaled Quail, mostly old birds. No sign of Bob White.

Kildeer abundant every place. Cliff swallow nesting beneath arches under flume.

Spend several hours at lake 4 ms. S.W. of Lakewood, this lake is formed by a spring that comes out just west.

Red wing and Coot nesting. If protected in early spring, would likely be attractive to ducks.

Fearful hot days.

[from the breeding bird report]

CARLSBAD RESIVOIRS

June 23rd and 24th Pecos Valley

I learn from the keepers of the two Resivoirs above Carlsbad, that there are very few water fowl about the Lakes in Summer. These

Gentlemen are both Federal Game Wardens. Prior to my visit, the Resivoirs were low, but the recent heavy rains have put the water to going around the Spillways, for the reason that these changes are so sudden and extensive. Water fowl can not successfully breed here.

I observe a few Coot, and Red wing black-bird, also quite a lot of Great Blue Heron. I see a few straggling ducks also.

My observation, coupled with information given me by the Resivoir Tendants is: The Resivoirs will never be a success as breeding sights for water bird. Owing to the sudden rise and fall of the water, the "irregularity of the shore-line. Kildeer nest, as they usually seek high ground, also marsh birds overcome some of the disadvantage.

[from the breeding bird report]

SEVEN RIVERS VALLEY

June 24th = 4 ms. S.W. of Lakewood.

Four miles South-west of Lakewood Station, in the Valley of the Seven Rivers. Is a small Lake, surrounded by marshes, the Lake is fed by springs that rise about a quarter, to the North-West.

This lake at present covers, I judge, 10 acres, and is filled with very rank Tula Grass, 10 feet high and over.

I find Red Wing black-bird here, in great abundance, breeding. Also about 20 Coot, some of these breeding. Meadow Lark and Yellow-throat also common.

This lake is supplied with fairly good water, and if protected in early spring, no doubt would be a favorite breeding site. There were no duck at all, when I visited the Lake.

I was told by hunters at Lakewood, that ducks do not breed in the vicinity.

The lakes Ligon inspected, except for Lake Avalon downriver, are now covered by Brantley Reservoir, as is the town of Seven Rivers, which played a role in the Lincoln County War and became notorious as an outlaw hangout.

Ligon perhaps had unrealistic expectations for the lakes in southern New Mexico, which are outside of the nesting range for many waterfowl species. Nonetheless, his observation that the varying level of the reservoirs limited nesting was valid. On the Bosque del Apache National Wildlife Refuge, southeast of Socorro, New Mexico, where water levels are maintained for nesting waterfowl and food species planted, the US Fish and Wildlife Service lists thirteen duck and goose species and twenty shorebird species that now nest in the area. Undoubtedly the Bitter Lake National Wildlife Refuge on the Pecos River near Roswell now has a similar array of nesting species. Many of these probably did not find much suitable nesting habitat along the Pecos River in 1913.

In these summaries, Ligon displays an awareness of the importance of habitat that places him perhaps ahead of his time. Biologists wandering the Southwest through the 1800s were interested almost exclusively in documenting new species. While distribution was of interest, they seldom wrote of specific habitat needs. Even as late as 1929, Florence Merriam Bailey, in *Birds of New Mexico*, does not use the word "habitat" in her writings or describe the finer details of habitat selection by species except, perhaps, for nest sites. Ligon, I believe, was among the earliest to use the word habitat in the sense we use it now—the vegetation, water, and space complex that satisfy the needs of a species—and he clearly discusses habitat restoration and management by 1927 in his *Wildlife of New Mexico*. Even Aldo Leopold, the father of modern wildlife management, failed to use the term in his 1933 textbook, *Game Management*, and discusses the needs of wildlife in a more general and somewhat agricultural framework.

According to the *Oxford English Dictionary*, the word had been used as early as 1762 to denote the locality in which a plant naturally grows. That the concept would be developed first for plants makes sense because, not moving, they are more easily recognized to have specific growth requirements. Elliot Coues used the word extensively in 1874, where he mentioned races of birds interbreeding where their habitats adjoined, as well as applying it to the needs of particular species (Coues, 1874). Caton (1877) used the word in its appropriate context for deer species as early as 1877, perhaps the first application to mammals. Ligon was probably more attuned to the literature of birds than to other natural history subjects. However, his sensitivity to habitat requirements was probably a result of knowledge acquired while growing up in the distinctly segregated riparian and desert landscapes of the middle Pecos Valley and his later wanderings through the Southwest.

Pecos Valley–Artesia to Santa Rosa

[from the diary]
June 25th—Wednesday

Insects a terrible pest.

Red wing and Meadow-lark common about the fields all up the valley. Much complaint about English Sparrows being injurious to fruit and garden truck. I am told by some, that ducks also do damage in fall, also black birds to the maize (milo maize) and Kaffir heads.

Stop for a while and investigate Clark Lake, 5 ms. South West from Lake Arthur. Perhaps 100 duck and coot here. No indication of duck nesting

Red wing very abundant, I find perhaps 25 nests, (new) one to four eggs, and the grass full of young. See first Pr. ______ Stilt, they two, breeding. Doves nesting on the broken over water grass. Camp north of Cotton wood creek, and mass of mosquitoes.

Ligon is headed back north now, passing Artesia.

[from the breeding bird report]

—CLARK LAKE—

June 25th 5 ms. S.W. Lake Arthur

This lake, which covers now, about 20 acres, is protected, more for the fish, than birds. The lake is almost round with thick Tula Grass all around west side, and also on the South. The lake has lately been drained down 4 feet, by a ditch being cut out. The lake is fed by artesian Springs that come up in the bottom and to the sides.

It is certainly gratifying to see the water birds here. Their presence being accounted for by the protection given the Lake. Otherwise the duck would not be here, as the main traveled road passes at its edge.

There are now, perhaps 75 duck, and 25 coot.

2 Pair of Black-neck Stilt nesting.

Coots nesting sparingly.

Red-Wing Black bird breeding in profusion, laying second sets I am convinced, as the grass is full of young birds, and in a few minutes time I find five nests 1 to 4 fresh eggs, many new nests half completed.

Kildeer abundant, nesting in the short stubby salt grass. 1 nest 4 eggs.

Dove nesting on the dry, broken-over Tula grass, many.

Here, I see too, the first gull that I have observed, 2 flying about over the Lake.

Many Yellow-throat and Meadow Lark.

I found no duck nests. The ducks were well bunched near center of the lake and did not seem to be wild.

Later—since I have found duck breeding the last of July, fresh eggs, in the Jicarilla Apache Indian Reservation. I feel confident that the ducks, some of them, are breeding since my visit to Clarke Lake.

> If permanently protected, I believe this small lake would be a great breeding ground, and I am quite sure its owner could be induced to protect it.

Here we get an insight into how Ligon worked. He was making entries in the report as he traveled but went back later and made additional entries, given space, as he gained perspective in other areas.

[from the breeding bird report]

PECOS VALLEY

> No doubt, at time passed, the Pecos Valley of New Mexico was a great breeding place for water bird; but that time has long been passed, for where the water can reasonably be used for irrigation purposes, it is utilized, and the valley to-day is, most places thickly settled, and cultivated in farms and orchards.
>
> Lakes and Sloughs are abundant, especially in rainy seasons.
>
> West of the river the country slopes rapidly toward the River Valley, while East toward and including the Staked Plains, there is very little, general fall, and among the sand hills and on the plains are wet-weather lakes that, to-day, afford better advantages to birds than the valley, especially, the Shore Birds. In this country, I know Duck, Curlew, Plover, Avocet, Stilt, and snipe to breed, but on my present round, it was impossible for me to visit this district. The Pecos Valley, where cultivation has been carried on for any length of time, and trees have grown to good size; has given the Song birds ample room for breeding and they have certainly taken advantage of these introduced conditions. Many are abundant that prior to the planting of trees, had few favorable breeding places in the tree-less valley.
>
> Today, cuckoo, Flycatchers, and Sparrows are abundant. I am sorry to say that the English Sparrow is far in excess in numbers, and reported to do very much damage to fruit and truck, while the House Finch, is almost as abundant, and is equally as destructive, and these two Pest, among the general public, cause all birds to be more or less condemned.
>
> I even meet many in the valley who argue that the ducks do a great deal of damage in the fall, to crops, and that they are a great detriment, and should not be protected. People, generally, in the South West, are ignorant, as to the value, and necessity of the birds and give them no credit for the vast good, and aid they give the farmer. Insects are a great pest in the Pecos Valley, and if the birds were exterminated, we should see a great increase in these pests. The Red-wing Black-bird and also the Meadow Lark, are abundant throughout the

farming districts of the valley, and it is hard to estimate the value these two species, alone, are to the farmers. They are to be seen in every meadow and Swamp, and through the Alfalfa fields. The King bird is another very, very abundant bird in the valley, and is a good insect harvester, And so is the Western Night hawk, and it too is to be seen every place.

The above essay is one of Ligon's more perceptive early reports. He is drawing on past experience as much or more than observations made during the 1913 survey.

[from the diary]
June 26th—Thursday

Little of interest along my route, Prairie Country. Prairie Dog com. In P.M. Reach the Alfalfa district of Dexter. Many Artesian wells.

June 27th—Friday

Pass west of Roswell, go around North Spring River, drop back to North East, Bitter Lake, and others. See two Prs. Stilt, not breeding, some wandering ducks. Much water, many lakes, but bad water.

See first rattle snake of my trip, below R. R. bridge, N.E. of Roswell.

While Ligon says he passed west of Roswell, he somehow managed to mail a letter there, dated June 26, to Nelson.[41] It is worth quoting in its entirety:

Replying to your letter of June 17th that I received while at Carlsbad three days ago. I will give you a brief outline of my round since leaving the Tula Rosa Valley.

I came over the Sacramento Mts. By way of Cloudcroft, and down the Penasco river, hit the Pecos at Artesia. I found Red wings at a few places on the Penasco, and quite a lot of yellowthroat, but no water fowl.

I went down on the East side of the Pecos from Lakewood, having left my pack animals at Artesia. Visited both resivoirs above Carlsbad, got all information possible, then from Carlsbad I came back on West side of the river. I found in this district, very few water birds, there being scarcely any on any of the big Reservoirs. And I will state here: My observations, connected with information received from the National

> Wardens at these places, as well as opinions of theirs interested. The storage resivoirs will be, and are, places of refuge and feeding grounds, but of little value as nesting sights, owing to the irregularity of the shore line. The resivoirs have been rather low, but a few days before my arrival, there was quite a flood over the valley, and the water was passing over the spillways, indicating what sudden and extensive rises the lakes are subjected to.
>
> South-west of Lakewood four miles is a lake and marsh. Here I found coot and redwing breeding, the latter abundantly but no duck.
>
> Five miles South-west of Lake Arthur Station, just yesterday, I came up with my first gull and snipe.—also coot and duck-blue wing teal principally. This at Clark's Lake. I could find no evidence that the duck were breeding, further than I found one egg, just back from the lake shore.
>
> I shall next investigate the lakes about Roswell, then work up the river to Santa Rosa, which will be my next mail station.
>
> Owing to the heavy rains, and insect pests, and the terrible hot weather in this valley, my progress has been a little slow, and disagreeable at times, but all considered, I think I am doing about as well as I could expect. I will send in some more bird skins in a few days.
>
> As to the labels being incomplete on the birds I sent in, I had no instructions at the time as to the way the Department required them filled. I have always, in individual work, filled them according to your instructions.
>
> I shall be glad to carry on the work thro next month; but not longer at present, as I have a little individual field work I desire to do down in Arizona.
>
> I am expecting to run up with many of the water birds, in the valley above Roswell.
>
> I have no instructions beyond Santa Rosa, and your mere reference that I would go to the northern part of the state.

Several places in his diary or report, Ligon prefaces his entry with "I will state here" to announce that what follows is a generalization, conclusion, or even hypothesis, informing the reader that he is moving beyond simple observation and submitting an opinion.

For a newly assigned assistant, Ligon sounds somewhat testy and independent. Seemingly, the problem in labeling stemmed from the fact that specimens he was collecting were the legal property of the USBS and required a different numbering system. His reference to past "individual" work is evidence that he had been sending specimens to the USBS before he was put on the payroll, no doubt being paid by the specimen. Ligon makes it clear that he considers himself a free agent and has work of his own that he feels is important. The intended Arizona work relates to his desire to try to locate masked bobwhites. He is also a little brusque in pointing out to Nelson that his instructions regarding where to go in northern New Mexico are incomplete.

I wonder if Roswell was located right on the Pecos River at the time and has moved westward. Going west of Roswell today would require a rather lengthy circle. The Bitter Lake area is now a national wildlife refuge, managed for waterfowl. I visited it on March 7, 2008, and saw pintails, mallards, ruddies, buffleheads, and an egret (greater?). I heard sandhill cranes. In March, I would be seeing wintering birds along with, perhaps, some resting migrants heading north.

[from the diary]
June 28th—Saturday

Go up river to mouth of Salt Creek, where I find many lakes and marshes. Find Black Neck Stilt nesting. See several Great Blue Heron, Probably nesting west of River in cotton-wood that grow along the river (scattered) here. Cliff Swallows abundant. Go up Salt Creek five ms. to bridge and Ft. Sumner road. Blue Wing Teal breeding below bridge. Many lakes freshly filled, north of Salt Creek, ducks, but only wandering bands. Prairie dog abundant.

I suspect present-day US Highway 285 follows approximately the old Fort Sumner road. In passing through this country, I followed this highway, hence traveled several miles west of the Pecos River. Seemingly, Ligon did the same for several miles. I saw no prairie dogs.

[from the breeding bird report]

SALT CREEK

June 28th—18 ms. North and north-East of Roswell—

Although, near its mouth, where it reaches the Pecos River, Salt Creek, contains very bad water. It is quite a water and marsh bird district.

North of the channel to the creek is a vast Swampy, Tula Flat, fed by springs that rise back against the foot-hills. This water forms several lakes and sloughs, thickly overgrown, with rank water grass. Here I find but very few ducks, but with some indication that they are nesting. Black neck Stilt nesting in the valley above where the small, salty lakes have barren shores. Red wing blackbird, Yellow throat, and Kildeer nesting, also Marsh Hawk [Cooper's written first and crossed out] in the rank grass. Cliff Swallows abundant, no doubt nesting in the cliffs East of the river. Also Western night-Hawk very abundant. I traveled out the creek for several miles, to where the most of the water comes up in artesian springs. There must have been an overflow previous to my visit, and I find that high water destroyed most of the nests, eggs, and young-birds, hence the birds were rebuilding and laying the second nests. Duck rare.

North of Salt Creek, I find several large, wet-weather lakes, filled by the recent rains. Quite a lot of Ducks. Stragglers, floating about over them. But at this date June 29th no sign of nesting—still some of them are apt to nest later.

[from the diary]
June 29th—Sunday

I am on the road early. fine grass. Lakes play out. I strike trail of hail storm. Carcasses of Jack rabbit and cotton-tail, every where, killed by hail stones. By the absence of bird life, they have surely suffered too.

In P.M. I meet a deluge of rain, that wets some of my outfit. Make my bed for night on bed of mesquite brush. and thanks to a few little limbs and roots of mesquite that makes it possible to boil coffee. Road leads over rolling hills, a monotenous stretch of land. No cattle, occasionally a few sheep.

Horned lark and Meadow Lark common after leaving hail trail.

This is the first rain I have experienced this year

Heavy hail at this time of year is certainly an unusual phenomenon, and I have to wonder if Ligon isn't following the track of a tornado. He must have had a good pad to put between himself and the mesquite brush. Not many plants have sharper spines.

[from the diary]
June 30th—Monday

Very hot and Sultry in early morning. I find breeding Curlew.

Road muddy late when I pack up and break camp. Kill big rattle snake, country changes slightly more prairie. Fine grass. Jack rabbits abundant. Count 12 at once in old sink, also cotton-tail abundant.

Grass better in P.M. Many varieties—gramma, mesquite, needle, tabosa, burro, and others. In late, P.M. I strike rolling sandy country. Many "squats" land holders about but none show prosperity. Mosquitoes and little black ants bad. Hardly enough wood to kindle a fire.

Ligon is passing through stabilized sand dunes here. His comment about lack of wood is interesting—these dunes are now covered by low-growing mesquite.

[from the diary]
July 1st—Tuesday

Heavy dew. 8 ms. to Ft. Sumner. I foard river below town, (no bridge here) it almost gets me down, as it is up. Stop in cotton wood below the town. Find Red head woodpeckers here, a surprise to me. I write some and send of[f] bird skins.

Leave for Santa Rosa in late P.M. beautiful prairie country for a ways, carpeted with green mesquite grass. Camp 8 ms. out. 40 ms to Santa Rosa.

Ligon camped in the vicinity of Bosque Redondo but mentions nothing of the history of this site, which had been an Indian campground long before gringo arrival. Both Spanish explorers Francisco Vásquez de Coronado and Antonio de Espejo may have used it, but it attained infamy in 1863, when Kit Carson, under the orders of Major James H. Carleton, forced six hundred Apaches and seven thousand starving Navajos to settle the area (Julyan, 1998). Both tribes suffered hardship and severely damaged the environment over a four-year period. The Apaches fled the area and resumed raiding; the Navajos pledged peace and were allowed to return to their homeland. Such high human densities must have left impacts on the area that would have still been visible when Ligon passed.

A stand of large, old cottonwoods exists along this reach of the Pecos River today, as do irrigated farmlands. I saw a field full of feeding long-billed curlews on April 6, 2008. Ligon passed west of the river, in the prairie, probably near the present highway route and in the vicinity of Sumner Lake. Ligon seems to be more competent in his identification of grasses than he was earlier in naming shrubs in the Tularosa basin.

[from the diary]
July 2nd—Wednesday

I get on the road fairly early. Hot in early A.M. beautiful prairie country, low abrupt rim on East side, Pecos River several miles West and much lower. About out of prairie dog country. Many rabbits. See new wood pecker's (2) in Alamogordo creek.—

Young sparrow hawks and Western Horned owl on Arroyo San Juan, where noon. Horned lark very abundant. One nest with three very small birds. Many Meadow Lark, Western Night hawk, not so common as below. Visit rain water Lake, 16 ms. S.W. Santa Rosa, Some duck and coot, none nesting. Strike an other new bird—

On big prairie East of Puerto de Luna, rather abundant, Males singing, rising and as they come down to ground sing. 35 ms. to-day. Fine day, S.E. wind.

Alamogordo Creek is one of the main tributaries entering present-day Lake Sumner. Ligon is following the approximate route of US Highway 84. His statement that he is leaving prairie dog country reflects the changing terrain, rather an unusual way to acknowledge it. He is climbing now into a rockier and juniper-covered country, with a mixture of mesquite. The Pecos River is running through more of a gorge and becoming more of a mountain stream.

I'm not sure where this rainwater lake is, but it is probably on a private ranch. His comment on "striking" another new bird is confusing. The following paragraph seems to apply to it, and the behavior he describes is that of male horned larks, yet he has been recording horned larks all along the way. He may have been seeing lark buntings here.

Throughout this stretch, Ligon is mainly covering dry country, with the lakes around Santa Rosa his next wetland area to be visited. His observations are pretty limited.

[from the diary]
July 3rd—Thursday

I pack up and come in to Santa Rosa (5 ms.) early, Get mail. Camp on river above R. R. bridge, talk with Mr. Thurston—Game Warden, and others about breeding birds. None of them know of breeding Duck in country about. I visit Lakes, West side of River, S.W. of town, In P.M. Coot fairly common in two lakes. Find some of their old nests, made of wild water flag blades, and floating, but no new nests or young, tho' I wade and search thro' the marshes. See three duck on these lake, one Blue Wing Teal acted as if it had nest.

Country has Changed Character. River has quite a Gorge below and above the town, Broken country about, cut by abrupt canyons, Hills covered with cedar and Pinion.

Hot day, with Hot S.W. wind. First hot wind of season

Here, Ligon must be visiting Blue Hole and Rock Lakes, and possibly also Hidden Lake. He is definitely entering foothills country.

[from the diary]
July 4th—Friday

I, guided by two boys visit Artesian lakes South East of Santa Rosa, In A.M. Observe 9 coot at "Twin Lakes, a very deep lake (as it is one now) located in sink, water stocked with fish, boat in lake and much visiting, as it is near public road. A few red-wing, no other birds.

In P.M. I move about 5 ms. up the river, follow out road, East side, and then drop back on bluff over the Gorge. Cotton-tail very abundant here.

Cliff Swallows nesting.

Prairie Falcon and many Turkey Vulture.

No sign of water fowl on river. It is just getting back normal after about 10 ft. rise several days ago.

I visited the Santa Rosa vicinity on July 16–17, 2009, trying to locate the lake Ligon had photographed. The lakes near town, with the exception of Blue Hole, are on private property, and access to them is restricted. I was able to gain access to Hidden Lake, but it does not match Ligon's photograph. Ligon probably photographed Twin Lakes, probably from the boat he mentions. The entire area is densely urbanized and fenced.

Ligon camped near present-day Santa Rosa Reservoir, which is now a heavily used recreational area administered by New Mexico State Parks. I spent a Thursday night camped at one of their developed campsites and was kept awake well into the night by prowling vehicles. By morning, perhaps half of the available campsites were occupied, and a large troop of Boy Scouts had commandeered the primitive camping area. Many of the campers had large boats or skidoos and were preparing for a weekend of play. No doubt this reservoir is used by migrating waterfowl during the fall and winter for resting and feeding. I doubt that it provides much nesting habitat with all of the summer disturbance by recreationists and the fluctuating shoreline as water is drawn off for irrigation.

[from the diary]
July 5th—Saturday

I make round out in valleys, to East to get on to River above. See two Cowboys, that ride this range, they tell me no duck breed in the country. I strike river below Hick's farm. Lookout cottonwood groves below. No more Red Head Wood-pecker here.

Sparrow hawk has young in hole high in cotton-wood. I see parent bird bring in Stripped Lizard.

A lake south of Santa Rosa, New Mexico, 1913

> I foard river above Hick's Farm. Camp still higher up, West side. Insects a pest, especially gnats.
>
> Showers to north. Hot.

Ligon is approaching Colonias. I'm not sure where Hick's farm might have been.

> [from the diary]
> July 6th—Sunday
>
> I move out of River valley to S.W. edge of rolling plains country. Camp near small tank in a draw. Many Horned Lark—Montizuma. Find two nests. Make quite a study of their habits. The birds undoubtly rear two broods in a season, and I find that the male shares incubation with fm's.
>
> Weather fearfully hot.

In *Birds of New Mexico* (1928), Florence Merriam Bailey considers the horned lark summering in central New Mexico to be the Montezuma subspecies. However, she does not show this subspecies in her *Handbook of Birds of the Western United States* (1902), so Ligon used another source for some of his names. He may by this time have received a copy of the American Ornithologists' Union Check-list of North American Birds.

[from the diary]
July 7th—Monday

I stir out early, cover my camp, go on my horse to Santa Rosa for my mail. Get instructions to proceed to the Jicarilla Indian Reservation to study the breeding Bird there. See breeding Long billed curlew near road, also Horned Lark very abundant.

I reach my camp at sun-down. Find my pack animals near and camp unharmed. Very hot sultry weather.

Seemingly, Ligon's burros routinely ran free around his camp. It is interesting to me that he could have ridden Red away from camp without them following him. Yet they did not wander away. I wonder what harm Ligon feared for his camp. Possibly his own burros seeking food? Or range cattle? Or humans?

In Santa Rosa, Ligon received confirmation of his second appointment, for the month of July. Along with it came a letter from E. W. Nelson with more detailed instructions:[42]

From your letter of June 26th you appear to have covered the country pretty well in the section you are working in. The work we wish you to do during the month of July is to proceed from Santa Rosa to the Stinking Springs, La Jara and all other lakes on the Jicarilla Indian Reservation, Rio Arriba County, New Mexico, to ascertain the breeding birds there. Of course, the water fowl are the ones we wish especially to know about but all others are important. I see by the railroad maps that you can proceed from Santa Rosa direct to Santa Fe, and thence north from Santa Fe to Conejos, Colorado, and thence west and south by rail to the immediate vicinity of Stinking Lake where it will be best for you to begin work. I trust that you will be able to get into this country at once and have time during July to visit all of the lakes in that section and make a good thorough job of determining the bird life there. You should secure a lot of extremely interesting records and spend all of July in this Lake country.

I wrote you recently to Carlsbad and if you have not received the letter I would suggest that you have it forwarded from the postoffice there.

Please send in specimens of red-winged blackbirds as well as anything else of interest.

Ligon had paused near Santa Rosa for the mail extending his appointment. He immediately replied to Nelson and also sent a short confirmation of receiving his extension to Henshaw. To Nelson, he writes:[43]

> According to the tone of your letter, you do not understand my mode of travel. I have saddle horse and pack outfit as suggested by Mr. Vernon Bailey. My outfit is now twelve miles north west of here. So I presume it will be satisfactory for me to go on with the present conveyance. Since it is so much better to have my own outfit, to move at liberty, and since there is so many Rail Road changes and delays. I really gain time when once on the ground.
>
> I shall designate
> Lumberton
> N. Mex.,
> As my next Post office, and I can have it changed when I once get there if desired.
>
> Mr. Nelson, I wish you would please send me another bottle of ink to use in making my report. The stopper came out of the bottle I had, while traveling, and I lost my ink. I have ink but not of the best quality.
>
> I find very few water fowl in this district, many artesian lakes, and some marshes, few water bird breeding.
>
> Your letters to Carlsbad have all been received—forwarded here.
>
> I sent some specimens from Ft. Sumner. Will send others soon.
>
> I shall search out the new territory and do my very best to see all.

The difficulties in communicating become apparent here. Ligon had received Nelson's letter of June 17 and responded to it. Apparently, a second letter was mailed to Carlsbad, but it is not in the files. This may have been the mail from Engle finally catching up. Ligon's writing style actually improves in this letter. Perhaps the ongoing communication between him and his supervisors at the Smithsonian is taking effect.

Ligon's discussion with Nelson regarding his mode of travel does not end here. In April 1914, after Ligon has been hired to survey prairie dogs in northeastern Arizona, he writes to Nelson:[44]

> I wrote you in my letter about having two pack burros that I much preferred to the horse. Of course I would not let this little matter interfere with an agreement, but as I said, these burros have advantages over horses. I have been training these . . . time on the road, and for several reasons, I prefer these to a single pack horse. The two burros will carry much more, and do the work on less feed than one horse, they always stay near camp, and since I drive, in the place of lead them, they are

much less trouble in this respect. One pack animal cannot carry all the camp material one needs on a trip especially when supply points are so far between. I much prefer this, to two horses if it is satisfactory to you people.

In a letter dated July 11, mailed to Lumberton, Nelson confirms the above letter, concurs with Ligon's decision to stay with the pack animals instead of going by train, and acknowledges mailing a bottle of ink.

[from the breeding bird report]

—Artesian Lakes—

July 3rd to 7th near Santa Rosa

My next destination, as given by the Department, was the Artesian Lakes near Santa Rosa, In the Pecos Valley. I will state at the outset, these lakes are too near Santa Rosa for the good of the water Fowl.

The Principle Lakes on the East side of the River, Lie South-East of Santa Rosa, ½ to 1½ miles and are:

Twin Lakes. One on each side of the road a mile and a half from Santa Rosa. Very deep. Contain fish. Much fishing done. The two cover several acres. Observed many coot, none nesting. No ducks.

Black Lake, just North of Twin Lakes. No outlet, very deep, mostly surrounded by high cliffs. Covers perhaps 4 acres. No birds except Cliff Swallows, and a few Red-wing, both breeding.

Blue Hole, about ¾ mile East and a little South of Santa Rosa quite a stream flows out, half Surrounded by cliffs. Gyp water, but no disagreeable taste, almost round, perhaps 100 feet across. 97 feet deep, when the wind is not blowing the bottom of the hole is visible, provided the sun is high up, and shining. Contains no fish. No birds at all. There are many other Salty lakes and marshes about, also springs, but no birds except Red Wing.

—West Side— 3 to 4 miles to South-and South-west of Santa Rosa. Over here are several lakes, and quite a lot of marshy ground I find quite a lot of Duck, one Pr. nesting. Many coot, nesting sparingly. Red-wing abundant. Many Musk Rat.

The lakes have no protection from hunters. If they were protected, the ones to the South-west would be a breeding sight for many duck, I am sure.

Black Lake is probably the one now called Hidden Lake. Ligon's description of the Pecos Valley to this point is rather cursory. However, in

1918, he revisited the valley in a new role as predator control inspector. Although this new job did not require natural history observations, Ligon submitted a nine-page typed report entitled "Natural History Observations, Pecos Valley, New Mexico from June 16th to 21st, 1918."[45] This report draws from the 1913 trip as well as subsequent observations: "That portion of the Pecos Valley in New Mexico that lies between Ft. Sumner and Roswell appears at a glance to hold very little of interest to the naturalist, but in reality it is a region of varied and peculiar interests. My time was too limited by other matters—instructing hunters in predatory animal work—to go into very detailed study of the animals and birds, yet I feel that the observations made are worth recording."

This is the open rolling part of New Mexico—devoid of timber except along the Pecos River and for a distance of one to five miles out in some of the main draws where there are scattered cottonwoods. A stunted growth of mesquite covers most of the country, but there are long stretches of open flats—barren of everything but grass, and even this was lacking at this time. The mesquite grows twelve to thirty inches high, but attains somewhat larger size along the river proper. In the latter location the bunches of brush are larger—often big beds elevated by the collecting of sand.

From Fort Sumner to Roswell the eastern side rises abruptly from the valley. The western side slopes away very gradually toward the Capitan and Gallina mountains and the higher divide country to the north of these mountains. The Capitan Mountains are eighty miles distant from the river and are plainly visible from parts of the country, even at a greater distance.

The elevation ranges from 3,500 feet at Roswell to about 4,000 feet at Fort Sumner, which is a distance of about eighty-five miles. The country is so level and open that there is very little twilight, and in summer there is an almost constant breeze from the southeast. The water is all gyp and not fit to drink.

During my visit, there was desolation over the valley because of the long continued drought, and many of the cattle had been shipped out. A good rain had recently fallen at Fort Sumner, and for a distance of about twenty miles south, there was some short green vegetation. Before this rain there was hardly a vestige of green, and the stock that remained alive on the ranges had subsisted mostly on the small yucca and the salt grass along the water courses. The region was strewn with the skinned carcasses of cattle that had died of starvation.

In places the small yuccas and mesquite bushes were dying, so stubborn had the drought been. The scene was truly one of desolation. There were no indications that any of the wild mammals or birds had died of starvation. Both jackrabbits and cottontails were common, and in most localities extremely abundant. Where there had been no moisture, the rabbits were feeding on the mesquite bushes and yuccas, as well as prickly pears. The prairie dogs were found well distributed over this region west of the Pecos River—but in isolated villages. Bird life was confined in the main to favored localities, although the horned lark—desert dweller that he is—was found in the region generally.

Ligon goes on to provide a list of species for the Pecos Valley, which included a lengthy discussion of bison: "A herd of forty-five buffaloes is kept on the ranch of E. W. and R. E. McKenzie, 16 miles south of Fort Sumner. These are known as the 'Buffalo Jones' animals and were bought by the McKenzie brothers from the Jones estate at Portales, New Mexico. The McKenzie Ranch is of one hundred square miles."

Although bison were native to this part of New Mexico, they had been extirpated by 1860 (Findley et al., 1975). Charles J. "Buffalo" Jones had figured in saving the bison, starting in the 1880s by roping and raising calves. He was appointed game warden of Yellowstone Park in 1901, with the specific job of caring for the newly established bison herd. Jones hoped to make a fortune raising bison-cattle hybrids. In 1908, he established a bison herd north of the Grand Canyon. He died in 1919. We have found no information regarding Jones's estate at Portales or his relationship with the McKenzies, who owned the Hat Ranch in Texas and eastern New Mexico (Easton and Brown, 1961; McHugh, 1972).

At the time Ligon conducted his 1913 survey, bison conservation efforts had been underway for some twenty-five years by William T. Hornaday, Ernest H. Baynes, and Jones, along with many others. Prevention of the extinction of the bison is one of American wildlife conservation's success stories. Some five hundred thousand bison now exist on private ranches and national refuges throughout the United States (Redford et al., 2009), and at least three large ranches in New Mexico, owned by Ted Turner, are dedicated to raising bison. One of Turner's goals is identifying and isolating remaining bison herds untainted by cattle genes as a result of the interbreeding process started by Buffalo Jones and others.

Ligon continues the 1918 report with a discussion of bison behavior and problems they cause with ranch neighbors. It is in this unpublished report that Ligon also discusses the relationship of homesteaders to the decline of the pronghorn.

Other species discussed in this report include coyotes, rabbits, badgers, birds, great blue herons, long-billed curlews, kildeers, Swainson hawks, marsh hawks (which he said were nesting in the area), burrowing owls, turkey vultures, scaled quail, mourning doves (which he continues to call turtle doves), white-necked ravens, western night hawks, meadow larks, redwings, barn swallows, cliff swallows, blue grosbeaks, horned larks, Cassin's kingbirds, crested flycatchers, Bullock's orioles, mockingbirds, and English sparrows.

By 1918, his report is typed, his writing much more professional, and his descriptions vivid. Also, he appears to be aware of a much wider variety of species. Either he had made a dedicated effort to improve his knowledge, writing skills, and spelling (mockingbird is now spelled correctly), or he was now working with someone who was cleaning up his reports. Whatever the case, the change over five years is striking. But back to 1913.

Santa Rosa to Santa Fe

[from the diary]
July 8th—Tuesday

> I am up early, pack up and am on the road in good time,—off for a two-hundred and twenty-five mile jaunt. I get a rather serious kick from my horse that makes riding a misery to me. No water on the road, as the main traveled road leaves the Pecos at Santa Rosa, and does not strike it until Anton Chico is reached—35 ms. I see many young Horned Lark. Two nests by road-side. Very hot. I camp at Anton Chico.

Ligon does not mention passing Colonias, even though it was one of the oldest settlements in the area. Residents were said by Julyan (1998) to have used it as a base for hunting bison. Ligon is leaving what G. Emlen Hall has called the middle Pecos River Basin and entering the upper Pecos River Basin, two reaches of the river with distinctly different histories (G. Hall, 2002). Even by 1913, the middle basin below Santa Rosa, especially the portion near Roswell and Carlsbad, was bordered by lands owned by boosters with dreams of large farms and future growth and development. McMillan Dam and the Avalon waterworks had been providing irrigation to farms around Carlsbad for twenty years, and had already been blasted out by a flood in 1904 and rebuilt. Water conflicts were developing with downstream users in Texas, and these conflicts, in spite of various interstate compacts and lawsuits, continue to the present. Having grown up as a member of the agricultural community around Pecos, Texas, Ligon must have been aware of the conflicts, and we have to wonder where his allegiance might have resided. A key figure in these water wars, Francis Tracy, lived at La Huerta just northeast of Carlsbad. Ligon later settled in La Huerta and developed his private game bird farm there. He undoubtedly came to know the Tracy family, but nothing in his written works suggests interest or concern about the various water conflicts.

The middle Peco River Basin has continued to grow and develop, just as the Tracys and other early Americans hoped it would. The Pecos River flow is now regulated by Santa Rosa Lake, Sumner Lake, and Brantley Lake. Much of the countryside surrounding Roswell, Carlsbad, and Artesia is now covered with oil wells, with agriculture becoming a secondary economic force in the area.

[from the diary]
July 9th—Wednesday

> My wounded leg is sore this morning. From Anton Chico, I am in the hills—follow one of the old Santa Fe Trails. Much Cedar, and Pinion. Above Anton Chico 10 ms. strike some Pine. Awful rough, I cross to East side of river at a small Mex. Town.
>
> Not very many birds thro' here. Camp at Old San Maquil. Nothing but Mexicans since leaving Santa Rosa.

Mexican families had settled this stretch of the Pecos River by 1808, and the villages had served as outposts for Pueblo bison hunters and traders (Julyan, 1998). The river runs through a beautiful valley bordered by steep sandstone walls with farms along the bottom. Surrounding slopes are covered with stands of juniper. Ligon's Texas roots show here in his statement "nothing but Mexicans." He seems oblivious to the century of pre-Anglo domination of the area by Spain and, later, Mexico of this portion of New Mexico, although he notes that he is following one of the old Santa Fe trails. It had been under rule by the United States for only sixty-seven years in 1913. He passes Villanueva, which is probably the small town where he crossed the river.

His comment that the area has few birds would not apply today. Cottonwoods have increased since 1913, and the area along the river supports lush riparian vegetation with the attendant birdlife. Villanueva State Park provides protection for this stretch of the river and is a popular area for camping, fishing, and hiking.

[from the diary]
July 10th—Thursday

> Hit the mountains here at old San Maquil. East of Glorieta, I see first Mt. Prairie Dogs, these have very different habits to those living on the Plains. Hybernating thro' the winter months being one.—

They bark very little. Nights very cool. Camp near Glorieta, a region of many birds, but few can be observed along the road.

I collect a queer specimen of Horned toad, made so no doubt, to conform to the color of soil he lives in.

When Ligon says he "hit the mountains," he apparently means he departs from the river and heads cross country. From San Miquel, he is following an established road between Las Vegas and Santa Fe. He is now seeing Gunnison's prairie dogs. The species is still common in this area (Knowles, 2002).

[from the diary]
July 11th—Friday

Nothing of interest Reach Santa Fe about 3 P.M. Stay balance of Day. Many birds in Santa Fe. Mostly English Sparrow and House Finch Neither of very much economic value.

Ligon is now on the main Santa Fe Trail. During the day, he has passed (perhaps unaware) the old Pecos Pueblo, visited by Coronado in 1541 (Hallenbeck, 1950, 36). It was the trail used by early Indians to travel between villages on the Rio Grande and the Great Plains. The Spaniards used it for explorations, and Anglo and French Mountain men traveled it in the late 1700s and early 1800s. Exploration parties of the US Army—led by Lieutenant James W. Abert, Captain Randolph B. Marcy, and Lieutenant Amiel Weeks Whipple—traversed it and recorded their trips in detail during the 1840s and 1850s. US Army General Stephen Watts Kearny and Lieutenant William Hemsley Emory routed the Mexican Army near here in 1846, thereby taking the area for the United States (Calvin, 1951, 54–56). Ligon's campsite must have been near the location of the Civil War's Battle of Glorieta Pass, where in 1862 Union troops destroyed the supply wagons of the Conferate Army, sending it defeated back down the Rio Grande (M. Hall, 2000). So Ligon, while stating there was "nothing of interest," has been for the past two days riding through one of the most historically interesting landscapes within the continental United States. Either he is ignorant of history at this time in his life or he is intentionally limiting diary entries solely to matters that pertain to the survey.

Throughout this stretch, Ligon did not mention meeting other travelers. By 1913, the railroad had been present for thirty-three years, and automobiles had also entered the scene. His comment about not being able to see birds along the road may speak to the amount of traffic—railroad, automobile, wagon, horse—that was probably present. Reputedly, the first person to drive an automobile through Glorieta Pass was N. L. Dodson, who drove a "Locomobile" from Denver to Albuquerque in 1897.[46] The Locomobile of that era was powered by a steam engine, and the name derives from locomotive. The manufacturers were apparently unaware of the name's implications in the southwestern United States, where it might be construed as describing the mental state of the driver. By 1908, Albuquerque had its first car dealership and had established a speed limit of 8 mph. In 1913, railroad, wagon, horse, and some motorized vehicle traffic along the trail must have been constant, if not abundant.

In the Blachly interview (1952), Ligon reminisces about his stop in Santa Fe:

> You couldn't get accommodations very many places, you didn't have highways and camps and all that, but an interesting thing on that trip was when I got into Santa Fe where there's a big, fine garage today there was what we called a wagon yard then. Of course everybody knew about wagon yards if they had teams and . . . ah . . . I put these two burros in this wagon yard, but the stall that they selected for the two burros, it was a little dark and they had to go up a little kind of a ramp to get in there to the feed troughs. But Smokey and Albert these two burros they were not used to that. They got 'em into the shed but they didn't want to go into that small stall, so finally I was pulling, leading 'em and two of the attendants got behind 'em and pushed 'em and we got 'em up in there and finally tied 'em. So Smokey and Albert that was probably the only time they ever spent the night in a wagon yard.

Santa Fe, of course, is now another overgrown Southwestern city with all the attendant excesses of traffic, overbuilt housing, and abused wild landscapes. By 1922, only nine years after Ligon's stop, another long rider, anthropologist-to-be Clyde Klukhohn, complained that no wagon yard existed in Santa Fe and that in its place was a new garage (Klukhohn, 1927, 60). Things had changed to the point that Klukhohn had difficulty in finding a place to pasture his horses. To attract tourists, Santa Fe has more or less protected the Old Town portion, but in general, Santa Fe is now a busy and crowded place.

Santa Fe to Stinking Lake

[from the diary]
July 12th—Saturday

Owing to some difficulty in getting information and supplies, late when I get out of Santa Fe. Take the Espanolio road. Make 18 miles by camping time, mostly a barren, erosive country, no grass to speak of.

The trail follows the Rio Grande to Española. The river today has large cottonwood corridors along it, but the surrounding terrain is still barren. The big change since Ligon's time is the increase in human numbers. Española today, as well as the landscape between it and Santa Fe, is taken up with residences and businesses. Many of the residents commute to jobs in Santa Fe, not being able to afford the expensive housing within that city.

[from the diary]
July 13th—Sunday

Although it is the Sabbath, I keep beating on toward the North-West. Cross the Rio Grande at Espanolio. Head out the Chama River, where I encounter deep Sand for miles. One continual string of Mexican farms for 25 ms. up the Chama, To Abiquiu.

Near Mouth of Chama see my first crow. Old Mexican tells me they do great damage to crops in the fall. Chama River, a thick milky color, flows quite a lot of water, broad and sandy dry, no grass.

Ligon here acknowledges his religious background. He was raised Methodist; Trinity University was Presbyterian when he attended it. He has not been predisposed to rest on the Sabbath up to this point of the trip, so I wonder why he makes a point of it now. Perhaps he is trying to impress his supervisors at the USBS in that he takes no day off.

The Chama River is now lined with cottonwoods through its length and is moderately settled all the way to Abiquiú. We passed along it quickly in July 2008, and noticed no crows, although this species has apparently expanded its range in New Mexico since 1913. They are fairly abundant along the Rio Grande in southern New Mexico, and on June 4, 2009, Patty and I watched one at Wall Lake near the point where Ligon photographed prehistoric Indian ruins in 1913. For all the time he spent in the Beaverhead region, Ligon mentioned no crows, but in *New Mexico Birds* (1961), he notes expansion of the species southward.

At Abiquiú, the Chama River was dammed in 1963 to form Abiquiú Reservoir, one of the several larger bodies of water that have been developed since Ligon's time.[47] All of these have undoubtedly helped waterfowl and modified their distribution in the state. Ligon passes through the area quickly, finding little of interest for his breeding bird survey.

On one trip through, Patty and I stopped at Ghost Ranch, an establishment not present when Ligon passed. The ranch gained fame as the home of conservationist and philanthropist Arthur Pack and the long-term residence of artist Georgia O'Keefe. It now has a paleontological and archaeological museum which also gives passing recognition to local wildlife. Perhaps its main claim to fame from the standpoint of wildlife is that Frank C. Hibben was based here between 1935 and 1937, while he carried out his field study of cougars—the first effort at direct field research on the species (Hibben, 1937). Hibben later became a noted professor of anthropology at the University of New Mexico and was also a New Mexico game and fish commissioner and friend to Ligon in later years. He was among those responsible for importing a variety of exotic wild mammals into New Mexico, including Barbary sheep and the oryx, which now grace the Jornada del Muerto, San Andres Mountains, and Tularosa Basin.

[from the diary]
July 14th—Monday

> The valley, narrows and boxes in, above Abiquiu. Beaver rather plentiful up here. Also, the Mexicans tell me, in the Mts. that lie on each side of the river, are Turkey, deer, bear, and Lobo Wolves. The many high bluffs to the sides, are of high colors,—beautiful, orange predominating. Queer forms caused by erosion.

This reach of the Chama River is now within the Santa Fe National Forest and has a road along it leading to a monastery. Ligon's comment that beavers were plentiful is significant. This country was undoubtedly trapped heavily in the days of the mountain men, and by 1910, the beaver had been eliminated from many of New Mexico's streams. Beavers are a resilient species, given suitable habitat and a modicum of protection. The New Mexico Department of Game and Fish restored beaver to many streams between 1947 and 1958, and they are now abundant along streams throughout New Mexico—abundant enough to be a problem in agricultural areas (Findley et al., 1975).

[from the diary]
July 15th—Tuesday

My road fades away into nothing more than tracks in places. But as I was directed to follow the Chama River, that is what I am doing. Strike mouth of Gallina River in late P.M. Get Directions to Ranger Station, 13 ms. further on, from a Mexican who lives at mouth of Gallina River. Very little stock. A wild Region, now in the Jamez National Forest.

[from the breeding bird report]

—CHAMA RIVER—

July 13th, 14th, and 15th North-West of Santa Fe

The valley of the Chama River near its mouth, is a continuation of small farms, and Mexican huts, for 25 miles. Mostly a Sandy Valley, Cotton-wood Groves and scattered trees. Higher up, the River boxes up, with high Cliffs and Mts. on the flanks, covered with timber. I find crows especially abundant. See the first about 5 ms. up on Chama. The first I have seen on my round.

The Natives say, Late in the fall, during harvest time, or when the corn ripens, that the crows come down in great numbers and destry a great deal of their farm products.

Among ancient snarled Cotton wood a mile and more below the Village of Abiquiu, is a fine place for water and marsh birds, lakes and swamps, overgrown with grass and willow. Still, nothing in the form of birds greeted my ear, except the mournful squall of the young crow, and the Singing Red wing. No water bird at all could I stir. I was told by an old Man, who lives in the valley, who Speaks English fluently, that in "former years" Duck nested in these swamps in abundance, also, he said, the wild geese nested here years ago. But he added, "since there has been so much hunting, few duck and geese come." I am sure, from the character of the valley here, it has, in time past, been a favorite breeding site. Higher up the valley, I found some duck on the river, and also snipe breeding, as well as black bird. Crow very abundant clear out river valley. The natives tell me, Turkey are rather abundant here, in the Jemez Forest Reserve.

[from the diary]
July 16th—Wednesday

I follow West in Gallina River for eigh[t] ms. Then turn North. One of my pack animals gets down in quick-sand. This is, in the valleys, a sage brush country, Pine, Spruce, Pinion, and cedar on Mts. Cotton-wood along rivers. No stock to be seen.

I find no one at the Ranger Station, See no one to get directions from, follow some old trails north. Get balled up in deep gulches, in the valley, caused by erosion. Have trouble getting over some, make a lonely dry camp. Nothing about but my animals, and Jays, Crows, and Sparrow hawks, a coyote howls near after dark. I see a rattle-snake in late P.M. about 3 ft. long. 7000 feet elev. Most all old Spruce dead. Young timber looks thrifty.

Apparently, Ligon stayed with the Gallinas River to its northernmost apex. I'm not sure where the ranger station might have been. I've seen references to the Otero Ranger Station, forty miles south of Dulce (Tiller, 2000, 114). The area wherein this ranger station existed was incorporated into the Jicarilla Apache Indian Reservation in 1908, which may explain why no one was present when Ligon passed it in 1913. In 1928, it became the headquarters for a cattle operation operated by the tribe (Tiller, 2000, 99–117). The area had been used by an organization of Mexican ranchers before the Jicarilla Apache tribe moved from the Mescalero Apache Reservation to these lands in 1887. Non-Indian squatters continued to swarm the reservation lands even after reservation designation had been made, and livestock numbers soared to ten thousand head. Conflicts over land allocation limited any planned grazing of the reservation lands until 1908, when addition of the southern lands doubled the size of the reservation. Logging of the reservation began in 1908–1909, with a sawmill being established at Dulce in 1910. Grazing by non-Jicarilla Apaches continued, however, and the tribal members had little control of livestock production on their lands. At the same time, money derived from lumber went into trust funds for the tribe in Washington, D.C, providing no direct payments to the Jicarilla Apache people.

Why Ligon failed to see livestock in 1913 is a puzzle, because the tribal lands were apparently at a pinnacle of abuse by a variety of grazing interests.

[from the diary]
July 17th—Thursday

Not cool, but cold. I get early start. Keep guessing on North. See family of Magpie. First on my record. Come in to where forest fire has raged last winter perhaps. See coyote, but he is far from a prairie. About 10 A.M. I sight, down a draw that leads to N.E. a small amt. of water, I ride a little further out and see more, after going down for a mile, I see many small lakes among the hills. And so it turns out to be a portion of Stinking Lake, my goal, and Water Fowl dot the surface every where, and many strangers to me. I pass around to South, and camp on East near overflow, among hills and pine, and no trace of humanity. Except a blind dug on a crest, and perhaps a half bushel empty shot-gun Shells. I presume this hole is the slaughter hole—

We were unable to explore this portion of Ligon's route. On our first trip to the area, we had to circumvent it and we camped at El Vado Lake. I awoke to the calls of magpies the next morning, so this is seemingly near the southern extremity of their normal range now, as it was when Ligon passed.

On our second trip to the Jicarilla Apache Nation, we camped on the Santa Fe National Forest to the south and drove to Stinking Lake via Puerta Larga Canyon. This may have more nearly approximated Ligon's route of approach to Stinking Lake, or at least run more closely parallel to it. The tribal lands are still used for grazing and are heavily posted against trespass. They place no restriction upon visitors driving major roadways, but allow no hiking or camping without special permit.

One curious statement in Ligon's notes is his referral to the "slaughter hole." This sounds like something he had already heard about. If it is, we have to wonder what his source might have been. One of his glass plate negatives at the Denver Public Library shows it as a site heavily littered with shotgun shells, suggesting regular use by hunters from Chama to waylay large numbers of waterfowl.

The Jicarilla Lakes

[from the diary]
July 18th—Friday

I explore the shores and water too, find many nests, many young swimming. Little coot, just out of the eggs, following the parent birds. Wade to my arms examining nests and Tula Grass. Swim out and get one specimen I shoot.

I am in the Ornithologists Paradise.

In P.M. Gentleman Mr. Haynes Passes near on old Road. He gives me Key and Permission to stay at cabin of "Chama Gun and Rod Club." That stands near Lake, further up, and not least, gives me privilege to use Canoe. So I am eleated. Will go to-morrow to get some chuck. Showers about.

July 19th—Saturday

I start early to hunt me some chuck, as I am down to bed-rock. Go to the old Sawmill camp at El Vado, Chama River, as directed by Haynes. Get every thing I need and get back by 1 P.M. Move up to cabin, ½ mile by lake. Clean up and get established in P.M. The mice and rats have possession. The water birds keep up a constant racket. Rains some in P.M.

By horseback, El Vado was less than ten miles. It began as a crossing on the Chama River but became a logging community served by narrow gauge railroads. It is now beneath the waters of El Vado Reservoir (Julyan, 1998). We might guess that Mr. Haynes was associated with the lumber industry at El Vado and perhaps approved Ligon's purchase of supplies at the lumber mill.

July 20th—Sunday

Rather cold this morning. I visit the Grebes nesting sight and spend much time taking observations. Find new Ducks nest, See dead Water Dogs floating about on water, also one young coot dead.

In P.M. Visit Isolated lake to North E. Find many Ducks and Heron. Kildeer, Yellow-head black-bird, and Heron.

Showers in P.M. Get 3 new Specimens, 2 of Duck, one Heron. And one small Duck.

In July 2008, when Patty and I visited Stinking Lake and the other lakes on the Jicarilla Apache Nation, they were nearly full as a result of recent summer rains. Over the past decade, drought had nearly emptied them, and there was little emergent vegetation to provide the kind of nesting habitat Ligon describes. These lakes, especially Stinking Lake, have been surveyed for waterfowl several times over the past century. Rock Lake now shows up on maps as Stone Lake. From all appearances, even though now accessible by paved road, Stinking and Stone lakes are

Stinking Lake from the vicinity of the Chama Rod and Gun Club cabin, 1913

The Stinking Lake outlet, 1913

no more disturbed than they were in 1913. A crude campground exists at Stone Lake, but it is rarely used. Waterfowl hunting is strictly controlled by both federal and Jicarilla Apache Nation regulations, and except during regulated waterfowl or big game hunting seasons, the nation discourages non-tribal recreation on its lands. Non-tribal hunters must hire a tribal member as a guide to hunt.

Ligon was enraptured with Stinking Lake, and after his visit he attempted to have it declared a wildlife refuge. Conservationist Aldo Leopold later joined him in this effort. However, the fact that the lake was on Indian lands made assignment of refuge status impossible. Nonetheless, it seems to be now well protected by the tribal wildlife department.

During his stay, Ligon found many eared grebes on the lake. Subsequent biologists have also found it to be a haven for nesting eared grebes. However, when we visited the lake in 2008, we saw no eared grebes, but did see several western grebes, including birds on nests. Our visit was brief.

[from the breeding bird report]

—Stinking Lake—

July 17th to Aug. South-Eastern Corner Jicarilla Indian Reservation, Rio Arriba Co.

In this lake, we have the Star water fowl breeding ground of all New Mexico.

The Lake lies in a trough almost on the crest of the Continental Divide, a range of Mts. Along the East, dip West, gradually, abrupt on the East side. This ridge runs parallel to the Continental Divide, North and South for perhaps 26 miles, cut at intervals by outlets, canyons. At one of these outlets, to the North end of the trough, is Rock Lake, about seven miles South of it and at the West Gap lies Stinking Lake. I presume the largest Natural body of water in the State, Covering, I judge when up to the Spill way, four (4) Sections. The Main body of water lies to the North-West, connected by channel to the rest of the lake, that threads in lakes and channels through the cliffs and hills to the South and South-East. Forming two Islands, that are hills themselves.

The Lake has an Elevation of about 7000 feet. A depth, I am told, of 9 feet. It is said the lake is perminant, tho' at times, during dry seasons, gets low.

Included with it, is a Smaller Lake that lies East of the main portion of the big lake, about 400 yards. This lake is now about ¾ mile long, with average breadth of about 100 yds. Although at times, when full covers much more country. (Clear Lake).

In the Canyon, of the Overflow, ½ and a mile, are two more lakes, that are considerable size, when filled by the overflow of the main Lake. Owing to a great amount of Shore line—perhaps 12 miles and the abundance of rank water grass, this lake is peculiarly adapted to the breeding of water and marsh birds.

The Lake is filled with moss, most places it floats thickly over the surface. This and Tula Grass along the Shores, is of great aid to nesting birds, by holding the water steady, during strong winds.

The Pine to the East and South-East contains many song bird, while in the cliffs in the same place, Cliff Swallows nest.

Floating all thro' the deep water in the lake is little long moss leaves, green, about ¼ in long.

Timber growing near the Lake. Cotton-wood and willow — on the shore—not very much.

Red Cedar. Cherry near lake.
Yellow Pine (East side).
Blue Spruce
Fir—some high up in canyon heads
Quaking Asp.—very little
Pinon. Abundant
Sunflower

Summary of Stinking Lake and Estimate of Birds.

Area, when Full. (Lacks at present about 3 Ft. Being up to outlet) About 4 Square miles.

Shore-Line about 12 miles
Depth-am told-9 Ft. (Deepest)
Elevation 7000 Ft.

Birds, —Estimated-July 20th

Specimen no.	Name	No. of birds
34	Eared Grebe (2/3 nesting)	1000
36	Pied-billed Grebe (all nesting)	50
46	Coot (all nesting)	2000
44 and 47	Yellow-head and Black-bird (old and young)	1000
42	Red-wing—(mostly nesting)	100
Total		4150

Carried over		4150
	Great Blue Heron	3
41	Black-Crowned Night Heron	25
	(Many vacant nests in willows)	

—Ducks—

I judge 1 Pair out of every 50 birds, breeding. Perhaps, all tole 150 Pr. Nesting (breeding)

Total No of ducks	7500.
Yellow-throat and marsh wren	200
Total no of birds =	11878

In these No'.s I include the Isolated Lake North E. of Main Lake.—Clear Lake.

Bull-frogs are very abundant at Stinking Lake. Also at Horse Lake.

Water Dogs also, in all the Lakes, a great food of the Herons.

Whether or not the bull frogs were introduced is unknown. Degenhardt et al. (1996) note that the first New Mexico record of this species was from Santa Fe in 1885, but the origin of this specimen is uncertain. The water dogs, or salamanders, were undoubtedly tiger salamanders, listed in Degenhardt et al. as native and widely distributed in New Mexico.

Alexander Wetmore provided a more detailed description of Stinking Lake, which by 1918 had been temporarily renamed Lake Burford:

> Lake Burford, the largest natural body of water found in New Mexico, is situated in the Jicarilla (Apache) Indian Reservation in the northwestern part of the state. This lake for many years was known as Stinking Lake and is so shown on most maps, a name derived from the Spanish appellation, of "La Laguna Grande Hedionda" (so-called from a spring of sulphur-tainted water near the western side). Recently, the lake has been given much prominence as a possible breeding ground for water birds by various interested agencies, and it was decided that it would be fitting to give it a more euphonious name. On May 3, 1918, therefore, by petition of the Southwestern Geographic Society and the New Mexico Game Protective Association, it was rechristened Lake Burford, in honor of the late Miles W. Burford of Silver City, New Mexico, a gentleman who had been prominent as a pioneer in promoting the cause of game protection in the state.
>
> The trip to the lake [from Chama], made in a Ford auto truck, required four hours, a sufficient commentary on the state of the mountain roads, as the distance travelled was only about forty miles.
>
> Lake Burford is located approximately 7,000 feet above sea level

> and lies in a trough or depression extending north and south near the summit of the Continental Divide. The lake covers an irregular basin surrounded by rolling knolls that around most of the shore come down directly to the water. These are strewn with loose fragments of sandstone and overgrown with sage. In several places, rocky promontories of yellowish white sandstone rise abruptly from the water's edge. Near these the lake bottom is hard and firm; elsewhere it is composed of soft black mud that is deep and treacherous. The shoreline in 1918 was between fifteen and seventeen miles in all, and the water surface extended over between four and five square miles. The northern end of the lake is broad and open, while the southern part is cut by projecting promontories into several small bays. In the southern area are three small islands. The depth of the lake in the center varied from six to nine feet. Lake Burford receives its water supply from snow water and rain, and to some extent from springs. In extremely high water, it may overflow from a narrow east bay down a great cleft in the sandstone rock known as La Puerta Grande, which leads down toward the Chama (or Brazos) River, but within modern times the water content of the lake has not reached such a level. There is, however, an underground flow here that feeds two small lakes below the large one, and seepage continues on below these.
>
> The waters of Lake Burford are distinctly alkaline, though the alkali is not concentrated, so that sheep, cattle and horses water here without trouble. Where low flats bordered the shore a thin alkaline scale or efflorescence formed on the surface of the mud, and isolated pools in such areas were found to be strongly saline. There was a decided difference in appearance in the water of the northern and southern parts of the lake. That in the broad, open northern portion was gray, murky and opaque, so that objects four inches below the surface were barely visible. The water in the southern end was clearer and contained less sediment, so that the bottom might be seen at a depth of three feet. This difference may be due in part to the presence of springs in the southern end (though none were located) and in part to the fact that the wind sweeps strongly across the open north end, so that the waves usually run high every afternoon and evening, a condition that would tend to keep the water roily. (Wetmore, 1918, 221–247; 393–412)

Wetmore's description of the muddy bottom of the lake as treacherous draws attention to Ligon's diary in which he casually mentions wading in water up to his armpits in order to inspect nests. As with some of his climbing exploits mentioned earlier, Ligon was not adverse to risk, even when alone. Had he drowned while wading, no one would have known, perhaps for weeks or months.

The ruins of the adobe cabin used by both Ligon and Wetmore remain on the eastern edge of the lake. Only fragments of two walls are standing, and the wooden floor and beams, along with fragments of old bottles and cans, are scattered between it and the lake. It is interesting that an active rod and gun club existed in Chama in 1913. Chama was a railroad town that began in 1880 when the Denver and Rio Grande Western Railroad arrived. It became a supply center for ranches in the area and has continued to grow. Today, it is mainly a summer recreation area, rather a smaller version of Durango, Colorado, with the historic Cumbres & Toltec Scenic Railroad providing daily rides through mountain scenery.

[from the diary]
July 21st—Monday

I find there is an enormous lot of Ducks here, many varieties, but very few breeding, compared to the whole.

I find many nests in the Sage, and other brush, that appearance indicates that the birds never hatch. I believe the Skunk gets most of these eggs. Skunk are abundant about the Lake, also Badgers and they too, are bad after eggs. Before I moved into the cabin, of morning skunk tracks would be thick all in my camp. This would make it extremely dangerous for me to sleep out were it not for the fact that I have a heavy Tarp and put it over my head. As a matter of fact, I had rather be bitten by a rattle snake that [than] a Skunk.

I found coot nesting in great abundance, Young birds almost as big as the parent birds, down to nests not complete. Many Yellowh. Black B.

Skunks are feared, of course, as carriers of rabies. Ligon writes an assessment of predation on wildfowl in his breeding bird report, once again reflecting his tendency to categorize wild animals as good or bad:

[from the breeding bird report]

—Water Fowl Enemies—

Stinking Lake

Those birds that nest out of the water at Stinking Lake have little chance of hatching their young. From the great number of nest that I find that have been destroyed, I conclude few hatch their young out of water.

Skunk are very abundant all around the lake, Prowling in the grass along the Shores in broad day-light. They, I believe, the most serious enemy to nests, still—

Badgers are common about, and they too, are bad after eggs.

Coyotes are abundant here, and their tracks every place in the mud, and through the grass indicate that water is not all they seek.

Fox tracks are also common, and a Duck hawk? Occasionally swoops down for a bird. There are some very small snake, but I believe these do no harm, as they feed upon the frogs, as bull frogs are rather common. Abundant, in places, often fifty yards from shore in the short grass.

I had located a duck nest, five well-incubated eggs, 100 feet up on the Mountain side, East side of the lake, I went back two days later to get the mother duck, which was rather tame, and to get Photo of nest and eggs. The Skunk, I presume it was, had just beat me, and eaten the eggs, and scratched the nest to pieces. I had decided this was a Red-head's nest. The nest was in thick Shin-oak brush, made of leaves, with breast feathers among the leaves.

I find many nests out in the sage brush, that have like wise been destroyed. The alarming part is, the valuable birds suffer most.

In what appears to be a copied page of field notes, undated, Ligon states:

The lake is used for no commercial purpose, as far as I can learn, except during the months of May and June the country about is used for a lambing ground, and the sheep are then watered at the lake. Owing to the character of the lake shore, there are few watering places, many places the hills are too abrupt. Others are boggy or contain too much water vegetation. If the lake should be fenced, the watering places could easily be left open. During my stay, I don't believe, on an average, there has been more than 50 stock-horses watering here, no sheep or cattle. If set aside as a breeding [remainder of note missing]

On the reverse side of this page is a note:

Aug. 12th Some cattle watering west side of lake.

[from the diary]
July 22nd—Tuesday

I go around the main lake, in A.M. in boat.

Ducks, of many species in huge flocks, but wild, apparently, with no breeding inclinations.

I rather think this condition is brought about by constant disturbance. While I have been here, I have heard shooting across the lake.

The diving birds seem to pay little attention to firing of a gun, but with duck it is different. Keeping them on the wing much of the time.

From the Cabin, I observe a fierce combat, very often, among the coot. Very often 4 birds taking part, and usually brought on by an intruder fighting the young of other birds.

Showers every P.M.

Ligon perhaps overrates the effects of human disturbance on nesting in a place this isolated. While some disturbance certainly existed, Wetmore later more correctly interpreted the non-nesting birds as those headed farther north to nest, considering Stinking Lake as a stop-over for these species. Ligon was actually at the lake too late to catch peak nesting, if any existed.

[from the diary]
July 23rd–Wednesday

In early morning I make round in lake among hills, go to Spillway later and leave boat, walk ¾ mile to lower Lake in Spill-way, find nothing but coot and yellow-head Blackbird breeding here, altho quite a few small duck, Teal I believe. I get a good wetting before I get back to my slicker, But that matters little as I am wading in water two to four feet deep much of my time. But when I reach the cabin I do enjoy dry warm change of clothes.

Coyotes howl each night.

I can but admire the industry of a species of ant that are very abundant about here, they pile up great heaps of small sticks and trash, at their holes, making great mounds, some a foot high and 3 feet and more across.

Cooler to-night than usual, fire is comfortable.

The ant species Ligon mentions is probably *Pogonomyrmex* spp. It characteristically builds mounds of leaf stems harvested from nearby trees, often cottonwoods. Its nests occur consistently at the uppermost edge of moist soil around wetlands. They concentrate grass seeds as well as leaf stems, and their mounds become highly visible clusters of tall grasses, particularly alkalai sacaton.

[from the diary]
July 24th—Thursday

Very foggy in early morning, something I have not observed but twice for two years or more. I woke to see one foggy morning on the

Gila River early last Spring. After making a round in the lake, I eat my dinner, and pack up to go to Lumberton, for my mail. Over hills covered with very thick sage brush, my route lies. In about six miles, I come up on Rock Lake.

It is a plain round Lake with very little water grass—Tula—is not adapted to breeding birds. I see only a very few duck, several coot with young. I follow the abandoned Narrow Guage Rail Road, camp just over the Continental Divide. Elevation about 7700 feet Little grass. Fairly good Pine Timber, Mt. Prairie dogs abundant.

[from the breeding bird report]

—Rock Lake—Jicarilla Reservation

As Rock Lake, which lies north of Stinking lake about 6 miles, Elev. About 7200, has very little rank water-grass around on its shores, it is not adapted to the breeding of water fowl. The lake is almost round, and at present, I suppose it covers about ¾ of a square mile, perhaps a little less, and appears to be shallow.

July 24th I found a very few duck, and no sign of breeding. No Heron or Crain. Quite a lot of Coot with young, also Red wing and other Black Bird. (Speci. 57) but no yellow-head Blackbird.

By 1913, the narrow-gauge logging railroad built in 1910 had been abandoned on the Jicarilla Apache Nation lands, perhaps indicating the rate at which the area was logged. Rock Lake, now called Stone Lake, is one of the developed recreation areas on Jicarilla Apache Nation lands, with fee-use campgrounds. The Jicarilla Tribal Fairgrounds are just northwest of the lake.

On our visits, we saw no prairie dogs near Stone Lake, but Dale Stahlecker, who knows the wildlife of the Jicarilla Apache Nation lands well, says they are present, especially around Dulce, where a trapper works to control them. A small colony exists south of Stone Lake, and more colonies remain in the southern half of Jicarilla Apache Nation lands. Ligon's comment that little grass was present contrasts with what we saw in 2008. Although the bottoms of the valleys were covered with sage brush, they also had good stands of grass interspersed. This was in part due to the fact that we were there during a wet year.

[from the diary]
July 25th—Friday

Rather late when I leave my camping place, as my animals are quite a way off. Coyotes rather plentiful. I see them often by the road.

> Have no rifle with me. See first Indians and Teepees since I come into the reservation. Awfully bad water in the arroyos Stock will hardly drink it. Man can not. 12 O'clock when I get in to Lumberton. Get a lot of mail. Fix two boxes of bird skins for mailing in P.M. Answer letters by lantern light. Cold, almost cold enough for frost. No indication of rain at present.

Tiller (2000) noted that a small group of Jicarilla Apaches had a teepee village north of Stone Lake, apparently the same group seen by Ligon. Compared to Dulce, Lumberton is now almost a ghost town. Its livelihood was apparently tied to the timber hauled by narrow-gauge lines reaching into the forests.

By July 25, Ligon is synthesizing his observations and writing recommendations independently of his breeding bird report. Among USBS files, with no provenance, is the following handwritten recommendation. This is on letter-sized paper and shows signs of having been edited after arrival at the USBS office. I have eliminated the editorial comments, presenting only Ligon's original version. He must have enclosed this with a letter to Nelson, or with his report.

> Stinking Lake, New Mexico, for a Preser[v]e as a Breeding Place for Water Fowl
>
> I recommend Stinking Lake, in the Jicarilla Indian Reservation, Rio Arriba County New Mexico as a Candidate for a breeding Reserve for Water Fowl.
>
> -1- Because it is, practically, of no other value. Owing to its situation.
>
> -2- Because, owing to its altitude of 7000 feet, It attracts birds that are rare in this region, that otherwise would go much further north for the same climatical conditions.
>
> -3- It is peculiarially adapted to the breeding of water fowl, as it has a great amount of shore line, well bordered with water grass and contains a great amount of grass.
>
> My estimate is now, that there are 12000 birds here. Perhaps half of these are ducks of at least a dozen varieties. I consider only about one pair out of every fifty duck nesting. I believe, under more favorable conditions, the greater part of the number could be induced to breed, and many more would remain thro' the breeding season.
>
> My estimate is: when the lake is full up to the spill-way, it covers four (4) square miles. With, perhaps, twelve (12) miles of Shore Line.
>
> But, unless it was properly fenced, its appointment as a preserve would do little good, it is true, it would stop late, and I might add, constant shooting, which keeps the ducks moving. But they need the

grass for nesting, on the banks, but do not need the skunks, coyotes, badgers and fox. At present these varmints prevent most eggs that are laid out of the water, from hatching. It would require between eight and ten miles of fence to enclose it.

Stokley Ligon
Field Assistant
U. S. Biological Survey
Stinking Lake July 25th 1913.

July 26th—Saturday

Late when I leave Lumberton for Horse Lake, 16 miles to South-East. Scenery is good coming out canyon and even after I reach the high country where it is more of a rolling hilly, and valley country, with beautiful Pine. Much of the Jicarilla Reservation is beautiful country. I reach south end of Horse Lake in the late P.M. quite a lot of water bird here, not so very many duck. Magpie in great abundance here. I count 23 in one string flying over my camp.

A few robin. Prairie dog abundant even over the summit Elev. Nearly 8000 feet. Horse Lake is partly divided by Reservation line. A small saw mill to Eas[t] Big Public Road around South end and up West side, Lake now is about ¾ mile long, Perhaps average of 500 yds. wide.

Nelson had written Ligon on July 22, giving him official notice that his appointment would end on July 31.[48] He adds, "I hope you are having good success among the water fowl on the lakes of northern New Mexico. We wish very much to have summer specimens of the crow and also of the blue heron from that section; so I wish you would make special effort to try and get them. Please try and get two or three good specimens of adult blue herons."

Nelson continues with detailed instructions on how to prepare and ship heron and crow skins. Apparently, he had no communications after Ligon left Santa Rosa. Ligon notes that he replied to Nelson's letters, but no letter for this date is among those in the Smithsonian files. Nelson's letter had not yet arrived, so Ligon left Lumberton without seeing the official notice of the termination.

[from the diary]
July 27th—Sunday

For the first time since my appointment, I rest during the Sabbath day. Still I spend much of the time on the Lake Shore, observing the action of birds. Two Indians eat dinner with me. And then sleep in the shade half of P.M. Horse Lake has perhaps, all tole a thousand birds. Many Yellow-head Black-bird.

It has an elevation of 7670 feet. Saw mill on East Side. The line of the Indian Reservation divides the lake, north and south. This lake is very clear. Water fairly good to drink. Cold nights, some frost.

July 28th—Monday

I spend morning at Horse Lake. Taking notes and find nothing new. Pack up and start for Stinking Lake before twelve o'clock. About 15 ms. Back around road.

Get in late P.M. tired. Nice day, but cool.

[from the breeding bird report]

—Horse Lake—

July 26th and 27th Rio Arriba Co.

This Lake Lies North-East of Stinking Lake, air Line, about 12 miles. It is partly divided by the Line of the Indian Reservation. It is now, not quite up to its spill-way, about one foot below. The Lake lies almost on the crest of the Continental Divide, at an Elevation of 7670 feet, by authority of Geological Post near. The lake has an Eastern out-let to the Chama River.

At its present stage, it is a little less than a mile long, with an average width of ¼ mile. Is clear, and the water is fairly good to drink. Has an almost due North and South direction, open country to the North and North-west, but boxes in between mountains at South End. Public Roads on both sides. A saw mill on East side.

I estimate that there is 1000 birds here now. Many of this number Yellow-head Black-bird and some Red-wing.

Coot abundant with young. Eared Grebe, also fairly com. with their young in the middle of the Lake, diving for their food.

I see very few ducks, one mother duck leading her 8 young, half grown, about over the lake.

Magpie and Long-Crested jay, very, very abundant, also Crows.

Get in late P.M. tired. Nice day, but cool.

We did not visit Horse Lake on either trip to the Jicarilla Apache Indian Reservation.

On July 28, Nelson writes:

We are highly pleased with your interesting discovery of such a fine breeding place for waterfowl in northern New Mexico and look forward with much interest to your report on the same. I trust that you will give a very full and complete report of the character of the lake, its size and every other piece of information which you may learn that will be of interest in connection with the preservation of game there. How much shooting is done there? Do the Indians do much hunting, and if so at what season and how extensively; and also do white men hunt much about Stinking Lake?

Before you leave this locality I wish you could make a special effort to get us two or three specimens of the blue heron. Try to get good adults and also a specimen of the crane which you report is breeding there. We also desire several specimens of the red-winged blackbird, about three or four each, males and females. If there are any nighthawks in that vicinity, please send us a couple of specimens.

I note what you say about it requiring until about the tenth of August to complete your work about the lakes and regret that we did not know earlier in the season that you would strike such a rich field here, in order that your appointment could have been continued a little longer. However I trust that your work there will not be expensive so that you can do a satisfactory job.

What you say about having a reservation made of this lake in order to protect the breeding birds there meets with our approval and we will at once make inquiries as to what the possibilities are in this direction. For this reason, the fuller the information you give us concerning that section of New Mexico, the more likely we are to get some action.

I trust you will not fail to send us specimens of every breeding bird you find about the lakes.

It is clear that Ligon had written Nelson during his trip to Lumberton, apparently expressing some enthusiasm about Stinking Lake. Nelson finishes the letter by repeating the instructions on salting and handling larger bird specimens that he had given in his previous letter.

[from the diary]
July 29th—Tuesday

I spend early A.M. working on my report. Later on go on lake in boat, wade a great deal among Grebe Nests. My wading suit is jumper and overalls. And the water is cold chilling one for hours. I expose some plates on nests and birds.

In P.M. go to South end in Canoe. Get some interesting notes on habits.

See many Skunk in grass by shore. Kill two with rock. Many places they have trails through the grass. Showers some in P.M. quite a lot of wind.

To-night copy on my report and records. The birds down under the Cabin keep up a constant hollow and Splash. In the great sheets of fallen Tula Grass just under the Cabin, the Duck rest and spend much time, those that are molting. I catch many that can not fly, young feathers coming.

In August 2009, when Patty and I made our second visit to Stinking Lake, it was very low, indicating that its water level is almost totally dependent upon annual precipitation. The water edge was perhaps one hundred yards from the ruins of the old cabin, compared with the situation Ligon describes for 1913, wherein the waterfowl were concentrated just below the cabin. Even then, Ligon had noted that the water level declined without precipitation.

[from the diary]
July 30th—Wednesday

So late when I turn in last night, Late when I get up. Work on report until M. Go in boat in P.M. South end. See many little Scarlet-heads —Coot— just hatched. See quite a lot of young duck. One specimen. More skunk. Kill one. The lake shore in places has quite a growth of under brush, but now, this is a Skunk den.

The Eared Grebe are getting quite tame about their colony, allowing me to pass very near. About out of cartridges for my Shot Gun. Could not get them at Lumberton. Showers some. Wind blows. The lake rolls where there is no moss or grass.

July 31st—Thursday

Work on my records and report in A.M. See about my animals.

In P.M. I go to in Canoe to South End. Get Among the duck one Specimen, old Red-head. Showers in P.M. Wind blows. Water bird most all go into Tula Grass. My Grebe colony are hatching off now.

Find duck nest, two eggs, abandoned, seems.

Lake is falling rather fast. Late when I turn in. Work on my report.

I manufacture me some 16 Gauge Cartridges. Find some 12" in Cabin. Put Shot, Powder, and Primers in my 16 gauge shells. They do lovely. Quite a lift.

August 1st—Friday

In A.M. I go in Canoe, Get nothing of especial interest. Lake is falling, in time I have been in neighborhood. July 17th to August 1st It has dropped about 3 inches. Still, one can easily account for that, so much sun-shine, and no rains that make water run. I collect some specimens in P.M. Work on report until late in night showers in P.M.

Ligon was as yet unaware that his appointment had ended.

[from the breeding bird report]

Ducks At Stinking Lake, Jicarilla Reservation

Rio Arribo Co. N. Mex.

Aug. 1st. The ducks here have got me pretty well balled up, by their conduct.

Since July 17th, I have found many nests containing eggs of the Larger Ducks, that have been deserted.

Most of these, the nests are floating among the Tula Grass, in from one to 3 ft. of water, and as the nests are poorly constructed, and not being constantly built up, as with the coot. The nests settle and the eggs sink under water.

These nests have had from 1 to 13 eggs in them.

I am led to believe, if conditions were more favorable—If there were no varmints to molest them, these nests would be on the shore. I find many nests in the Sage brush, well up on the hills, that appear to have been robbed, in most every case.

Now too, the Ducks, since so many are moulting and do not fly, but run over the surface of the water flopping their wings, they are misleading. One often thinks they have young or are young themselves, and, unless one is careful, these will result, misleading records. In the Rank Tula Grass, there is around the Lake, two great resting places for the ducks. They have great beds of the grass beaten down, — or most likely, it has blown down, and there will be hundreds of them on this, which is generally back in the brakes of the grass, entirely surrounded. Some will fly out and away, others, that have very shaggy features, will run on the water or dive, and both, very often. Most of these secured at such places are matured birds-adults. That are merely moulting.

There are many of the larger ducks here, that I am sure have no young; although, doubtless, most of them have laid.

They stay in flocks, drifting about from place to place, at times 2 to 3 hundred to-gether.

The two eggs—F8/13 are samples of those found in nests, with no sign of being occupied.

Very likely my presence, and constant cruising about, has caused many to abandon their eggs. Shooting does not bother the coot, and diving ducks and birds, but it does put most all the ducks on their wings.

The large duck here are all very wild.

I am in hopes it will not be necessary to chouse the breeding birds here, any more, as I have done this season. At least the report of a gun should be prevented.

Stokley Ligon

This is a strange entry and reads more like a letter to Nelson. It is, in fact, written on a piece of paper from an unlined tablet, probably the same one Ligon used for correspondence, and inserted into the breeding bird report, apparently stitched in place with heavy thread or fine wire. In it he summarizes his observations at Stinking Lake. He sounds a bit defensive here, a feeling with which most isolated field biologists working far from headquarters can sympathize. He is overwhelmed with a large number of waterfowl and a variety of species in a lake with dense growth. In addition, some of the species are apparently in eclipse plumage and difficult to identify. And finally, Ligon has begun to worry about the effects of his own disturbance on the ducks, while feeling pressed to collect more specimens. For a relatively new employee working alone, the sense of uncertainty under such circumstances can be overwhelming. His correspondence with Nelson has already left him sensitive to criticism, and he seriously wants to perform well on this first job with the USBS. The above entry is an effort to justify any inadequacies in his report or collections.

[from the diary]
August 2nd—Saturday

I look through nesting colony of Grebe in A.M. My birds are getting tame, but seem very inquisitive While I am near their nests. They are hatching off rapidly, I presume the chicks turn to fish, as they are always out sight.

Quite a lot of the duck have left. These ramblers, make up the great flocks that one often sees in Aug, on the rain-water lakes far south of here. —In Tula Rosa flats and the Jornada. I begin preparations to go back to Lumberton.

Here, Ligon finally makes first reference to the migratory habits of the ducks, acknowledging that birds present at Stinking Lake have begun to drift southward. He is winding down his work and planning to depart.

> August 3rd—Sunday
>
> I get up early, pack up. Clean up the shack. Go for animals. Have a race over the Mts. After my saddle-horse, late when I get back and am all in. Get started about 11 A.M. Stop at Rock Lake and Inspect it. Find no duck this time. Quite a lot of Black-bird. I see several Indians. The first I have seen down here. They were looking about horses. No Teepees down in this district. As I think about Stinking Lake, it always comes to my mind, how it would improve the breeding birds condition to make it a Reserve, and fence it. I have planned the fence, its route, and selected posts to do the fencing. Still it is all but a plan of mine. Indians say no deer or turkey in this Region, still I find they do not confine themselves to the truth, with strangers.
>
> August 6th—Wednesday
>
> I spend the day at Lumberton, writing letters and fixing up mail. Showers about. Awfully dry here.

There is a two-day hiatus in his notes that is unexplained. He rides from Stinking Lake to Stone Lake on Sunday afternoon, then says nothing about either Monday or Tuesday, noting only that he spends all of Wednesday in Lumberton. Perhaps he was simply taking his time, exploring the areas around Stone and Horse lakes.

Ligon probably mailed specimens to Washington, D.C., at this time, but did not mail his written report until later, perhaps after he had returned to Chloride. In his mind, he was finished with his work, and he had already cleaned up the cabin. He may very well have planned to head home without returning to Stinking Lake. However, upon reaching Lumberton, he received Nelson's letters of July 25 and 28. Although he now knows he is on his own time from this point on, he returns to Stinking Lake for another five days, attempting to acquire the particular specimens that Nelson has requested.

> [from the diary]
> August 7th—Thursday
>
> I start early for Dulcie. 4 ms. On my way to Lake La Jara.
> Stop quite a while, talk with Government Authorities. Am told La Jara is a small and artificial Lake. So I decide to cut visiting it out. Go

to Dulcie Lake, 4 ms. South of Dulcie. Dulcie is the Jicarilla Agency. Find some duck, small ones with young.

Prairie dogs very abundant in the Canyon.

August 9th—Saturday

My animals are out of "Pocket", so I get late start. Stop for dinner north of Rock Lake. Indian eats dinner with me. Late when I reach the Cabin, Stinking Lake. Kill Porcupine. First I have ever found. Dry generally over the country. Lakes falling fast.

Ligon apparently spent August 8 at Dulcie Lake or in its vicinity. He fails to make an entry for the day in his diary. His notes appear in his report, however. His comment regarding the porcupine may be significant. By 1913, he had spent at least six years working and hunting in areas that would be suitable for porcupines, including forested areas of the Black Range and San Mateo Mountains. The porcupine is easily detected when present. For this to be the first one Ligon has ever seen bespeaks an extreme scarcity of the species throughout the state. Vernon Bailey (1931) stated that the species was common throughout the state in the late 1800s, and as late as 1904, he had found them to be abundant at both Horse Lake and Burford (Stinking) Lake. He also comments that they were known to undergo extreme population fluctuations. Ligon failed to mention the species in 1927. I remember porcupines being abundant on the Mogollon Rim in Arizona in 1956. I have yet to see one during ten years of making daily rambles in the Black Range near Kingston, New Mexico. Brown and Babb (2009) have presented strong evidence that mountain lions control porcupine numbers and that during years following heavy lion-control programs porcupines increased.

[from the breeding bird report]

—Dulcie Lake—Aug. 8th 1913.

4 Ms South, Dulcie, (The Indian Agency) Elev. about 6700.

At this little Lake, which is partly artificial, having a dam thrown across the canyon at the North end,—I found rather favorable breeding conditions. The Lake, when up to the Spill-way covers about ¾ Square mile, Surrounded by Mts. and canyons. I am told by the authorities at Dulcie that the birds are rarely molested here. Some ducks winter here. When the Lake is frozen over, they go to the creek, that runs out under the dam. The lake is fed by springs, and the water in Summer is used for irrigation. The lake now, is about 6 feet below the spill-way.

I found coot and ["Pied billed" is written in pencil by W. W. Cooke] young, Red-wing, and young Ducks with downy young, and Grebe, (No. 36) rather common, with young.

Kildeer with young.

(Perhaps 100 all tole birds here)

[from the diary]
August 10th—Sunday

Thoughtless of the day, I have made it an important one. Collect several specimens. See many young duck. Kill three Skunk, 2 very large ones, together on lake-shore, near Cabin. In places around the edge, the Lake has green scum. Bad water.

Weather is cool, nights cold.

At some point after his visit with officials in Dulce, Ligon wrote an assessment of hunting at Stinking Lake:

[from the breeding bird report]

—Hunting at Stinking Lake—

I am informed by the Federal Officers at Dulce, and others, that the Indians Never Hunt at the Lakes. They care nothing for birds, it is said, to eat, nor as sport for hunting.

But white people come great distances to Hunt the Water Fowl. Even from other states, and the vast Number of empty shells at the many blinds and along the shores are proof of the slaughter that takes place.

I desire to embody this thought in this report: The inhabitants rarely, if ever, decrease the game supply where they live. Those in such localities, are not generally very well supplied with Ammunition. And they use judgement. Kill only when it is needed for food, and usually make dead-shots. While the man from the city has a supply of ammunition, he shoots at any thing, generally, regardless of distance, or opportunity, hence, usually one half of the game is never gotten. The great number of Duck carcasses here are proof of the ["great" crossed out] waste. The hunting, if done in a reasonable way, would not decrease the game supply to any great extent.

The character of the lake and surroundings is peculiarially adapted to killing the fowl, since the Lake is chopped and cut by hills and ridges, several hunters having scattered over these, brings the birds to their Mercy—which is very scant. There could be nothing worse than this Club Cabin on the Shore, with no one for miles to interfear.

Considering the relative remoteness of Stinking Lake from major population centers, along with the difficulty of travel in 1913, Ligon's comments on hunting pressure are surprising. It would be interesting to know how heavy the pressure was and where the hunters originated.

Ligon's comment on the cabin at the lake seems disingenuous, since he has certainly been willing to work from it. He is confronting, perhaps for the first time, a conflict that anyone working in game management experiences—the hunter is the member of the public most interested in game species and most willing to pay for conservation. But the payback is the freedom to hunt. Herein are the beginnings of the complex system of licenses, wardens, biologists, surveys, and regulations that have evolved in order to have wildlife and eat it too, as it were.

[from the breeding bird report]

Stinking Lake August 10th, 1913

At Sunset this evening, I believe I am very moderate, when I place the number of water fowl, in sight, in front of the "Chama Rod and Gun Club" cabin, at 2500. And to-night there is a constant chirp, twitter, squeak and quack. And good too—I got more of the great robbers, this eve (Skunk) 2 the largest I have ever killed, in all my rounds. One mother duck, (Specimen. 65) with 12 young 2/3 grown. Many more young. Kill big porcupine—first one I have seen.

Stokley Ligon

Ligon has returned to the cabin in order to collect herons and other birds requested by Nelson. His comment on the large numbers of ducks on the lake is probably prompted by arrival of flocks migrating southward, for which the lake is serving as a resting place.

[from the diary]
August 11th—Monday

I cruise about in Main Lake (Stinking) see some new birds,—first migrants. Many young Eared Grebe, Riding mothers back. See two Blue Heron, but get none. Ducks swam out in West side of Lake. Showers in P.M.

Water [birds?] all seem to be much tamer, than when I came. Locate new Grebe nesting colony, west of old one, out in lake. Nests float on moss.

Rains some to-night.

August 12th—Tuesday

Spend much time trying to get on to Blue Heron, West side, crawl in water and push Canoe ahead. but no use. In P.M. kill fine one in Pine, East side. Migratory birds arriving here. and to-morrow eve. I expect to begin migrating toward the Gila Forest Reserve.

—Farewell—
To Stinking Lake and the many birds.

The diary ends here. Ligon sent a plant list from the vicinity of the lake, describing nine numbered but unnamed species. He submitted plant specimens with this list to be identified by the USBS.

Having fulfilled Nelson's request for a blue heron specimen, Ligon is ready to depart. He acknowledges that migratory birds are still flocking in. There seems to be a disconnect between Ligon's expectation of finding breeding waterfowl at Stinking Lake and his acknowledgment of southbound migrants beginning to arrive in late August.

CHAPTER FIVE

After the Breeding Bird Survey

Beginning a Career

J. Stokley Ligon departed Stinking Lake on August 13, 1913. He left little record of his trip southward, after completing the Jicarilla Lakes survey. According to Wells W. Cooke, in Florence Merriam Bailey's *Birds of New Mexico* (1928), Ligon followed the Continental Divide back to Chloride. As already noted, once he was finished with the survey, he made no further entries in the government diary, so this portion of his trip is unrecorded. I believe that he maintained a personal diary in addition to the one submitted to the US Biological Survey (USBS), but have given up hope of finding it.

Ligon looped through Putnam at Chaco Canyon on his way home. Then he went south to Thoreau and Ramah. This southward journey, especially the portion through the present Navajo lands, might well have been the most difficult part of his trip. This is an open, hot, and often dry landscape during August. How he found his way and located water remains unknown, but no evidence exists that he experienced any particular difficulty. In his report, he notes seeing golden eagles at Putnam, and he took a photograph which he labeled "Coming into Putnam," but failed to date the entry in his photographic journal. Putnam, in 1913, was the post office and trading post at Pueblo Bonito. He therefore diverted over thirty miles westward from the Continental Divide, apparently to see the ruins at Chaco Canyon or to visit an acquaintance. The fact that he spent two days in the area suggests he was enjoying his freedom to explore. He seemed to be in no hurry to head south. I have found no indication Ligon was visiting relatives or acquaintances at Putnam. By the time he arrived,

Looking toward Putnam, August 1913

Richard and Marietta Wetherill, Putnam's original traders, were gone (Wetherill, 1992). Richard had been murdered in 1910, and Marietta had moved to Cuba, New Mexico. Charles F. Spader was postmaster.

So far, I find no cover letter that Ligon mailed with his breeding bird report to the USBS, nor have I found any confirmation or comment from the biological survey regarding the report. Over the next few months, he carried on an increasingly congenial correspondence with E. W. Nelson of the USBS, expressing disappointment that Stinking Lake could not become a refuge, discussing plans to revisit the lake on his own volition the next year, and disclosing his desire to write a definitive book on Texas birds. He again expressed concern about the status of the masked bobwhite and divulged plans to take a personal trip into Arizona and Sonora to determine the status of that species. He responded heatedly when Nelson chastised him for sending a specimen collected on USBS time to the Peabody Museum of Natural History at Yale University. Shortly later, he apologized for his reply and acknowledged that he had been rightfully criticized. He submitted some of his photographs taken during the survey to Nelson, and perhaps more important, he collected the first specimens of Mexican spotted owl that the USBS had ever received. He continued to sell specimens to the USBS as a private collector.

Rock spires near Ramah, August 1913

In Nelson's replies, he informed Ligon that ornithologist Harry C. Oberholser was writing a book. He expressed interest in Ligon's plans to revisit Stinking Lake and to study masked bobwhites, and suggested that the USBS might be able to provide some support for these efforts. He thanked Ligon for the spotted owl and Mearns quail specimens, as well as the photographs, and complimented him on his field skills, at the same time again criticizing the quality of his specimens. He also downplayed the seriousness of Ligon sending the horned lark specimen to the Peabody Museum, noting that he merely wanted Ligon to be aware that specimens collected while employed by the USBS legally belonged to that agency.

At this point, Ligon informed Nelson that he was writing a report on the Black Mountain district, which lies northwest of Beaverhead Ranger Station, recommending it as a breeding preserve for wildlife. He further noted that he was working on a report on game management in the national forests. These both were independent and unfunded projects and demonstrate that Ligon was already thinking critically about the handling of wildlife by government agencies. Although somewhat of a neophyte in the USBS, he was bold enough to tackle potentially controversial subjects. Nelson acknowledged receipt of the Black Mountain report and expressed interest in the national forest report. Nelson also encouraged

The rock spires, August 2009. (Photo by Steve Albert)

Ligon to send more spotted owl specimens and observations, noting that this was a new species for the survey.

In collecting spotted owls for the USBS, Ligon initiated a process that culminated in the listing of the species as endangered some seventy years later. It has become an icon of the Endangered Species Act of 1973 and has been used to protect thousands of acres of old-growth timber on national forests in the United States. Similarly, Ligon became involved with the masked bobwhite, a species he may have helped save from extinction. His entry into the politics of wildland management at this time seems a bit prescient, considering that the national wildlife refuge system had hardly begun. He was obviously confident in his knowledge and not afraid to speak his mind, and his ideas often ran counter to his own family culture. I have not seen the Black Mountain report or any correspondence that Ligon might have submitted with it. That it was submitted was acknowledged by Nelson on January 16, 1914, with a request that Ligon try to learn more about the history of elk in the area. He states that he had been told that elk existed in the Black Mountain area as late as 1883.

Nelson discusses the politics of attaining refuge status for Stinking Lake, noting that the upper Pecos River valley was destined for such protection. He then chides Ligon once again on the poor quality of his museum specimens and offers to send examples of properly prepared study skins. He ends by praising Ligon on his enthusiasm in fieldwork, his experience with pack animals, and his ability to get about in the country.

With the completion of his Black Mountain and US Forest Service manuscripts, Ligon went to Texas for Christmas. March found him once again in the San Mateo Mountains collecting spotted owls and Mearns quail for Nelson, and probably hunting or trapping wolves for bounty. In spite of his plans, he did not return to Stinking Lake nor search for masked bobwhites until later in his career. In April 1914, the USBS hired him to survey prairie dogs in northeastern Arizona. They then placed him in charge of predator control in New Mexico.

Ligon was obviously enthralled by the diversity of waterfowl at Stinking Lake. However, he did not know ducks well enough to identify all of them. Ligon notes in his diary that the ducks at Stinking Lake have him "all balled up" by their conduct. However, he does not record unknown species, but seemingly relegates all of his unknowns to the broad category of "duck." Ligon tallied only seventeen wetland species at Stinking Lake, compared with thirty-two to thirty-four for the subsequent observers. Alexander Wetmore's survey occurred five years after Ligon's, so no major change in bird species composition was likely to have occurred over that time.

Species that Ligon missed at Stinking Lake, but that all the other surveyors saw, included Wilson's phalarope, American merganser, baldpate (widgeon), green-winged teal, cinnamon teal, shoveler, canvasback, and greater scaup. Ligon had noted Wilson's phalaropes at more southerly locations during his survey, so he could have identified the species had it been present. The remaining six species are ducks. A check of his specimens at the Smithsonian shows that he did not collect any of these species, something you would expect him to have done in order to have them identified, had they been present.

Ligon finally returned to Stinking Lake in July 1916. By this time, he was employed as an investigator in the USBS's Predator and Rodent Control Branch. If a report of this visit was written, I have not found a copy, and only the records cited by Florence Merriam Bailey in *Birds of New Mexico* (1928) remain for this trip. In addition to those who subsequently did waterfowl surveys at the lake, Aldo Leopold visited there in 1915 and described it eloquently in the Christmas 1915 publication of *The Pine Cone* (Leopold, 1915). He, too, promoted it as a national wildlife refuge in 1918 in an article "The Popular Wilderness Fallacy" in *Outers' Book–Recreation* (Leopold, 1918). David E. Brown visited the lake with Neil Carmony in April 1989 and found it still relatively unchanged (D. Brown and Carmony, 1990, 31). Patty and I made two trips to the lake while researching this book and found it undisturbed, although in 2009 the water level was extremely low due to drought conditions.

CHAPTER SIX

The Significance of the Breeding Bird Survey

Exactly how the decision to hire J. Stokley Ligon for the breeding bird survey in New Mexico was made remains unclear. Other prominent ornithologists at the time were occupied with duties and tasks elsewhere. Florence Merriam Bailey and Vernon Bailey were fully occupied in a biological survey of North Dakota. US Biological Survey (USBS) employee E. W. Nelson was apparently involved in administrative duties in Washington, D.C., and doing little fieldwork. Alexander Wetmore and A. K. Fisher were both present, but perhaps did not have the abilities to cover the terrain on horseback. Wells W. Cooke was up in years and was operating more as a coordinator of volunteers and freelance collectors than as a field biologist.

Compared to the work of other USBS biologists of the time—the Baileys, Nelson, E. A. Goldman, Wetmore, Cooke, and Fisher—Ligon's efforts seem amateurish, but he was a capable woodsman, horseman, and packer, with the ability to travel and work alone. While he knew more about birds and other wildlife than most Western residents, his writing skills were limited, and he consistently ignored the smaller warblers and sparrows. What he contributed, more than anything else, was a confirmation that New Mexico hosted large numbers of waterfowl during the summer, either for nesting or for resting during migration. He clearly stated his opinion that Stinking Lake was especially valuable for the number of wildfowl it hosted. However, detailed identification of species using it and assessment of their breeding status had to await the more professional ornithological skills of Wetmore in 1918.

Ligon's primary assignment was to fill in gaps of knowledge regarding waterfowl and shorebirds that nested in the state. Vernon Bailey and Nelson outlined the places he was to visit, based upon their earlier travels and Cooke's recommendations.

In his breeding bird report, Ligon recorded 99 species observed over a three-month period, during which he covered some 1,200 miles on horseback. With the possible exception of the bird he called a scarlet ibis, nothing particularly unusual turned up during the survey. For comparison, a pair of ornithologists recorded 155 species during a single-day bird-a-thon in June 2009. Their survey covered a circular route from Las Cruces up the Rio Grande to the Silver City highway (New Mexico State Highway 152), then west to the Mimbres River valley, south to Deming, and back to Las Cruces, less than two hundred miles. They were traveling by vehicle and therefore could not record bird songs or scrutinize habitats between their various stops.

Ligon recorded only the common names of birds in his diary and report, and the binomials in the report were added later by Cooke. The common names he uses generally match those in Florence Merriam Bailey's *Handbook of Birds of the Western United States* (1928), although his consistent misspelling of some names leaves his source open to question (appendix, table 1). I am not sure if he was relying entirely upon his accumulated knowledge or if he was using Bailey's or some other field guide.

From all appearances, Ligon was using three numbering systems for his specimens. He had been collecting commercially prior to being hired for his survey, with eighty-five specimens recorded before May 31. He continued using his personal numbering system through June 3, then began numbering specimens collected for the USBS at number one after that date. He used a different numbering system for eggs. Once he started numbering for the USBS, he proceeded sequentially with these specimens, collecting a total of sixty-nine bird specimens during the summer (appendix, table 2).

Ligon completed most of his report before leaving the Jicarilla Apache Indian Reservation, although entries regarding eagles at Putnam and jays north of Thoreau suggest that he did not mail it until he returned to Chloride. The breeding bird report has two components: descriptions of specific sites of special value to birds, and accounts of the species he observed and collected. In a sense, although it was written to satisfy the USBS's requirements, its format suggests that he was already envisioning the long-term outcome as a book on New Mexico birds. As noted in correspondence with Nelson, he had hoped to write such a book covering the birds of Texas and was usurped in this effort by Harry C. Oberholser, although Oberholser's book was not published for several decades and posthumously. Ligon must have known that Cooke and Florence Merriam Bailey were working on such a publication for New Mexico. His

New Mexico Birds (1961), a meager effort compared to Florence Merriam Bailey's book, became a life-long project. In it, he depended upon many observations that had been made on the 1913 trip, so early in his career. As with Oberholser's Texas book, *New Mexico Birds* was published posthumously.

By the time Ligon left Stinking Lake, he was beginning to think more as a manager of wildlife than as a traditional naturalist. Previous USBS biologists had been mainly interested in classifying new species and adding to the collections of the Smithsonian and the USBS. While conservation was slowly becoming part of the American ethic, naturalists of the exploration and territorial eras within the West were largely resigned to the demise of wildlife as the land was converted to farming, ranching, and towns. Ligon was one of the first to voice the possibility that wildlife might be given some priority and that other, more commercial, land uses might compromise. His brief essay in the breeding bird report on "duck's rights" was prescient by perhaps fifty years.

CHAPTER SEVEN

Ligon's Later Career

In 1914, J. Stokley Ligon was hired by the US Biological Survey (USBS) to survey prairie dog populations in the White Mountains of Arizona. Prairie dogs at that time were considered undesirable, and the dog towns Ligon recorded were slated for eradication with poison. In 1915, he was sent to the Poe Military Reservation in Wyoming to help develop a predator control program for that area. The fact that he was now in a position of planning and training suggests that he had already been involved in predator control programs, and that his organizational abilities were valued. This is further substantiated by his appointment that same year to the position of inspector of predatory animal control for Arizona and New Mexico, a job which kept him constantly on the move. For at least some of these trips, he continued to use his pack animals: Gila Red, Albert, and Smokey. In November 1915, his position was expanded to inspector at large, a job which allowed him to be assigned to special duties throughout the United States.

Ligon met Rose Kunz in Albuquerque in July 1918, and somehow amidst his travels managed to carry on a courtship. They were married in 1921 while he was on an assignment in Michigan. He continued to rise in the ranks of the predator control branch of the USBS until 1923, then took leave from that agency to carry out a statewide survey of wildlife for the New Mexico Department of Game and Fish. He spent a large portion of 1924 traveling the state by automobile, recording game animals, game birds, and predatory animals. He continued collecting birds during this time as well. He spent much of 1925 and 1926 compiling his survey results, and published *Wildlife of New Mexico* in 1927.

Beginning about 1920, Ligon also became involved in a growing conflict over the Black Canyon deer herd of southwestern New Mexico. Although not as well known as the North Kaibab deer conflict of the 1920s and 1930s, the Black Canyon deer overpopulation and range depletion paralleled very closely that more famous Arizona circumstance and lasted through the 1920s and into the 1930s, ending in a controversial herd-reduction doe hunt (Warren, 1997).

In 1926, Ligon wrote a special report entitled "Bears in New Mexico and Why They Should Be Protected." This was a plea for restraint in killing black bears, wherein he recommended eliminating only those that were proven killers of livestock. His efforts resulted in both black bears and grizzly bears being elevated to game animal status by the 1927 New Mexico Legislature (Ligon, 1927). By 1927, Ligon was also promoting the creation of the La Joya Refuge on the Rio Grande near Socorro. This area is now a state waterfowl refuge.

In 1928, Ligon's efforts began to gain him national recognition, and he received the *Outdoor Life* Medal for Wildlife Conservation from *Outdoor Life* magazine. In 1929, he and Rose started a private bird farm in Carlsbad, where they raised a variety of game birds for use in propagating them in the wild. In 1934, Ligon returned to employment with the USBS, this time as the regional supervisor covering New Mexico, Arizona, Oklahoma, Kansas, Texas, Arkansas, Colorado, and Utah. Rose continued to run the bird farm. In 1938, Ligon became a wildlife biologist in the federal aid branch of the USBS, serving, apparently, as the first coordinator of Pitman-Robertson Wildlife Restoration Act funds for wildlife. From that time on, his primary interest was game bird study and propagation, which included writing a monograph on Merriam's turkey (Ligon, 1946a) and another on methods of game bird propagation (Ligon, 1946b).

To recognize his lifetime achievement, he was awarded an honorary doctorate from the University of New Mexico in 1952.[49] In the late 1950s, he was still involved in efforts to protect and restore the masked bobwhite, traveling to Mexico and locating a rare extant population.

Ligon died in 1961, and his book, *New Mexico Birds* (1961), was completed by Bill Huey of the New Mexico Department of Game and Fish and Rose Ligon and published by the University of New Mexico Press.

Ligon, Leopold, and Changing Philosophies

Compared with Aldo Leopold, a contemporary, Ligon remains difficult to characterize. He broke from his family's traditional ranch-oriented lifestyle early in his life, seemingly determined to make a living as a freelance naturalist. Through sheer persistence, he carved out a career in wildlife management.

Ligon first met Leopold in November 1916 at a sportsmen's meeting in

Magdalena, New Mexico (Meine, 1988; Sweet, 2002). Leopold had arrived in Springerville, Arizona, in 1909, but worked mainly in the northern end of New Mexico with the US Forest Service. Leopold's 1913 bout with nephritis removed him from New Mexico for sixteen months, so he was not present at the time Ligon made his waterfowl survey. Leopold returned to New Mexico in 1914 and was assigned by the US Forest Service to a newly created game protection and recreation project for that agency in 1915. In this role, he traveled widely, holding meetings with sportsmen's groups, and he was functioning in this capacity when Ligon first met him. By 1915, Leopold had already begun to shift his views on predator control, writing mournfully of the death of a grizzly on Mount Taylor—one that had been killed by Ligon and his brother, Ed.

Leopold began his effort to organize a New Mexico game protective organization in January 1916 (Meine, 1988, 151). This organization was intended to represent middle-class sportsmen and provide a political force opposing the drift of New Mexico game laws toward the European system of ownership of wildlife by the wealthy landowners. Leopold began his campaign in Silver City and created the New Mexico Game Protective Association within two months. I find no record that Ligon was involved with this effort, although he was working in the vicinity of Silver City at this time, controlling wolves and other carnivores for the benefit of the livestock industry.

Much has been made in the literature of Leopold's change of heart toward predator control, usually attributed to his experience in the shooting of a wolf in 1909. However, Leopold did not change instantly and, as Meine points out, did not speak openly against unlimited predator control until about 1925, after he had seen its effects on Arizona's North Kaibab deer herd and New Mexico's Black Canyon deer herd. By this time, Ligon was questioning bear control, but shifted his views regarding other carnivores more slowly than Leopold and apparently never developed the broader ecological philosophy of Leopold. Nonetheless, Ligon formed an experience-based understanding of the habitat needs of wildlife and noted the value of riparian and alpine habitats in the Southwest more clearly and much earlier than Leopold (Ligon 1927, 44–49).

Ligon was aware and documented clearly that the low point in Western wildlife populations was exacerbated by the small rancher and homesteader during the initial surge of settlement, roughly from 1880 to 1935. The failure of the Homestead Act, because of its tendency to put families on arid acreages too small to support them, has been written many times. To some extent, an American myth has grown up around it wherein the big rancher wanting too much land persecutes the smaller and impoverished citizens, trying to drive them from the land. In the American myth, the little man fights back and ultimately wins. In reality, it was simple ecology and economics that defeated the little rancher. Only in the best of times would the small homesteads support a family. Bad times, when they came, drove them out, and the bigger ranch, often supported by money from the eastern United States or Europe, absorbed the small holdings.

But while the small homesteader was present, land and wildlife suffered. Deer, pronghorn, elk, bighorn, waterfowl, and gallinaceous birds were all seen as God's gifts to be exploited to support conquest of the undeveloped landscapes. Once the land was made agriculturally productive, these wild species were no longer needed, and their passing represented the success of the American way of life (which was a continuation of the European way of life). Breaking of the soil for farming, grazing by too much domestic stock on small acreages, and overuse of waters destroyed habitat and, ultimately, the wildlife that depended upon it. At the same time, impoverished homesteaders, barely surviving, killed and used any suitable wildlife inhabiting areas surrounding their lands. By the time Ligon rode through New Mexico in 1913, pronghorn were nearly gone from the state's prairies, elk had been eliminated from the southern mountain ranges and the Mogollon Rim, turkeys were greatly diminished, and species at the margins of their range, like masked bobwhite, were gone.

While those species were destroyed due to their usefulness to humans or to loss of habitat resulting from human use, others were being intentionally destroyed due to the damage they caused. Settlers relentlessly killed wolves and grizzlies, and some became specialists in trapping or hunting these large carnivores, augmenting their income with bounties. As a supervisor of federally employed trappers and hunters, Ligon presided over the demise of wolves and grizzlies in New Mexico. He developed an extremely efficient strategy of concentrating his hunters and trappers in areas where ranchers were complaining of livestock losses to predators. In more than one case, he brought such worthies as Ben Lilly, Jack Thompson, and Albert Pickens, along with less-well-known trappers and hunters, into single camps and focused trapping and hunting on the area of concern for several weeks, literally "cleaning out" the wolves and grizzlies. This strategy was not new to Ligon, resembling the Ligon family hunts in the San Mateo Mountains and Black Range between 1909 and 1912.

The efforts by Ligon and his hunters came at the end of at least four decades of efforts by the independent settlers to eliminate predators. Much of the damage had already occurred, and Ligon's troops were essentially a mop-up team. They effectively eliminated the grizzly, sent the wolf well along its way to extirpation, and would have destroyed the cougar and coyote had it been economically or biologically possible. Only the resilience of those two species saved them. Ligon also aided in the destruction of prairie dogs and apparently felt no remorse in the use of poisons, either against prairie dogs or predators.

Yet Ligon was an astute observer, and he had an independent mind. Unlike many of his contemporaries, he was able to recognize and acknowledge mistakes. He was one of the first to oppose extirpation of the black bear. As a result of his own observations, he concluded that only a few individuals of this species became serious killers of livestock, and he put a stop to efforts to remove every black bear in the woods. He opposed, early on, the killing of most raptors—at a time when any hawk was considered a "chicken hawk" and a target for elimination.

Ligon was a late-bloomer. He was thirty-four when he was hired to do the breeding bird survey and thirty-nine when a photograph of Miss Rose Kunz appears in his photographic journal. While he and Rose did not marry until 1921, when he was forty-two, his movements and ambitions began to change with their meeting. Unlike some of his wildland contemporaries, such as Ben Lilly and Nat Straw, he was able to transform from his early wild and independent lifestyle to a functional role within society. Straw and Lilly, like so many of the hunters and trappers who persisted in their perceived independence, ended as paupers, cared for by the state or caring neighbors, yet they attained more popular acclaim, simply as a result of their eccentricities (Dobie, 1950; Davis, 2003). J. Stokley Ligon proved himself early on to be as capable in the woods as any of the backwoods recluses, but he was able to apply the skills and knowledge acquired as a "gentle mountain man" and to contribute significantly to the developing discipline of wildlife management.

Appendix

An Assessment of Species Distributional, Behavioral, and Taxonomic Elements of the Breeding Bird Report

I have quoted Ligon's descriptions of various locations from his breeding bird report along with the presentation of the diary in the text above. His accounts of nearly one hundred species of birds observed and collected are given below, along with limited annotations, with the hope that they will hold historic value to future ornithologists and wildlife biologists.

Ligon did not identify many of the species in his report. Instead, he provided his notes and descriptions along with the specimen number. The species were then identified, and the scientific names shown here were inserted into the report by someone other than Ligon, most likely Wells W. Cooke. Formatting of the entries below duplicates that of the original report as closely as possible. For species not identified by Ligon, I have inserted common names in square brackets. Common names for those he identified have no brackets.

Species Accounts from the Breeding Bird Report

—Birds—

Colymbus nigricollis californicus Speci.
Eared Grebe No. 34

First met with July 17th Stinking Lake. Jicarilla Reservation.

July 19th North-East side of stinking Lake, Under "Chama Rod and Gun Club" Cabin, Colony of nesting birds. Nest mound-shape, floating among Tula Grass. This colony of nests is about 150 feet long, 25 feet wide. about 25 feet from land. Extends to open water. Nests in water 1½ to 4 feet. Birds keep up constant Racket day and night.

July 20th Passing among the nests I count 210 with eggs. I miss at least ⅓ of the nests. Making at the least 250 nests containing eggs. 1 to 6 in number. generally 3 as compliment. Many nests not complete. I am confident there are 600 breeding birds here. Although I see many birds to South of this place, Lower end of Lake, I find none nesting. They are constantly swarming through the nesting grass. Although the grass is thick, from one stand I counted 30 nests with eggs. The birds, when they have time, completely cover eggs before leaving nests. They rarely fly or run on water, always dive. Some duck and coot nesting among them. The birds rarely fight, seemingly very sociable.

July 26th I find the birds rather common at Horse Lake, most all here have young. Feeding in the Lake. 1 to 3 young to the pair. For a while, the young,—very small ride on the back of one parent, while the other dives and brings up the food. Then they leave the little mights floating and both bring up the feed. I observe some here half grown. They too dive, but do not remain under so long.

I notice too, where there is but one young, generally one old bird, although, I observe one young to the bird, only of good age,— half grown.

August 1st Along the center of the Colony, no eggs are to be seen now-all hatched but the nests have been extended each way, and many fresh eggs. All the nests contain moss in their construction. I believe 350 nests here.

—34 concl.—

Aug. 11th I see very plainly that I have estimated these birds at half. at Stinking Lake, ¾ mile west of colony previously reported, for ½ mile, through the West Center of the Lake, I count to-day, 275 nests, 1 to 4 eggs mostly fresh. Nests in grass no. 2, that grows scattered for ¾ mile, North and South, in, generally, about 4 ft. water, nests floating on moss. all eggs covered, that birds had time to cover. I am sure there are 300 nests here in this new colony, with eggs. others being built.

I find, the young that have hatched at the old colony, scattered over the lake ¼ to ½ mile West and South-west of the colony. Specimen, young, that was riding on its mothers back.

In his book *New Mexico Birds* (1961), written through his last years, Ligon relied heavily on his memory. He acknowledges Stinking Lake (Burford Lake) as the most important nesting area in New Mexico for the eared grebe. He states: "Here on one occasion, in mid-July, the author counted 250 nests in a single colony. . . . On a return visit a short time later another colony, containing 200 or more nests, with others under construction, was found some distance from the one previously located." If we assume that he was recalling his 1913 survey, he has become very conservative about the number of nests on the lake. By actual count, recorded in his breeding bird report, there were more. Also, in his book, he fails to provide the numbers of eggs in the nests, even though he describes the numbers clearly in his report.

Cooke drew heavily from Ligon's report while preparing his and Florence Merriam Bailey's *Birds of New Mexico* (1928). Cooke's contributions are provided separately from Bailey's. Bailey drew more heavily from later observers, especially Alexander Wetmore, in describing the population and its behavior at Stinking Lake.

When we visited Stinking Lake in August 2008, we saw abundant western grebes, some nesting, but no eared grebes. Ligon did not mention western grebes at the lake in 1913. Eared grebes are known to vary drastically in numbers and distribution over their range as a result of El Niño southern oscillation events (Jehl et al., 2002). A comparison of the nesting behavior of the two species as it varies over time would make an interesting study.

Podilymbus podiceps
[Pied-billed Grebe] No. 36

July 17th First met at Stinking Lake. Fairly com. Birds with young half grown, nests with eggs.

July 20th nest near Colony, (No. 34) Containing 8 eggs, 3 young chicks, just out of shell, one takes to water, other two tumble about over eggs, Parent birds, near, flopping and hollowing. Nest floating in three feet of water, rather large, mound-shape, cavity about 4 in above water. Made of half rotten Tula Blades and trash. The swimming chick, when mother came near to her, tried to crawl on her back. Young almost black with white stripes length-wise, Red back of eyes and over head.

July 29th 3 young half grown following old birds in lake. 5 young ⅓ grown with old birds near the shore. Both old and young dive. About sun-down I run up on nest of young and old birds at nest, came to roost, these young ¼ grown, and were piping (squeaking) while the old birds would barly show their bills above water occasionally.

Aug 7th and 8th I find these birds rather Abundant at Dulcie Lake, all have young, ⅓ to ⅔ grown. fairly tame.

Aug 10th This bird is much more com. than I first thought, after I have worked the Lakes well, I learn that by easing along the shore I am constantly getting sight of old and young birds. Clear Lake and Stinking Lake.

Erismatura jamaicensis
[Ruddy Duck] No. 37

July 17th First met at Stinking Lake. Very abundant. Ovary of specimen contained yelks [yolks?] of eggs 1/3 grown. Males chug, thro' the water, and also chouk with a sort of a grunt at the end of the chouk, very showy and proud while courting his mate. Rarely fly, but dive and never re-appear seemingly. but come up in the grass generally, float about in bands of 2 to a dozen. usually in pairs.

July 29th 2 young half grown with old birds.

July 31st These birds are very abundant, in small bands all around the Lake, where there is rank Tula, but it seems very few, comparitavely, are breeding, Yet, by their conduct, one concludes that is their object. While I am on the shore, they give my presence little regard, never halting their love-actions, but when I appear in canoe they scatter and go under, this is the case with most all the birds here, the canoe seems to frighten them.

July 31st Male bird examined showed to be breeding bird.

Aug. 10th Clear Lake, North-East Stinking Lake, 400 yds. Jicarilla Reservation. Elev. 7000. Old bird, out in lake with five young, when I shot, all went under except the wounded one and one more. Mother kept diving, showing only head and back, the remaining 4 young bunched up, floated about out in the lake, never diving or showing any inclination to come to the rank Tula Grass near the shore.

For this species, Ligon relies on later observations, as late as 1956, in *New Mexico Birds* (1961). He also acknowledges Wetmore's 1918 survey of the Jicarilla Lakes. For some reason, he doesn't mention his 1916 observations.

One of the curious aspects of *New Mexico Birds* is Ligon's handling of references. He has no bibliography, although he does provide a discussion of the ornithological literature within the introductory sections. Ligon was certainly, by this time, aware of referencing protocols for technical literature. He had been a member of the American Ornithologists' Union since 1912 and therefore received their journal. One can only wonder why he decided not to use standard referencing protocols. Possibly, he considered his audience to be amateur ornithologists and bird-watchers who would not bother to access the more technical papers. His primary stated reason for publishing his book was the unavailability of Florence Merriam Bailey's *Birds of New Mexico* (1928), long out of print. Ligon died before his book was published, so perhaps the error is one of transcription.

Ligon does provide brief biographical sketches of some of the early naturalists who influenced New Mexico ornithology, and he acknowledges the work by Florence Merriam Bailey. He also notes an earlier list of New Mexico birds that was created in 1911 by Fanny Ford (Mrs. Arthur Sloan) and published as *The Natural Resources Survey of the Conservation and Natural Resources Commission of New Mexico* (Ford, 1911). A Miss Fanny Ford of the State Agricultural College, Mesilla Park, New Mexico, appears in the report on the 30th meeting of the American Ornithologists' Union as having been elected an associate member. She was one of 183 elected at that meeting. Others of note who were elected that year included Ira N. Gabrielson and Stokley Ligon. This meeting was held in November 1912. Ligon's address was given as Pecos, Reeves County, Texas (American Ornithologists' Union, 1913).

Ligon's description of the behavior, especially the diving behavior, of the ruddies seems directly opposed to Florence Merriam Bailey's later description. She does not note the diving, and in fact observed that the birds tended to remain calm while other ducks were fleeing. Ruddies are known to be competent divers, hence Florence Merriam Bailey's failure to mention it is puzzling—a case of different observers giving significance to different things.

Anas platyrhynchos
[Mallard] No. 35

July 17—Common at Stinking Lake, Specimen shot at nest. Nest was in rank grass, out of water. built of grass blades, and a few feathers. Ovary contained soft-shell egg.

This is the same Species of duck as No's. 6 and 7, young from V + T Meadow, June 6th. The birds seem tame, that is the female, as they are always in attendance.

Mallards are more common along smaller and high-elevation streams than any other duck species. Seemingly, Ligon would have seen them in such places as 74 Draw and Hoyt Creek, but does not note them. Perhaps they were so common as to be unworthy of mention.

Ligon collected them at V + T Lake, and in *New Mexico Birds* (1961), he notes that they winter there, using the stream below the lake. However, none of the book entries seems to use information from this survey. His discussion in his book is much expanded on this species and acknowledges their presence in many other parts of the state, as well as in the White Mountains of Arizona.

Since Ligon's visit, Wall Lake has been constructed near the mouth of Hoyt Creek, and it provides resting habitat for mallards as well as other small-lake-adapted species. We saw a mallard pair with young at Wall Lake on June 4, 2009.

Florence Merriam Bailey's discussion is more detailed than Ligon's. In citing Ligon's 1913 survey, Florence Merriam Bailey (or Cooke), as did E. W. Nelson, mistakenly refer to V + T Lake as Beaver Lake. Cooke gives the date as June 6, when Ligon was at V + T Meadow, after camping the evening before at Beaver Creek (Bailey, 1928). Nowhere, however, does Ligon refer to Beaver Lake. In fact, in a later correspondence, Ligon corrects Bailey, noting that he is referring to V + T Lake.

Marila americana
[Redhead] No. 38

July 21st This duck seems to be rather abundant here at Stinking Lake. Specimen was swimming with 6 very young. Collected at North End of isolated lake. Mother bird was tame, allowing me to make second shot before I secured her. They were in shallow water, that was full of moss, all persisted in staying to-gether, until I crowded up, then they scattered and began to disappear under water.

(Perhaps Same as No. 50)

Anything goes, it seems, for the cause of science. Ligon does not point out that in killing the mother redhead, he most certainly doomed the entire brood of six young as well. In *New Mexico Birds* (1961), Ligon notes Florence Merriam Bailey's record of this species at Stinking Lake (Burford Lake) in 1904 (based upon Bailey's first visit?) and says that they were the most abundant large duck present in 1913. He also mentions observing them nesting there in 1916.

Querquedula discors
[Blue-winged teal] No. 40

July 20th This duck is very com. at Stinking Lake. I have observed several families of old and young. Specimen had young half grown. As I shot old bird, they disappeared like a flash in the grass.

July 30th See several families to-day, among channels to South of main lake, The small, isolated lake has but few other kinds of duck, but these are abundant in it tamest of all the ducks here. The bands of young are hard to see, remaining under dense cover, occasionally showing at edge of lake-open water, very closely bunched.

Aug. 7th At Dulcie Lake, Elev. 6700, While walking from one End to other of the Lake, West side— Saw. old Duck and 8 young, half grown, Old duck 6 young, 1/3 grown old Duck 4 young 1/3 grown. not wild.

Aug. 10th This little duck is very abundant at Stinking lake with young, Especially in Clear Lake

Ligon's *New Mexico Birds* (1961) notes the species as common and widely distributed in the state, but makes no mention of it at Stinking Lake, even though he noted it as very common there during his survey. Like the mallard, it is still common throughout the state.

Marila Americana
Red Head Duck (No. 50)

I find these the most common of the larger duck, at Stinking Lake, although I have not identified any, for sure, with nests or young, actions of them warrant me listing them as breeders.

One of the first ducks nests I found, I decided it was a Red Head.

July 18th In a bunch of Shin Oak brush, about 50 ft. up on Mt. side, to South East of the Lake, The bird was not very wild. Nest was made of the oak leaves, with feathers from the ducks breast mixed. Contained 5 well incubated eggs.

Two days later I returned to get her and a Photo. of nest. A skunk had beaten me. ate the eggs and scratched the nest to pieces.

(Possibly same as no. 38)

I'm not sure why Ligon has a second entry on this species. Ligon's limited knowledge of botany shows again here. I doubt that there is any shin oak in the area.

Chaulelasmus streperus
[Gadwall] —No. 65—

This duck is very abundant at Stinking Lake, and is breeding quite Freely, Scattered all around the Lake in the Tula Grass. This specimen, no. 65 col.

Aug. 10th Was with her 12 young, that were about ²/₃ grown, near the shore, they swam directly out in the Lake, the mother came back near the shore flopping and quacking, After I had secured her, the young were out of range.

In *New Mexico Birds* (1961), Ligon provides a date of his observation of this species (August 10, 1913) at Stinking Lake, suggesting he had some access to additional notes. He is very uneven in this, and it is difficult to assess his record-keeping methods.

Fulica Americana
—Coot— (No. 46)

—young—
May 23rd Migratory birds on V + T Lake Gila River Forest Reserve.
June 11th Fairly common, Rio Grande Valley,—Las Palomas Springs. Sierra Co. Breeding.
June 15th A very few at Mal Pais Spring. Tula Rosa Flats.
June 24th 4 ms. S.W. of Lakewood station, Pecos Valley, about 20 birds, at small lake nesting.
June 25th At Clark Lake, Pecos Valley, South West of Lake Arthur 5 ms. Many, some nesting.
July 3rd Artesian Lakes, near Santa Rosa. Both sides of River (Pecos). A few nesting on west side, no nests on East.
July 25th Very abundant in the Jicarilla Indian Reservation. Breeding, perhaps 500 Pair at Stinking Lake, Also abundant at Horse Lake, Some few with young at Rock Lake. Lay 5 to 12 eggs. Floating nests, usually well out in water, in Tula Grass. Continues to build up under eggs, as nest settles. Young take to water soon as they leave the shell. Have scarlet Heads. I see many combats among them, often 4 participating.
July 30th Stinking Lake, Abundance of young, some about grown. Many nests with eggs.
Aug. 8th Dulcie Lake Jicarilla Reservation. Elev. 6700. Many coot with young. Some almost as large as old birds.
Aug. 10th Young birds hatching. Nests with eggs. Stinking Lake.
Aug 12th The coot, certainly has the nest-building problem solved, by constantly re-constructing their nests, and in the first place, locating them.

Ligon's description of the coot in *New Mexico Birds* (1961) is rather general, with no acknowledgement of his 1913 survey. Florence Merriam Bailey, on the other hand, relies heavily on Ligon's 1913 observations.

I saw no coots on October 16, 2007, at the V + T Ranch meadow, and as stated earlier, V + T Lake was dry. On October 14, however, Patty and I observed perhaps fifty coots at Wall Lake, so they are in the area. On June 5, 2009, the wet meadow at Slash Ranch headquarters had been recently grazed and had only a very shallow covering of water toward its center. Habitat for coots or other waterfowl was not present.

Oxyechus vociferous
Kildeer

Winter of 1912–13 Kildeer observed fairly common, Alamosa River, Socorro and Sierra Co's. Also on the East Fork Gila River. Seen constantly thro' winter.

Apr. 2nd at V + T Lake, They had arrived in abundance. Socorro Co. Elev. 7000.

May 8th Very young birds at Palomas Springs on the Rio Grande. Sierra Co.

May 22nd V + T Lake, young abundant. Abundant over Gila River Reserve.

June 15th to 30th Abundant and breeding over Rio Grande and Pecos Valleys. (All New Mexico)

July 25th Old and young at Stinking Lake and Horse Lake. Jicarilla Reservation.

Again, Florence Merriam Bailey provides more of Ligon's various observations than does Ligon himself. She relies not only on his 1913 survey but also on later observations. Obviously, even after Ligon was officially a member of the USBS's Predator and Rodent Control Branch, he continued recording birds and submitting records. In quoting him, Bailey cites "(MS)" at the end of some paragraphs, apparently referring to his breeding bird survey report.

Scarlet Ibis

Apr. 28th 1913, At V + T Headquarter Ranch, Gila River Forest Reserve. In meadow near Ranch House. Elev. about 6900 feet. Socorro Co.

—Note—

This was the first of these birds I have seen, but I am quite sure it was the Scarlet Ibis. In size, about the same as a Long Bill Curlew, with Same bill, would pass for one, except, It was almost Black beneath, with red or Scarlet back. It was alone, very tame. I had no gun there at the time. It left in Late P.M. went North. The Ranch-boy said it had been there several days.

[At the top of this page, above all entries, is a note in brackets, very faint, saying "not to be copied," suggesting that Cooke or Bailey had rejected this identification.]

This is one of Ligon's most curious records. He saw the ibis before he started the official survey, and apparently got a good look at it. However, other than this particular comment, I find no other acknowledgement of this observation elsewhere. His description does not match a scarlet ibis, and by 1961, in *New Mexico Birds*, he states that neither it nor the white-faced glossy ibis have been recorded for the state. Florence Merriam Bailey mentions the scarlet ibis for the state, but the only record is much older and tenuous, from a partial specimen examined by

Elliott Coues. Bailey does not mention Ligon's note. Also, she apparently considers the white-faced ibis and the glossy ibis as a single species. By 1961, Ligon was aware of the distinction between the white-faced and the glossy. According to Sibley, only the white-faced ibis commonly occurs in New Mexico (Sibley, 2000). I have searched literature on Latin America and even European birds and do not find anything that comes close to Ligon's 1913 description. Ford (1911) recorded the scarlet ibis as a straggler to the state, citing the American Ornithologists' Union Check-list of North American Birds.

Great Blue Heron

Winter 1912–13, Rather common on Alamosa River, Socorro and Sierra Co's. Elev. about 5500. Also, on East Gila River, Socorro Co., all winter, Elev. 6200. Breeds on Main Gila.

June 30—Common on Pecos River from Carlsbad to Ft. Sumner, Breeds about and below Sumner in the Cotton-wood

July 2nd Common North-west of Ft. Sumner, to Porta De Luna. Breeds here.

July 4th I am informed that it breeds here at Santa Rosa Elev. 4600. Fairly Com.

July 8th observed at Anton Chico.

July 18 3 at Stinking Lake, Jicarilla Reservation. Alti. 7000.

This bird is rather abundant along the Rio Grande.

Aug. 7th Specimen at Dulcie Lake, Elev. 6700. Jicarilla Res. only one bird seen.

Ligon apparently failed to place a header at this point in the report, giving the appearance that the following entry was the continuance of the great blue heron account. However, the specimen number, along with the diary entries, makes it clear that he was writing about black-crowned night-herons.

[Black-Crowned Night-Heron] (No. 41)

June 11th one at Palomas Springs, Sierra Co. Rather common at Swamps along Rio Grande.

July 20th I estimate 25 of these birds at Stinking Lake. Elev. 7000. Many nests in the willows on the Lake shore. I presume these are their nests. The birds, now, mostly young sit about in the thickest, rankest Tula Grass in the Lake. Stay to-gether, rather wild. Hollow at night, and Late P.M.

I presume they feed off the Bull-frogs, that are very abundant here at Stinking Lake. The frogs are always found back of the Shore, out of water in the short thick grass.

Little Brown Crane

[This is another entry that has a note at the top of the page saying "not to be copied," suggesting that Cooke disagreed with the identification.]

I have never found a nest or young of this bird. Still, in Summer. I have several times noted it at Palomas Springs. The fact is, I never hunted to find it breeding, as opportunity never admitted.

June 11th I observed one at Palomas Springs.

The little brown crane is a subspecies of the sandhill. Florence Merriam Bailey considers it to be a separate species, but then notes it as a synonym for *Grus canadensis*. She also lists *Grus mexicana* as the binomial for the sandhill, so the taxonomy at the time of her writing seems confused. In more recent literature, Sibley (2000) notes the sandhill crane and the lesser sandhill crane, a subspecies.

Himantopus mexicanus
[Black-necked Stilt] (no. 22)

June 25th First met at Clark Lake, 5 ms. S.W. of Lake Arthur Station, Pecos Valley. 2 Pairs here Breeding.

June 27th 6 Ms., North E. of Roswell. I think these were breeding birds, tho' am no[t] sure. 2 Pr. here. 1 Specimen. These were at a small alkali Lake.

June 28, at Mouth of Salt Creek, 18 ms. North-East of Roswell, 3 Pr. nesting. These were at the shallow Lakes, very bad water—in the open valley, 2 ms. from the Pecos River. one nest, built on salt grass hump. About 30 ft. from water. Slight depression, with short stick in bottom. 4 eggs. Birds run about, some distance away, flopping their drooped wings, as I draw away, the[y] rise and fly about hollowing. Elev. about 3500.

Ligon gives a general discussion of the black-necked stilt in his book, with no reference to his early sightings. Florence Merriam Bailey acknowledges the above records and also notes a record provided by Ligon from the Jornada del Muerto in 1905. This is my first clear note of his presence on the Jornada that early. It also suggests that he was corresponding with the US Biological Survey and perhaps submitting specimens prior to 1907.

Actitus macularius
[Spotted Sandpiper] (No. 31)

July 15th This Snipe is Probably the same as Specimen no. 11. [" = yes" is written in pencil here, undoubtedly a note by Cooke] I find them fairly common Along the Chama River.

To-day Collect this Specimen 20 ms. West of Abiquiu, on Chama River, on Sand Bar. Had 2 very small young that resembled little kildeer. These ran about among the gravel, trying to hide from me.

July 20th Fairly Com. and breeding at Stinking Lake.

Actitis macularius (No. 11)

June 10th I find these Snipe common on the Rio Grande, along the Sand Bars. 3 years ago [1910] I found young, 2 miles below Elephant Butte.

Male often seen gliding upward over water and Sand Bars. hollowing as he drops and circles, seemingly, parading for his mate.

Numenius americanus
Long-Bille[d] Curlew

June 30th First met with, coming up the Pecos Valley 35 ms. South of Ft. Sumner. Near the River, West side—Elev. 4000. Breeding here, one Pair, in the low marshy river flat. Bird met me on the hill a mile away, running about hollowing and drooping about in the grass, as I came near, it flies near, running about flopping its wings.

July 1st I am told they breed about Ft. Sumner.

July 5. Breeding North of Santa Rosa.

July 8th Breeding, in prairie country 5 and 10 ms. North-W. of Santa Rosa. Elev. 4800.

Texan Bob-white
Colinus virginaianus texanus

June 24th Although I keep a look-out for Bob White in the Pecos Valley about Carlsbad and North, I see no birds. I am told by hunters and others at Lakewood, that Previous to a heavy snow-storm of some 6 years ago, Bob-white were to be seen here,—at Lakewood, even on the west side of the river. They say, however, few survived the winter, and none have been seen in the valley since. The Bob White are common, East of the valley, in the Sand Hills and extend well into Texas in the Sand and Shinnery to the Texas and Pacific Rail Road, Touching the Pecos at, and about Dixie Land Texas, but no more, until one reaches, The mouth of Solio Creek, East of Ft. Stockton Texas.

(Letter from W. R. Owen, Ex. County Clerk of Eddy Co. N.M. Relative to Bob White in the Pecos Valley, of N.M. Inclosed)

(Bob-White in the Pecos Valley N. Mex.)

[Written on lined tablet paper and attached to report page]

Carlsbad N. Mex.

June 30—13

Mr. Stokely Ligon
Santa Rosa N M
Dear Sir

Replying to your enquiry, of June 25th will say that the natural range of the Bob White Quail is on the East side of the Pecos River. I would say from about the Chavez Co. line South, very few coveys on the River but quite numerous in the sand east of the River say from 15 to 20 miles east. The farther East you go the more plentiful, as to any ducks breeding here I have never observed any.

Yours very truly
N. R. Owens
(Jake)

Ligon failed to find bobwhites himself in 1913 but notes their former occurrence near Carlsbad. In his 1927 *Wildlife of New Mexico*, he noted small populations east of Portales and on the Cimarron River. Florence Merriam Bailey considered them essentially gone from the state, due to loss of suitable habitat. The drought of the late 1920s and early 1930s undoubtedly pushed them to extirpation in the state. Bobwhites now occur in the eastern one-third of New Mexico (Kamees et al., 2008).

Callipepla squamata
Scaled Quail

Scaled quail are fairly common in New Mexico, from the Central part of the State South, although they reach pretty well north, they are not abundant.

June 9th Coming East from Gila Reserve. first seen East side of Cuchillo Mts. Elev. 6300.

June 14th Abundant in San Andrea Mts.

June 19th East side of Sacramento Mts. First observed 2 ms. above Elk. Penasco River. Elev. 6500. Very abund East on Penasco.

June 24th 6 ms. Above Carlsbad 3 coveys, young, ¼ grown.

June 25th In alfalfa fields about Artesia.

July 6th Bunch very young 10 ms. N.W. of Santa Rosa. Com about Santa Rosa.

July 12 Com. in Pecos Valley to old San Miquil.

July 14th Rare North-West of Santa Fe. A few observed on Chama River below Abiquiu.

Aug. 14. Observed at Haynes, Rio Arriba Co.

The August 14 location (Haynes) would have been between Stinking Lake and Pueblo Bonito. Julyan suggests it was very near the county line of Rio Arriba and San Juan. It therefore was probably somewhere near the present-day location of Lybrook or Forty-Four Store. The scaled quail is the most widely distributed quail in New Mexico (Kamees et al., 2008).

Lorphortyx gambeli
Gambel's Quail

I have never observed this quail East of the Rio Grande valley. It is generally speaking, a bird of the watered courses. Very abundant in the Rio Grande Valley North to San Marcial. Elev. about 4000. and west on its tributaries to Ojo Caliente, Socorro Co. and to Fairview, in the Foot of the Black Range. Elev. 6200. on the Gila, East Fork, to mouth of Beaver Creek Elv. 6400.

June 10th At Cotton-wood Spring Cuchillo Creek, 12 ms. West of Elephant Butte, I find it very abundant. Many in pairs, also in bunches of a dozen, no young observed yet.

Gambel's quail now occurs well onto the Jornada del Muerto, at least. It is common throughout the San Andres Mountains. From all appearances, it has either expanded its range or become more abundant in areas where it existed in Ligon's time. Removal of grazing and protection of the San Andres Mountains from hunting may have been factors. Ligon, in *New Mexico Birds* (1961), notes that by 1960 or so, the species was established in the foothills of the Sacramento Mountains. It now occurs in south-central Lincoln County and north-central Otero County (Kamees et al., 2008).

Meleagris gallopavo merriami
Merriam's Turkey

Nov. 1912 Several bunches along West Slope of San Mateo Mts. Socorro Co. N. Mex.

Jan 1913. North of Haut [Hoyt] Creek, Black Range, Socorro Co. I find this turkey abundant. A high divide, covered with Pine, Pinion, and Juniper timber runs Parallel to Haut Creek. Elev. about 7500. A good mast of Pinion nuts, the great food of Turkey. Several bunches here, one of about 50 birds. Also 2 bunches range on South side of Haut. Distributed pretty well over Gila Reserve. Begins gobbling in this district Mar. 25th. Its great enemies are, to— nests, Skunk and Cats, to old birds, Golden Eagle, one of the worst enemies out of thick timber.

June 19th in Sacramento Mts. fairly Com.

June 22. I learn that turkey are no more to be found in the Guadalupe Mts. A few years ago they were in these mts.

—Food of the Turkey—

Acorns, while they last are a favorite food, but these are usually soon gathered up being a universal food for all game and rodents. Pinion, when a mast, is the principle food, comes in in Sept. and lasts until June. Where these cannot be had during winter, The turkey survive on Juniper Berries. These are not fat producing, a mast of long duration.

Feb. 10th Haut [Hoyt] Creek Black Range Socorro Co. Elev. about 7200. Turkey hen, crop contained 76 juniper, 25 pinion, 6 acorn, 30 Soft worms an inch long, grass blades and some rock. Killed at roost.

Mar. 25th Black Mts. Socorro Co. Elev. 8000. Gobbler. Shot at sun[down?] weight about 30 Lbs. Crop. 30 pinion, 215 Juniper berries. Tail feather 17 in. Spurs 1 in. Whiskers, 10 in. bunch of 50 birds. Snow on ground.

In *New Mexico Birds* (1961), Ligon notes that he believed about five hundred turkeys existed on the west slopes of the Black Range in 1912–1913. Even in 1960, however, he is still recommending control of skunks, eagles, and, especially, coyotes. He is also a proponent of supplementary feeding in poor years. My impression is that turkeys within the Black Range and other national forest lands are about as abundant as they were during Ligon's time, if not more so. Reduced grazing has probably helped. Managing the forests for a more open condition than presently exists would probably allow the species to increase even more.

When Ligon (1946a) wrote the first book to be published on the Merriam's turkey, the species had been restored to the Guadalupe Mountains in Texas, bordering New Mexico. Turkeys apparently never were extirpated from the Sacramento Mountains, and they might have re-populated the Guadalupes. Guadalupe Mountains National Park now lists them as present in the forests higher on the mountains.

Band-tailed Pigeon
Columba fasciata

Sept. and Oct. 1912. These birds are rather com. in the San Mateo Mts. Socorro Co. Where there is mast. While at rest they stay in the high peaks, 8000 to 9000 ft. Among the Spruce and Pine.

Jan. 1913, Most common in the high Divide north of Haut [Hoyt] Creek, Black Range, Socorro Co. where there is abundance of mast. Often observe the birds on Pinion trees picking the nuts from burs. Water in box of canyon—Haut Creek.

March 1st. Pigeon have been seen all the time this winter, on Haut Creek. Also, I observe them now, at different Places, over the Range. May 1st on Middle Gila. Elev. 8000. see several.

June 3rd, 1913 In Monument Pass Black Range, Sierra Co. find them nesting. Quite common here. One nest, 1 egg. Nest 10 ft. up in tall Sugar Pine on Horizontal limb, in crotch. Nest made of nothing but dry twigs. Birds fairly tame. Make coarse, mournful sound when cooing-males, in nesting time, also, often heard in winter. They usually do this while perched in top of dead Pine.

Food consists entirely of Pinion nuts, when these can be had. They also eat the Dwarf Cumac [Sumac?], when these are to be had.

June 19th. Some pigeon in the Sacramento Mts.

June 22nd. Pigeon fairly common in the Guadalupe Mts. New Mex and Texas.

July 31st. I Have observed no pigeon in the North Part of the State—Pecos or Jemez Forest Reserves.

In *New Mexico Birds* (1961), Ligon gives the distribution of band-tailed pigeons as forested regions throughout the state. He also mentions a heavy concentration of bandtails on the west side of the Black Range in 1913, feeding on a good pinyon crop. While he notes the presence of bandtails in the 1913 breeding bird report, he does not consider their numbers as remarkable. Only in retrospect, after years of observation throughout the state, has he realized that the 1913 concentration was perhaps unusual. He also states that the birds remained throughout the winter in the area.

Zenaidura macroura marginella
Mourning Dove

Jan 1913. Observed one dove on East Gila River below mouth of Beaver Creek.
Apr. 1st. 1 Corduroy Flat, Gila Reserv. 7200 ft.
" 5th. 1 V + T Ranch. " " "
" 7th 5 V + T " " " "
" 15 Rather Com. over the Reserve.
May 5th 1913, Nest with 2 fresh eggs. 1 mile East of Chloride. In Pinion bush, 6 ft. from ground. Elev. 6200.
July 9th on Pecos River, 15 miles above Anton Chico. Nest in Pinion tree, one fresh Egg.
July 31st Fairly Com. Jicarilla Reserv. I have found them generally destributed over the entire State, but it seems few nest. Generally in pairs.

Mourning doves were common in 1913, as they are now, and even wintered through much of the state, at least during mild winters. Perhaps more unusual than Ligon's observations of mourning doves during his survey is his lack of observations of other columbids. If he were to cross the Rio Grande now, he would also note white-winged doves, Inca doves, and collared doves. White-winged and Inca doves have expanded their ranges significantly, with white-winged doves occurring at least as far north as Albuquerque, and Inca doves common in Hillsboro. The collared doves are a relatively new arrival in the Southwest, but have expanded range and numbers rapidly. In 2005, we were seeing them at the Hubbell Trading Post on the Navajo Nation in northern Arizona.

Cathartes aura septentrionalis
Turkey Vulture

Spring Arrival.

Apr. 2nd 1 Gila River Reserve, near V + T Ranch. Elev. 7000.
Apr. 5— 2. Apr. 8th I see many above V + T Ranch.

—Range—

May 25th Com. about Cliffs, Chloride Creek, Sierra Co. N. Mex.
June 19th Rather Rare, Sacramento Mts. Nesting, James Canyon, East of Cloudcroft. Elev. 7000.

June 20—abundant on Penasco River, West of Hope, and to Lower Penasco. Nesting in cliffs along the canyons, among the barren hills.

July 7th from Carlsbad to Santa Rosa fairly com. At Santa Rosa and in the Gorge of the Pecos North. Very abundant, nesting in the side canyons.

July 18 Rather com. on Chama River and in Jicarilla Reservation—

For years, when we lived in Chino Valley, Arizona, we expected the vultures to arrive about April 1, corresponding closely with Ligon's observation of an April 2 arrival in 1913. In recent years, my impression is that vultures have begun to arrive in Arizona and New Mexico earlier, in early March. I don't know whether anyone is tracking this change.

Circus hudsonius
Marsh Hawk

I have no record of its occurance in the Gila Reserve.

June 25th Coming up Pecos Valley, see first bird, 4 ms. South of Lake Aurthur, on Cotton-wood draw.

June 27th observed, about Roswell am North East.

June 28th Com. on Salt Creek N. of Roswell, Nesting in Salt Marshes near mouth of Salt Creek 18 ms. N.E. of Roswell. Elev. about 3600.

Aug. 4th One Rock Lake, Jicarilla Reservation. Seemed to be after the Black bird, put them all on hills in Shin-Oak brush.

Buteo borealis calurus
Western Red-tail

Observed throughout winter in Gila Reserve.

Apr. 4th 4 ms. North of V + T Ranch Gila Reserve. Socorro Co. Elev. 7000. Nest fifty feet up, on shelf of Perpendicular Cliff—2 Slightly Incubated eggs. also, mile above this, nest near top of tall Pine. Nest was about 80 ft. up.

June 19th Sacramento Mts.

July 15th Upper Pecos, fairly com.

July 31st In Pine, Stinking Lake, Elev. 7000. Young continually wailing for food. They have a lonesome scream—the young.

In the Gila Reserve, in Monument Pass, Sierra Co. Elev. 8000. I also have Record, Downy young in nest, Dead Spruce 60 feet up, side of canyon

May 20th Nest with three young at Chloride, in Pinion tree.

May 4th Elev. 6200.

Buteo swainsoni
Swainson's Hawk

Fairly com. in Summer in the Jornada Valley, Sierra and Dona Ana Co's. And in early fall, It is very abundant, Moving over the flats and hills in great flocks, here, feeding on the big Grass hoppers. I consider this hawk a very useful bird. As far as I know, it bothers nothing of value to civilization.

June 15th Tularosa Flats, 25 ms. West of Tularosa. Nest 4 feet up in Scrub Mesquite 2 very young birds. Scraps of snakes in nest, 1 whole young ground squirrel, one piece. Ants very thick in nest and on little fellows. Mother bird at nest.

June 19th Nest with young, 50 ms. North of Roswell, in Cotton-wood.

July 1st Nesting north of Ft. Sumner, in Cotton-wood.

One of the most interesting of the phenomena involving Swainson's hawks was missed by Ligon and the Baileys alike. At the lava caves on the Jornada del Muerto, now within the boundaries of the Armendaris Ranch, Swainson's hawks gather each evening during the summer to hover in the evening flight of bats leaving the caves, grabbing them out of the air and at times consuming them without landing. Seemingly, such should also occur at Carlsbad Caverns. Because Ligon lived and worked on the Jornada when young and spent the last two decades, at least, of his life at Carlsbad, his failure to mention this behavior is curious.

Falco sparverius phalaeria
Sparrow-Hawk (western)

Observed all winter, In Gila River Reserve.

April 6th Common.

May 1st Begun to locate nesting places. Common over Gila Reserve.

May 12th At Cotton-wood Spring on Cuchillo Creek, 12 miles West of Elephant Butte, 2 Pairs have nests, 4 eggs each, fresh. One nest in base of rotten-snag, near top of tall Cotton-wood, 1 nest about 30 feet up in short at end of limb.

June 19th Com. In Sacramento Mts.

July 1st Very abundant at Ft. Sumner. Elev. 4200. 25 ms. North-West, find young in trees out of nest.

July 10th Young below old San Miguel Pecos Valley.

July 31st Common Every place I have been, where there are hollows for it to nest in. Very com. here in Jicarilla Reservation.

[A pencil note here says "add p 77."]

Aguila chrysaetos
Golden Eagle

Abundant in the San Andrea Mts. Feeds Principally on Jack Rabbit.

Dec. 20th Rather numerous in and about the San Mateo Mts. Socorro Co. Many old nests in the high cliffs in the Box of Alamosa River above Monticello. Birds roost here. Come to the cliffs about sun-set.

Jan. 10th Fairly com. In Gila Reserve. Very often Catch them on Steel traps set for wild animals. Most abundant about V + T Lake. Where it gets a wounded Duck occasionally.

Mar. 15th Nest on Chloride Creek, 5 ms. above Chloride. 300 ft. above Canyon Bed, on Cliff, 100 feet high. Nest 20 feet below top on shelf, Huge construction, made of sticks, cavity contained fresh Spruce tips for lining. Bird was rather tame. one egg bad doubtless been chilled as it contained no young. the other (2 eggs in nest) was about 10 days incubated. The nest was on the South face of Cliff, north side of Canyon. It also nests fairly common on Corduroy Canyon Gila Reserve. always in Cliffs.

June 24th Observe one at Resivoir-Lakewood. Eddy Co. I have seen no Golden Eagle in Northern Part of the State.

Aug. 9th Beautiful Specimen of the bird to-day, on hill South-east of Rock Lake, 6 ms. North, Stinking Lake.

Aug. 16 and 17. Several observed at and near Putnam (Pueblo Bonito) San Juan Co.

The golden eagle nest in Chloride Creek mentioned is the same nest that Ligon raided for eggs when accompanied by Raymond Schmidt. Possibly, the visit to the nest described by Schmidt in chapter 2 occurred as late as March 1913. The August 16 and 17 records confirm that Ligon definitely visited Chaco Canyon on his way to Chloride from Stinking Lake. His comment that he had not seen the species in the northern end of the state is immediately contradicted by his records on the Jicarilla Apache Indian Reservation. By the time he wrote *New Mexico Birds* (1961), Ligon acknowledged that the species occurred statewide. In his discussion of the golden eagle in *New Mexico Birds*, Ligon perhaps most nearly discloses a growing ambivalence about predator control. While he acknowledges the need for "local control" to protect wildlife or livestock, he also states that the good done by eagles in eating jackrabbits, etc., far outweighs the value of livestock it kills. He also notes that eagles were abundant at times when bighorn were also abundant on the San Francisco River, perhaps for the first time suggesting that predator control is not necessarily needed to benefit ungulates.

Haliaeetus leucocephalus
Bald Eagle

Feb. 2nd. At head of East Gila Socorro Co. I observed a beautiful specimen of the Bald Eagle, the first I have ever noted in N. Mex. This is at the junction of Taylor and Beaver Creeks. I am told it has been a constant resident here this winter.

—Later— In March I observe 2 of the birds at this place, but they disappear.

May 12th I am informed by Montoya's who live at the mouth of Diamond, East Gila, that the "White Head" eagle nests four miles from their ranch, in Pine Tree, Bed of Canyon.

July 31st Jicarilla Reservation. In all my rounds in New Mexico, the above are the only records I have of Bald Eagle, N. Mex.

Bald eagles must have been low in numbers in the state between 1907 and 1913. Given the amount of time Ligon spent afield during this period, it seems inconceivable that he saw so few of these birds. Ligon felt that the bald eagle had increased significantly by 1960, although even then he has only two records of nests. Bald eagles are now quite common at the Bosque del Apache National Wildlife Refuge in the winter.

Falco mexicanus
Prairie Falcon

Apr. 6th In cliffs above V + T Ranch, Gila Reserve, Elev. 7200—about. Nest containing 5 fresh eggs. Nest about 50 feet up in shear cliff. 35 feet from top. Birds fly by hollowing.

Apr. 29th Cliffs above V + T Ranch (Same as above) Nest 4 incubated eggs.

May 1st. Near nest found Apr. 6th Nest 4 fresh eggs. Very likely second nest of this pair.

May 3rd Observed on Continental Divide, North West of Fairview, 20 ms.

July 5th Old and young in Gorge of Pecos River, 4 ms. above Santa Rosa. Elev. 4700.

Apr. 1st One Specimen 5 ms. above V + T Ranch, Socorro Co.

Here is another situation where Ligon had climbed down a cliff to investigate a nest, no doubt, although he doesn't describe his activity. Without Raymond Schmidt's description of his egg collection at the eagle nest in Chloride Canyon, found in chapter 2, we might not realize that Ligon regularly climbed over cliffs and into relatively tall trees to observe nests and collect eggs. Schmidt mentions that Ligon climbed trees barefooted—like a monkey. The dates of these observations, with the exception of the one near Santa Rosa, all precede his official appointment to the survey. He adds an interesting anecdote or two in *New Mexico Birds* (1961), and he calls prairie falcons "enemies" of the lesser prairie chicken.

Falco fusco-caerulescens
Aplomado Falcon

In 1908–9—While I was working at the -+ Ranch, Sierra Co. I found several nests of this Falcon In the Jornada, north of Las Cruces. In this valley is the only place I have records of it in N. Mex.

June 17th 1909, 10 ms. East of Rincon. Nest in tall "Soap weed, 20 feet up. Well protected, In the crotch where the Soap-weed forked. Contained 2 feathered young, and 2 rotten eggs.

Nests here, always in the Soap weed. The Falcon Feed in the Late P.M. on the Bats, as they begin to stir from their hiding places in the Soapweed. They are also bad after the Scaled Quail.

The aplomado falcon was extirpated in New Mexico. In *New Mexico Birds* (1961), Ligon still felt it was present in limited numbers. He notes a nest southwest of Deming as late as 1952. The species has recently been restored to a site on the Armendaris Ranch, northeast of Engle. The success of this restoration remains uncertain but looks hopeful, with records of successful nesting in 2009.

If the falcons were taking scaled quail, it was most likely the young. These are relatively small falcons, and a mature scaly would be a talonfull. However, the falcons planted on the Armendaris are fed corturnix quail until they become independent enough to hunt on their own. They are capable of flying away with a corturnix carcass in their talons.

Desert Sparrow Hawk

Observed sparingly throughout winter in Gila River Reserve (Reported on page 71).

I'm not sure why Ligon repeats the species here, since he had already written it up earlier.

Bubo virginianus pallescens
Western Horned Owl

To be met with over the entire state, where there are trees.

Apr. 12—Middle Gila River, Elev. 7500. Nest containing 3 young begun to feather—one runt. Nest in Sugar Pine, in Bed of deep Canyon, 40 feet from ground.

Apr. 26th See nest, Middle Gila, bird on. 50 feet up in cave on wall of perpendicular cliff. eggs, or very small young.

May 2nd 2 ms. Above Fairview nest with downy young, In Pine.

May 17th Chloride Creek, Sierra Co. 2 young almost feathered, one flew out. Nest in Sloping Cliff, in round-hole. no nest, white dust and remains of food-rats-rabbits, birds.

July 3rd young flying, Alamogordo Creek above Ft. Sumner. Pecos Valley.

Interestingly, in *New Mexico Birds* (1961), Ligon does not mention the horned owl's propensity for gophers, even when he is heralding its beneficial nature. Great horned owls are one species that profits by limited urbanization. Trees planted around villages and towns provide nesting sites, telephone and electrical poles make good perches, and watered yards attract gophers and other rodents.

Otus flammeolus
[Flammulated owl] (No. 4)

I have only one record of this owl.

June 3rd Haut [Hoyt] Creek, 30 ms. West of Chloride, Socorro Co. Elev. 7000. A dead Pine Snag, about 40 feet high stood in the canyon bed. I observed a House Finch nest half way up, partly projecting from a hole. Also a Chestnut Back Bluebird was building a nest higher up. I climbed up to see these, as I reached the ground, I looked up in time to see the owl fly to a pine tree near. I secured her and climbed back to her nest hole. The nest was in an [?] hole, one hole about Flicker size, reached down about 8 in. from this was a hole, to the center of the tree, in which was the nest, this cavity was about 10 in. deep. Contained 2 Slightly Incub. eggs. Nest was quite a collection of Cotton-wood twigs and bark. and a few of the birds feathers. Her breast was entirely bare.

Geococcyx californianus
Road-Runner

I find this Bird fairly well destributed over the Southern half of the State.

July 7th I observed it 10 ms N.W. of Santa Rosa.

It is fairly com. on the Rio Grande to Engle. I note it in the Gila Reserve to 7000. It is common no place. yet its peculiar tracks, two toes pointing back two forward, are a familiar mark in the dust, where there is brush of any kind. The Striped Lizards are its favorite food. also snakes. and it is a robber too. steals other birds eggs and young. It lays as many as 9 eggs, but so deposited that they hatch at intervals of a week or more.

Ligon's report seems to follow an accepted taxonomic structure, but the roadrunner, while perhaps appropriately following the owls, does not belong among them. However, the report is handwritten, and he may simply have gotten ahead of himself in space allocation.

Speotyto cunicularia hypogaea
Burrowing Owl

This bird is common in the Prairie Dog towns in the Jornada, north of Las Cruces, to the North End of the Jornada. Elev. 4000 to 4600. It is very abundant South of the Sacramento Mts. and about Orange, and west to Northwest.

June 19th to 23rd Very common from Elk, on the Penasco River, Otero Co. Elev. about 6800, to Artesia.

June 23rd to July 4th Common from Carlsbad to Santa Rosa.

July 13th A few North West of Santa Fe. to mouth of Chama River.

I consider it a harmless, yet very valuable, bird, as it destroys many bugs, mice and etc.

By 1961, in *New Mexico Birds*, Ligon was acknowledging that poisoning of the blacktailed prairie dogs had greatly reduced the burrowing owls. He felt that it was due to loss of holes and does not mention the possibility of actual secondary poisoning of the owls. Burrowing owls are now relatively common on the Armendaris Ranch north of Engle, where prairie dogs have been reintroduced and kangaroo rats are abundant, both providing holes for the owls.

Coccyzus americanus occidentalis
California Cuckoo

First observation—May 22nd 1–4 miles above V + T Ranch. Elev. 7200. Socorro Co. N. Mex.

It is fairly common on the Rio Grande from Las Cruces to Elephant Butte, among the Cotton-wood.

June 24th observed in Cotton-wood at Clark Lake, 5 ms. South-West Lake Arthur, Pecos Valley.

June 26th 4 ms. N. East Roswell, in Cotton-wood Borendo Creek. Several here.

This is now called the yellow-billed cuckoo. Ligon's observation four miles "above" V + T Ranch seems unusual. This would place it at or near V + T Lake, which Ligon had described as barren. This area is at the south end of the San Augustine Plains and does not presently have significant riparian vegetation, nor, from Ligon's photographs, did it then.

Ceryle alcyon
Belted Kingfisher

I observed this bird in the fall and winter 1912–13, on Alamosa River, Sierra and Socorro Co's. Although the water was generally frozen along the edges, mornings and night, and at times most all over, I see the birds dive under and come up with their fish.

In Jan. and Feb. I noted it constantly on the East Gila. But as nesting time drew near they disappeared. I think however, they moved down the River. I have not observed it on the Pecos no[r] Chama Rivers.

The fish in Alamosa Creek in 1913 were probably Rio Grande suckers and Rio Grande chubs. It is possible that carp were present by this time as well.[50]

Sphyrapicus thyroideus
Williamson's Sapsucker

It is fairly common in winter, in the Gila Forest Reserve. But not noted during breeding Season.

Dec. 31st 1 Specimen. Divide North of Haut [Hoyt] Creek, Gila Reserve, Socorro Co. Elev. about 7500.

Melanerpes erythrocephalus
Red-headed Woodpecker

July 1st Find the Red-Head fairly abundant just below Ft. Sumner. on the Pecos River, among the big Cotton-wood, breeding. Pair with nest in dry limb in green Cotton-wood. Getting food in the alfalfa fields.

July 3rd I am told it is resident about Santa Rosa, but I failed to substantiate this report.

Ligon's discussion of the red-headed woodpecker in *New Mexico Birds* (1961) notes the role of the Canadian and Dry Cimarron rivers as corridors from its habitat farther east. This is one of the few examples I've found in the literature of the connective function of the Canadian River between eastern and western forest. Scissor-tailed flycatchers may be another.

Sightings of red-headed woodpeckers are relatively common along the Pecos River and Rio Grande in New Mexico (New Mexico Ornithological Society).

Dryobates villosus
[Hairy woodpecker] (No. 33)

July 9th First seen near Old San Miquil,—10 ms. to South- East, Pecos Valley, among Pinion on East side of River. Elev. about 5000. My next records are in the Jicarilla Reservation.

July 17th 5 miles South of Stinking Lake where I am sure this bird was a breeder. Elev. 7200.

July 31st In willows, Lake Shore-Stinking Lake. Elev. 7000.

Asyndesmus lewisi
[Lewis woodpecker] (No. 28)

I first Struck this bird on my round of the state at the mouth of the Chama River—5 miles from the Rio Grande.

July 13th There is a large grove of big cotton-wood here. The birds were nesting,—had young, in holes in the cotton-wood. One nest 20 feet up in dead cotton-wood snag. One nest in big green cotton-wood both had young.

July 15th Observed all way up Chama River.

July 25th Abundant in Pine Northern Part Jicarilla Reservation.

July 26th Most abundant at Horse Lake, often a dozen in sight at one time.

—Migration—

Inc My Spring Migration Notes

I have only two Records.

May 2nd 2 Birds. at Mud-holes, 15 ms. North-West Fairview Socorro Co.

May 3rd one Bird near Fairview Sierra Co.

Melinerpes formicivorus
Bairds Woodpecker [Acorn woodpecker]

Very abundant in the San Mateo Mts. Sierra and Socorro Co's. Resident at High Altitudes. Never seen out of Mts. and Pine.

Abundant in the Black Range Sierra Co. Lowest down. 6 ms. West of Chloride, Elev. about 6400. Mar. 15th I stopped hole, at dark, where I had seen a bird go in. this was about 8 ft. up in oak. The next morning I found there was six (6) of the birds in this one hole.

Nesting the Last of May, in high dead Pine.

It's interesting that Ligon notes six birds in a hole in March but mentions in *New Mexico Birds* (1961) only an instance in which he found five in a hole in December. Again, this is evidence that much of *New Mexico Birds* was written from memory, not notes.

Colaptes cafer collaris
Red-shafted Flicker

Very abundant in the Gila Reserve,—constantly.

May 17th Mile East of Chloride. Elev. 6200. Nest in Scrub oak, 4 ft. from ground. nest hole 2 feet deep. 4 fresh eggs. The bird staid near while I was at the nest.

June 3rd Monument Pass, Black Range Sierra Co. Elev. 8000. Nest in oak, 4 Skinny young.

June 5th Nest on Beaver Creek. Elev. 6500. Socorro Co. In dead walnut that leaned over water, contained small young.

June 8th Chloride Creek, Sierra Co. Nest in cotton-wood, young almost feathered.

Abundant in all the Mt. Ranges. Also nests on the Rio Grande below Rincon.

July 31st Abundant in the Jicarilla Reservation. feeding at roots of Sage brush. Often caught by hawks.

Autrostomus vociferus macromystax
Stephen's Whip-poor-will

Rare where I have been.

May 18th While camped in Monument Pass, Black Range, Sierra Co. N. M. Elev. 8000. After dark a little I heard some-thing new. it seemed to be in a tree. — "whip! whip! whip-poor-will! whip-poor-will," and hushed. This was the first I had ever heard,—in my life—.

June 7th 10 ms. West of Monument Pass. Sierra Co. Elev. about 7200. I hear them on both sides of my camp, between sun-down and dark. No other records.

Phalaenoptilus nuttalli
Poor-will

First noted—

Apr. 16th V + T Horse Camp. Socorro Co. Elev. 8000.

Apr. 18th Observed on Middle Gila River. Elev. about 7500.

May 5th Abundant at Willow Springs. Foot-hills of Cuchillo Mts. Sierra Co. Elev. about 6300.

June 13th Common in San Andrea Mts.—Sulphur Canyon.

June 23rd 5 ms. above Carlsbad on Pecos River.

July 5th On Pecos, in Cedar hills 12 ms. above Santa Rosa. Common here.

Chordeiles virginianus henryi
Western Nighthawk

Migration records—

June 6th Observed first—6 on head of East Gila River. Elev. about 6500. (I find Later Record)

May 24th 1 On Beaver Creek Sierra Co. Gila Reserve, Elev. about 6500. A rare bird West of the Continental Divide, In the Gila Reserve.

June 10th Cotton-wood Spring Cuchillo Creek. Sierra Co.

June 17th Rather Com., Tula Rosa Flats, Otero Co.

June 24th Com. about Carlsbad Resivoirs. Resting in day-time on fence post, wire and half dead cotton-wood.

July 4th Abundant in Pecos Valley to Santa Rosa.

July 5th Kill bird under scrub cedar 10 ms. north of Santa Rosa. [Ligon wrote the symbol for male here.] Stomach, which is large, was filled with large Grass-hoppers and a Green Chinch bug.

July 8th 14 ms. North West of Santa Rosa, on rolling hilly country. Elev. about 4800. Nest containing 1 egg, apparently fresh. (no nest rather—containing one egg). egg was on hill, barren grown. bird very tame.

Observed to Jicarilla Reservation, from Anton Chico, in Pecos Valley, but rather rare, but observed each night.

July 28th In late P.M. Flying over Stinking Lake in great numbers, feeding on insects.

Aug. 15 Migrating through Navajo Reservation.

Chordeiles acutipennis texensis
Texas Nighthawk

First Records—Spring—

May 6th Heard two Flooting 1 mile North of Palomas Spring, Rio Grande Valley.

May 10th See 1 on hill 2 ms. South of Elephant Butte.

June 10th I observed Pr. at Cotton-wood Spring Cuchillo Creek, 12 ms. West of Elephant Butte. I am sure these were breeding birds, and I believe this marks their North- and North-West Range Limit.

June 14th Abundant in Tula Rosa Flat, North of White-Sand, Otero Co.

June 15th I see several at South End of the Mal Pais, Otero Co.

June 24th observe them rather Common In Pecos Valley 5 miles North of Carlsbad. Near the Lower Carlsbad Resivoir. I believe this about their Northern limit in the Pecos Valley, as I saw nor heard them any more as I came on up the valley.

It is abundant in Summer on the Rim of the Rio Grande and on the edge of the Jornada Valley, at Detroit Station, below Rincon. Dona Ana Co.

Aeronantes melanoleucus
White-throated Swift

Arrival. Spring—

Mar. 22nd 6 seen, at Box on Taylor Creek, Head East Gila River, Socorro Co. N. Mex. Elev. 6600.

Mar. 23rd. observe more, at same place.

The glide of these birds, back and forth, by the face of the cliffs where they nest and seek shelter—is interesting. Reminding me of nothing so much as a bunch of good performers gliding over hall on Roller-skates. Compared with the Cliff swallows, which they are often seen with, it makes the flight of the Swallows appear laborsome.

May 19th 2 ms. above Chloride, Chloride Creek, Sierra Co. Elev. 6300. I swing off cliff on rope, and chisel into crevice, where two Pair are going in and out. I find the nest, made mostly of feathers, about completed, but no eggs. The nests are hard and compact.

They are to be seen about all the high cliffs in the Gila Reserve going in and out at cracks and crevices. So quickly do the[y] enter and leave the nesting sight, that one is puzzled to locate the entrance. Their nesting sights are generally at dazzling heights.

June 17th 2 seen, West of Cloudcroft, in foot of Sacramento Mts.

July 9th Breeding in Cliffs on Pecos, 8 ms. above Anton Chico, Guadalupe Co.

July 16th on Gallinia River, Rio Arriba Co. Jemez Reserve. See many about cliffs, for 6 ms. out the River from Chama River

Sayornis nigricans
Black Phoebe

Arrival—Spring

Mar. 21st 1 Seen at head of East Gila River. Elev about 6400.

Mar. 22. 1 observed, near same place. Rather common on Gila and watered canyons, any place it can get under a hanging rock to build nest.

May 18th 1½ ms. above Chloride, Chloride Creek, Sierra Co. Elev. 6300. Nest under cliff near the water. 4 fresh eggs. Nest about 6 ft. up. well protected by hanging cliff. Made of sandy mud, lined with grass and hair.

May 20th Nest with young, Head of East Gila River, in cave near water.

May 21st On Taylor Creek, Socorro Co. Elev. about 6600, nest in cave, not quite completed.

A rather common bird along streams in the Gila River Reserve.

Myiochanes richardsoni
Western Wood Pewee

Very abundant bird all over the Gila River Reserve (Perhaps bird no. 25, the same Species). [A note penciled in alongside this says " = yes."]

The small compact nests are a familiar sight. stuck to the upper side of horizontal limbs-usually, along the creeks, and canyons, the tree selected is a walnut. The nest cavity is small for the bird. other birds that chance to come near, are quickly attacked—

May 25th I found several nest, under construction but none with eggs. on Beaver Creek. Socorro Co.

June 1st 1½ ms. above Chloride, in Chloride Canyon, Sierra Co. Nest on drooping limb of box Elder. 3 fresh eggs. Nest Made of Dead grass, lined with yellow-tops, of fresh grass.

[Penciled at bottom: "add p. 103."]

Tyrannus vociferans
[Cassin's Kingbird] (no. 18)

June 20th Very Com. on Penasco River.

June 25th Very abundant in Pecos Valley, nesting every Place. Brackets, telephone and Electrict wire Poles. In town and out. In V formed by mile brands on telegraph Poles along Rail Road South of Roswell. Scarcely a mile post but what has a nest.

July 5th On main Street, Santa Rosa. A nest with young. Among net work of Telephone wires.

July 20th Com. to Head of Pecos, also, up Chama River. some.

Ligon does not list the western kingbird in his report, and I suspect that he failed to distinguish between the Cassin's and western kingbirds that he observed. Both species would undoubtedly be common.

Penciled at head of notebook page 103 is "Add to page 101." This is a continuation of the notes on the western wood pewee.

(no. 25)

This Fly catcher is rather com in the Cotton-wood along the Pecos.

June 27th At Roswell. In Cotton-wood Borend Creek

July 5th Above Santa Rosa. on Pecos.

July 10th I observe it in suitable places out to Glorieta.

Pyrocephalus rubinius mexicanus
Vermilion Flycatcher? (My no. 85 individ.)

First observed

April 2nd 1½ ms. South V + T Ranch, in edge of Corduroy Flat, Elev. about 7000. Socorro Co. N. Mex. In open pine glade.

April 4th Seen at same place with mate.

May 24th At Same place I secured the male, by his action I am sure the mate was on the nest, but I could not locate her.

This little fellow, at times would wobble high in the air twittering as he did so, I think, as a kind of courting parade.

Male [Ligon uses symbol] L = 5¼, E = 9¾, W = 3¼.

(This bird will be sent in later to have this record verified.) Stokley Ligon Aug. 10th 1913.

Horned Lark [Very faint, apparently written in by Cooke. No scientific name is given on this page.]
(no. 9)

June 9th Coming East from Black Range, first met on Mesa Land East of Cuchillo Mts. where it is breeding Sparingly.

June 13. Very abundant with young in Jornada Valley, from Engle South.

June 14th A few in the Tula Rosa Flats. West of Tula Rosa Winters on the Planes North Side Gila Forest Reserve.

Dec. 20th observed on Alamosa River. All the year in the Jornada.

Otocoris alpestris leucolaema
[More horned lark] (no. 19)

June 20th Coming East from Sacramento Mts. first observed East of lower Penasco, with young. Males usually sit on low bush or tuft of grass and sing. Also fly high in the air, floating about singing, all hours of the day.

June 21st. Very abundant between Hope and Artesia.

June 30th Very abundant in Pecos Valley. Especially from Roswell to Santa Rosa.

July 8. North-West of Santa Rosa Elev. about 4800. Very abundant many very small young by road. Several nests. 1 to 4 eggs, mostly incubated eggs. always on North east side tuft of grass. well sunken into ground. Lined with grass. birds fly up, and away, rarely appearing near while one is about nest.

(very *likely* same as no. 9)

July 11—observed as high up as Glorieta.

July 15th Mesa Country. 15 ms. west of Abiquiu, Chama River quite abund.

Pica pica hudsonia
Magpie.

July 7th Santa Rosa. I am told, by good authority, that the bird occurs about Santa Rosa.

July 17th I first see this bird coming North-West. In Jicarilla Reservation, 5 ms. S. of Stinking Lake, family of old and young.

July 18th at Stinking Lake, observed often. Feeding of bird carcasses at my camp.

July 25th At Lumberton.

July 26th Most abundant about Horse Lake, Elev. 7670. Very abundant here. Visits my camp, prowls about over bed and camp kit. Fights the crows.

Ligon says in *New Mexico Birds* (1961) that the bird winters as far south as Socorro. I wonder if it still does. I've certainly never seen it that far south. According to Florence Merriam Bailey (1928), one specimen was taken from the Mimbres River valley west of Hillsboro Peak, and the bird had been recorded regularly south of Albuquerque. Winter sightings on the Bosque del Apache occurred as late as the mid-1970s, and a sighting as far south as Isleta occurred in 2003 (New Mexico Ornithological Society).

Cyanocitta stelleri diadeniata
Long-crested Jay

Abundant in all the Mts. of N. Mex: Black Range, San Mateo's. Sacramento. Upper Pecos. Jemez. Not often seen below the Pine Belt.

Apr. 26th Nest, one egg. East Side Middle Gila River, In Mts. Socorro Co. N. Mex. Elev. 8000. Nest in Juniper, 15 ft. from the ground.

Apr. 27th Nest almost completed, in Pine, on Rim of Indian Canyon. Socorro Co. Elev. 8000.

May 30th Head of Chloride Creek, Sierra Co. Elev. 7500 Nest with young almost feathered.

It is resident where found.

Aphelocoma woodhousei
Woodhouse's Jay

Abundant in the Central Ranges of the state. resident. usually found among Pinion and Scrub Oak. Destructive to the nests of small birds—eggs and young. I consider this bird the cause of the rarity of many Small birds that try to nest in the Mts.

June 1st in Chloride Creek, Sierra Co. from Chloride, west, in the Canyon. I found this Jay depredating on eggs and young of the Fly catchers and Vero's. One nest, Black Phoebe, 2 dead young with bill prints in head. Many nests torn to pieces. That the Small birds are constantly quarreling after them is evidence of their robbing habits. I had collected a set of Phoebe eggs. put them at root of walnut while I walked a little way down the Canyon. on my return, altho' the eggs were in a few feet of my camp, a Jay had destroyed but one, I watched, in a few moments he returned, but for his last time.

Apr. 20th Nest. 4 fresh eggs. East side Middle Gila River. Elev. 8000. Nest in Scrub Oak. From this date I found many of the nests here, in every case the nests were in Scrub Oak.

May 4th East side Cuchillo Mts. Nest by the road. two young 4 days old Elev. 6800. Sierra Co.

May 5th East of Willow Spring 2 ms. Nest. 5 well incubated eggs. Elev. 6200. This in Cuchillo Mts. Sierra Co. Nests always in Scrub Oak.

Aug. 18th about San Antonio Pass North of Thoreau-McKinley Co. fairly common

Florence Merriam Bailey (1928) quotes the above record of depredation on flycatchers directly from Ligon's notes. She shows the bird scattered throughout the state, missing only in the very open prairies.

Corvus corax sinuatus
American Raven

Found in the Mts. All over the State, Resident where found. It is generally, in winter, seen flying about in Pairs. Among the high peaks its distant squak is familiar. Feeds off of carcasses of cattle and deer Left by wolves and Mt. Lion in Gila Reserve.

Apr. 3rd In Cliffs, 4 ms. above V + T Ranch, Socorro Co. I took set of 6 fresh eggs. Nest in Pocket, in wall of cliff well protected. Built of sticks lined with cows hair. Nest halfway up, in Cliff 75 feet high. Elev. 7200.

July 10th Family of young near Glorieta.

July 15th Com. on Chama River.

July 20th Most common, In Jicarilla Reservation. observed almost constantly about Stinking Lake, and Horse Lake.

Aug. 16, Observed in Navajo Reservation

Corvus cryptoleucus
White-necked Raven

I have observed it every month in the year in the Jornada South-East of Engle, Sierra Co., I[t] nests here in great abundance, in the high Soap-weeds. They are almost equal to Vultures as scavangers, Along public roads, where there is camping, they watch the camp, as soon as the traveler moves, they visit the camp ground and pick up the waste. Eat coyote or any other carcass. One Record, Jornada, 2 ms. East of Engle, May 2nd 1908, 7 fresh eggs. May 26th 1908, nest 5 fresh eggs.

June 9th First met 30 ms. West of Engle. Sierra Co. Elev. 6000.

June 12. After I cross to East side Rio Grande, and reach the rim of the Jornada. Very com. The Jornada is the greatest white Neck Raven Region I have ever seen.

June 14th Tularosa Flats, Ravens rather rare here. one nest with small young, 35 ms. West of Tularosa. In Soap-weed. 12 feet up.

June 16th 6 miles West of Tularosa, nest in mesquite. small young.

June 21st Between Hope and Artesia I see several Raven.

(—No Records North of this—)

Corvus brachyohynchos hisperis
Crow (no. 32)

July 13th My first Record in the State. Chama River, about 5 ms. from its junction with the Rio Grande. 2 old birds followed by 5 squaking young. Near Mexican farms, among large Cotton-wood.

July 14th Many with young about Abiquiu, Chama River. I am told by old gentleman here that crows come in by thousands in the fall and destroy much feed stuff.

July 16th Abundant Chama and gallina Rivers

July 25th Very abundant all over Jicarilla Reservation

Nucifraga Columbiana
Clarke's Nutcracker

Resident, tho' scattered, over the Black Range and San Mateo Mts. West of the Rio Grande. Always in high altitude. From 7500, up.

April 27th Black Mt. Gila Reserve, Socorro Co. Elev. about 7800. Family of the birds.

July 11th Near Glorieta saw one.

Aug. 4th A few on high points near Stinking Lake.

Aug. 5th observed near Lumberton Rio Arriba Co.

The bird eats meat, I having had them to eat off of deer hams hanging in trees.

I have found it most common on the highest points of the San Mateo Mts. Socorro Co.

A rather noisy bird, and inquisitive.

I have yet to see one of these in the Black Range. The New Mexico Ornithological Society online database shows only two records of Clark's nutcracker for the Black Range, one in 1969 and another in 2004 (New Mexico Ornithological Society).

Cyanocephalus cyanocephalus
Pinon Jay

Constant Resident, West of the Rio Grande, San Mateo and Gila River Forest Reserves. All ways in bunches. in winter, in flocks. nests in colonies. Roosts in thick tall Pine, in Canyons, generally. The most noisy bird of the South-west. When persued by hawks, they go into thick tree-tops.

Feb. 10th They show nesting inclinations—flying 2 and 3 to-gether.

Feb. 17th on Grassy, steep, Canyon side, among scattered Oak, I find one nest about complete. Others under construction. Birds in Pairs, and flocks. mingle and scatter. There was more than 50 birds flying about noisily. This at elevation of about 7500. South West side, Black Mt. (not Black Range) Socorro Co. N. Mex. Gila Reserve. Snow on half the ground.

Mar. 3rd I returned and found nests in almost all the Scrub Oak of sufficient size. Never 2 nests in one tree. Snowed many times since my first visit. Nests damp where snow has melted. Most all nests now contain full compliment. 4 eggs, except one set of 5— Birds continually going and coming to feeding ground, where the main body stays bunched. Very slow to leave nest, then do so noisily.

Mar. 4th South of Black Mt. Nesting colony, not so many birds. Nests contain compliments, many incubated slightly. Altitude about 7500

Mar. 28th 3rd Colony South-East Slope Black Mt. Elev. 7500. Just began to lay, many nests started. perhaps 150 birds here.

Nests always in Scrub Oak about 8 ft. up. I have but one record of exception, one nest South-East side Black Mt. nest half complete in Juniper Tree. Nests made of coarse sticks, always an inner lining of soft, velvety weed, lined with grass, sometime, grass roots and a few feathers.

Apr. 7th V + T Ranch, on Canyon side, young out in trees. Many.

May 5th Eastern Limit, willow Spring, Cuchillo Mts. Sierra Co., young here, many. Next met—

July 3rd at Santa Rosa, with young large as old birds.

July 8th 30th over entire distance from Santa Rosa to Stinking Lake, Jicarilla Res. with young.

Aug. 9th observed 3 miles north, Stinking Lake.

Aug. 18— Very abundant about San Antonio Pass, and South to Thoreau. McKinley Co.,

I have yet to see them near Hillsboro, but they are common around Hermosa. The New Mexico Ornithological Society online database shows only one record for Hillsboro, in June 1998. One record each exists along the Rio Grande at Elephant Butte Lake, Caballo Lake, and Percha Dam state parks. The database shows ten records scattered over Socorro County. The south end of the range for the species seems to be near Hermosa.

Molothrus ater obscures
Dwarf Cowbird

Well distributed over the state where there are watered valleys and streams. Rather common on the Upper Pecos.

July 6th 8 ms. above Santa Rosa, fresh egg, in nest of Black Chin Sparrow.

July 15th on Chama River. Rio Arriba Co.

Rather Common on the Rio Grande.

On Chloride Creek, June 1st egg in nest with 2 Vero eggs. Sierra Co. Elev. about 6300.

Cowbirds have become important in recent years because of their nest predation on endangered species such as the willow flycatcher. Current thinking is that with the disappearance of the bison, they have concentrated near cattle and horses, so the distribution of livestock now potentially affects the distribution of the willow flycatcher, even though they are not in competition for space or food.

Xanthocephalus xanthocephalus
Yellow-head Blackbird

No Spring Migration Records, in The Gila Reserve.

July, 17th First found at Stinking Lake, in abundance, with young, Feeding young a species of Dragon Fly (Snake Doctor) that they secure on shore and out over water among the Tula Grass. These, the old birds collect, not one, but many, then they go to the young, that are sitting about in the high Tula.

July 26th Many at Horse Lake, Jicarilla Reserv. Elev. 7600.
Aug. 6th Some at Dulcie Lake, Jicarilla Reserv. Elev. 6700.
(I have collected several Specimens, not quite sure that all are this species. All at Stinking Lake.)

[A note written in pencil at the bottom says "Add to this p 122."]

Yellow-headed blackbirds occur the lengths of the Rio Grande and Pecos River, so it seems unusual that Ligon had not seen them prior to reaching Stinking Lake.

Agelauis phoeniceus
Red-wing (no. 13)

June 15th I found this bird nesting in abundance at the Mal Pai Springs, 25 ms. North-West of Tularosa. Young were very abundant.
June 25th I have found it fairly com. from Carlsbad to Lake Arthur, in the Pecos Valley. I have no record above Lake Arthur.

Red-wing (no. 20)

June 24th I found these birds nesting in great abundance in the Valley of Seven Rivers Eddy Co.
June 25th At Clark Lake, South-West of Lake Arthur 5 ms. Most abundant breeding colony, in a little whle I found perhaps, 20 nests, not completed, to full compliment of eggs. and the Tula Grass was full of young birds. I am quite sure the old were laying second clutch of eggs.
July 5. Com at all marshy and suitable places. to Santa Rosa.
July 14th Rather Common on Chama River about Abiquiu.
July 30th Breeding at Stinking, Rock, and Horse Lakes, Jicarilla Res.
Aug 6th At Dulcie and Dulcie Lake with young.
(Wheather these all represent one species—my specimens must tell)

[A note written in pencil here says "add to page 119."]

(no. 48)

Very Likely same as Yellow-head Blackbird-killed in bunch of 50. Very abundant, bunching now. July 30th Stinking Lake.

Icterus bullocki
[Bullock's Oriole] (no. 10)

June 7th I find this oriole nesting fairly com on East Fork of Gila River. Nests made of Black hair. Swing on branches of big Cotton-wood.

June 10th At Cotton-wood Spring Cuchillo Creek. 12 ms. West of Elephant Butee, There are three huge Cotton-wood here. Perhaps there are 8 nests in them.

June 11th Fairly common on the Rio Grande.

June 25, Observed on Penasco River also on Pecos, where there are cotton-wood.

Icterus parisrum
Scoots [Scott's] Oriole
(Black and White)

This oriole is rather common, West Slope of the San Andrea Mts. In the edge of the Jornada Valley. I have found many nests, but never found one except swinging to the blades of the Soap Weed, usually pretty high up. A rather Rare bird, and a beautiful one (males).

July 8th South-East Anton Chico, Pecos Valley, I observed two old birds, followed by young that was continually begging.

July 9th observed 5 ms. North-west Anton Chico.

Sturnella neglecta
Western Meadowlark

A very few on Middle and East Gila Rivers, Socorro Co. N. M. Feb.

Apr. 27th Nesting notes and songs, Cooney Prairie, Sierra Co. Elev. 7500 to 8000.

May 1st at V + T Adobe ranch, Elev. 7500. Socorro Co.

June 13th Common, West Slope San Andrea Mts. Nests in rank grass.

May 26th nest, 7 miles East Engle. 3 fresh eggs. 1908.

May 29th 15 ms. East of Engle, 2 nests, 4 eggs each 1 set. fresh 1 incubated.

June 15th Tula Rosa Flat, and Mal Pai Spring. many, young flying.

June 16th in Alfalfa fields Tularosa.

June 25th, All the Way down Penasco River. Com.

July 1st Com. In fields and Marshes, Pecos Valley, all the way up.

July 3rd Very abundant at Santa Rosa.

July 13th 18 ms North-W. Santa Fe. caugh[t] one young out of nest.

July 15th Com. on Chama River.

July 20th Com. Jicarilla Res. Many young at Stinking Lake.

Abundant in the Mts. every place there is grass, to 8000 ft. Providing, the timber and brush is not too thick. Abundant here along the Continental Divide 8000 ft.

Euphagus cyanocephalus
Purple Grackle? [Brewer's Blackbird] (no. 57)

Apr. 20th V + T Horse Camp, Socorro Co. Elev. 8000. 12.

Apr. 23rd 2 Same place.

June 6th Nesting at V + T, Meadow, about 12 pairs. 3 nests in short thick meadow grass, where grew a few scattered willow bushes. one nest 6 very small birds. one 4 well incubated eggs. one 4 rotton, and one pipped egg. Nests rest on ground, made of grass and weeds, lined with black horse-hair. Elev. 7000.

June 19th one pair ½ mile East, Mayhill, Sacramento Mts. Elev. about 7200.

July 20th Chama River, near El Vado, Rio Arriba Co. many old and young just out of nest.

July 27th Very abundant, perhaps 100, old and young at Rock Lake. Elev. 7200 Jicarilla Res.

Aug. 1st Com. old and young at Lumberton (just West), and South of Dulce, and at Dulce Lake Jicarilla Res. Elev. 6700.

Ligon has misidentified this bird and demonstrates his uncertainty with the question mark following the name. The scientific name, added later, shows it to be Brewer's blackbird. This misidentification suggests strongly that Ligon had no field guide during his survey. Florence Merriam Bailey's *Handbook of Birds of the Western United States* (1902) does not show the purple grackle, a bird of the eastern United States, occurring in New Mexico.

Carpodacus mexicanis frontatis,
House Finch

Very abundant near and on all Mts. in Southern half of state. And observed to the Norther Part. — Jicarilla Res. Rio Arriba Co., A pest to growing truck and fruit about Tularosa La Luz. and in the Lower Pecos Valley. A rival, in most every respect, to the English Sparrow, which its appearance, tone of hollowing, action and habits resemble.

May 15th Several nests Chloride Creek above Chloride, Sierra Co. N.M. Nest all in the joint of cigar cactus. Elev. 6100 to 6300.

Passer domesticus
English Sparrow

Abundant in every Village and Town, and in the inhabited districts, Injurious to Garden truck and Fruit every place it is grown. Much complaint in the Pecos Valley, about Artesia Carlsbad and Roswell.

In *New Mexico Birds* (1961), Ligon made a strong pitch for eliminating this exotic species. Obviously, any resulting efforts were ineffective.

Zonotrichia leucophrys
White-crowned Sparrow

Winters abundantly on Alamosa River, Sierra Co. N. Mex. Elev. about 5500. About the field fences, in rank weeds and brush.

Apr. 8th 2—V + T Ranch, Socorro Co. Elev. about 7000.

June 7th I saw one, doubtless a breeding bird, head of East Gila River. Elev. about 6600.

In *New Mexico Birds* (1961), Ligon states that the bird only nests in the northern half of the state. Either he changed his mind about the June 7 observation or forgot it.

Spizella atrogularis
Black-chin Sparrow.

Abundant in dry Regions, among Greasewood and Black brush.

June 9th Nest in Grease-wood, by road, East of Cuchillo Mts. Elev. about 6000.

June 13th West Slope San Andrea Mts. Very abundant. young and nests, observed to the Summit of the Range about 6000.

June 15th Very abundant in Tularosa Flats, West of Tularosa. Breeding every Place, nest to-day not completed.

June 20th Penasco River Country.

July 6th North-West Santa Rosa 8 ms. Nest with eggs, also young. Elev. about 4800.

Chonestes grammacus strigatus
[Lark Sparrow] (no. 61)

First observed—

Apr. 28th Houghten Canyon, Gila Reserve, Socorro Co. Elev. about 7500. Later, very abundant all over the region.

June 9th East Slope Cuchillo Mts. edge of mesa.

June 20th observed on Penasco River. None between Cuchillo Mts and Sacramento Mts.

July 1st Common in Pecos Valley.

Aug 1st Fairly common in the Jicarilla Reservation.

Progne subis
Western Martin

First observed—

Apr. 18th at V + T Horse Camp, Socorro Co. Elev. about 8000.

Apr. 26th Several edge Cooney Prairie Socorro Co. Elev. about 8200.

June 8th Scattered well over Gila Reserve, nesting high in dead pine in wood-pecker holes. Socorro and Sierra Co's.

June 17th Rather Com. East Slope Sacramento Mts. James Canyon. Nesting.

Aug. 10th observed at Stinking Lake

This bird is always recorded at high altitudes.

Petrochelidon lunifrons
Mexican Cliff Swallow

(Authority: —Ind. Speci. Sent in, from Chloride)

Very likely Specimen no. 8 is this species. ["Page 161" was entered here later.]

The Species, —Specimen, Identified & collected:

May 9th 2 ms. above Palomas Springs on the Rio Grande, Sierra Co. Elev. about 4300. There was about 500 birds, and had just begun to lay. The nests that had eggs, were old nests, some having been slightly repaired. While above these a little way (100 yds.) the birds were buisy building new nests, getting mud just across the River opposite. The nesting sight was hanging concrete cliffs, water beneath (Rio Grande) nests 5 to 10 feet from water. nest material—very scant, a few grass blades and mesquite leaves. Nest measurements = average length 7 in. Enterence $1^3/_8$ Diam. Cavity inside rather large, almost Round. The enterence to nests drooped down.

Tadycineta thalassina lepida
Violet-green Swallow.

First observed—
Apr. 10th at V + T Horse Camp, Middle Gila River. Socorro Co. Elev. about 8000. Observed constantly afterward.
May 23rd Abundant over Gila Reserve. Seeking nesting places in dead pine.
June 7th See nest in Cliff,—in hole—head East Gila. Many nests in trees in old pecker-wood holes
June 17th Sacramento Mts.
July 11, Com upper Pecos.
July 16th to 25th Abundant in Jemez Forst Reserve and Jicarilla Reseration, breeding every place.

The V + T horse camp was located about 15 miles west of the V + T Ranch headquarters.

Hirundo erythrogastra
Barn Swallow

May 8th First Seen at Palomas Springs on the Rio Grande Sierra Co.
June 9th Nesting at Cuchillo in Adobe houses, Sierra Co.
June 17th Nests in old half-wrecked adobe building in Luz. Otero Co.
June 24th Com. and nesting, where found in Pecos Valley
June 28th Nests with fresh eggs under Salt Creek bridge 18 ms. North of Roswell. Where an overflow had swept over a few days before. No doubt destroyed nests at same place.
July 9th All way up Pecos, Com. at Anton Chico.
July 13 and 14 Com. North-West of Santa fe. Com. on Chama River, one place living, and nesting in adobe hut where family of Mexicans lived. All using the same door-way. It and the Mexicans seem to be best of friends alway. It raises war with hawks.

It is interesting that he was at Palomas Springs on May 8, so he had been away from Chloride for a while prior to the survey, yet he was there in April.

Petrochelidon lunifrons
Swallow, no's. 15 16

June 19th Penasco River East of Mayhill. Elev. about 6800. I found this Swallow nesting all along the River in the Lime-stone Cliffs. One colony contained about 500 birds old nests white with Gyp. huddled and jammed. I do not think these were hatching, but a short distance below, they were, I saw the birds carry shells out and dropping them.

June 24th Nesting under Flume, Carlsbad.

June 27th Abundant N.E. Roswell.

July 7th Many nesting on Pecos at Santa Rosa, young out on wire fences.

July 31st Young in nests at Stinking Lake. Species I think the same.

Ligon believed these to be a species other than cliff swallows, apparently, and gave them a separate entry. Whoever later identified the specimens classified them as cliff swallows. In *New Mexico Birds* (1961), Ligon places the cliff with five hundred birds two miles below Elephant Butte Dam.

Geothlypis trichas occidentalis
[Yellowthroat] (no. 12)

June 10th Fairly Com. on Rio Grande at and near Palomas Springs Serra Co., In marshy places, usually about Tula Grass.

June 17th Observed in La Luz Canyon Otero Co. In marshy branch.

June 19th 20th Penasco River, from Mayhill to Lower Penasco.

June 28th From Carlsbad to Salt Creek, 18 ms. North of Roswell, about all lakes and marshes.

July 10th Below Pecos on Pecos River.

July 28th Com Stinking Lake, Horse Lake, Dulce Lake. Jicarilla Res.

—Note—

This little Bird is generally found where Red Wing Black Bird reside.

Here Ligon confirms that he passed through or near Pecos, the settlement. He has no comment on the old pueblo.

Mimus polyglottos leucopterus
Western Mawking Bird.

Apr. 27th First noted in South-East edge of Cooney Prairie, Gila River Reserve. Socorro Co. Elev. about 8000.

June 12th Rare in Gila Reserve. a very few East Gila River.

June 8th Common about Chloride, Sierra Co. Elev. 6000 to 6500. North-East of Chloride 1 mile, nest, 1 egg.

June 9th Cotton-wood Spring, Cuchillo Creek, Sierra Co. many. Nest 3 eggs. A very abundant bird in the Jornada Valley. and all over the San Andrea Mts. in Summer. Com. Tularosa Flats.

June 20 Com. on Penasco River. Many dead young in nests, killed by rescent heavy hail-storm.

July 12. Common throughout the Pecos Valley.

July 14th a few on Chama River, not Com.

July 21st Rare in Jicarilla Res. old and young observed North-East of Stinking Lake.

Ligon uses "mawking bird" consistently throughout his notes for what is correctly spelled "mockingbird." This, along with a few other strange spellings, leaves us wondering if he was using a field guide or AOU species list of any kind.

Toxostoma curvirostre
Curved Bill Thrasher

June 1st Nest half mile below Chloride, Elev. 6200. Nest about 10 feet up in Box Elder, bed on Canyon. Contained 4 well incubated eggs.

June 9th 1 Mile North-West of Willow Spring, Sierra Co. East of Cuchillo Mts. Nest in Cactus. 4 almost fresh eggs. These birds are rather rare in this region. These being the only ones I have observed.

Toxostoma curvirostre
(no. 17)

June 20th I find these Thrasher com—among the Desert Roses,—jointed cactus, that grow in thickets Penasco River, East of Lower Penasco. The wide smooth valleys between the hills are full of these cactus. The birds nest in the cactus. Make bulky nests of sticks, lined with grass. A terriffic hail storm had proceeded me about ten days. I found many young dead in nests. Last July I found these bird nesting abundantly West of the Guadaloupe Mts. about Orange N. M. and North-West, always nest in the cactus.

Troglodytes aedon parkinansis
(no. 52)

Aug. 1st. I find this little water wren very abundant at Stinking Lake. Jicarilla Reserv. Rio Arriba Co. Always found near the water in the Tula and other tall grass or near it. Especially where there are willows. Its flight seems laborsome.

July 26th I found it fairly Com. at Horse Lake. Elev. 7670. I have noted it no other places.

Aug. 6th Com. At Dulce Lake. Elev. 6700. Jicarilla Reservation. 4 ms. S. of Dulce.

The description of habitat and behavior here suggests that the scientific name assigned to the specimen is in error. This is almost certainly the western marsh wren (*Telmatodytes palustris plesius*). Whoever assigned the trinomial at Smithsonian misidentified this specimen (no. 52), which unfortunately does not show up in the Smithsonian files.

Heleodytes brunneicapillus couesi
Cactus Wren

A common bird on West side San Andrea Mts. where it breeds in the desert Roses and bushes. as late as.—

Aug. 27th 1912. I found nest with fresh eggs, 20 miles South-East of Engle (ENGLE) Elv. About 5600. Their nesting period has a long range.

June 16th Com. Tularosa Flats.

June 20th Lower Penasco, Rather Com. breeding.

I am not sure what wren the next entry applies to. It is across the page from Rock Wren and Canyon Wren, and it could be the house wren. No scientific name was assigned by the US Biological Survey.

[Unknown Wren] (no. 1)

June 3rd I found this little wren nesting on Chloride Creek, Sierra Co. Elev. about 6500. Nest in snout of cotton-wood. Made of sticks, lined with grass and feathers. 6 fresh eggs. and above this nest 2 ms. found one in wood-pecker hole, oak tree, about 5 ft. up. 6 slightly incubated eggs.

It is rather common on both sides of the Black Range, and over the Summit of the Range.

In *New Mexico Birds* (1961), Ligon seems to mention these nests in his entry on house wrens.

Salpinctes obsoletus
—Rock Wren—

Very abundant in the Gila River Reserve, in Places. At V + T Lake Gila Reserve, Socorro Co. Elev. About 7000. It is very Com. about the Low Cliffs.

July 6th Com. about Santa Rosa.

Aug 1st I find it rather Com. about Stinking Lake, Jicarilla Res.

Ligon treats the unique nesting traits of this bird in *New Mexico Birds* (1961). He must have not yet seen a nest at the time of the survey.

Catherpes mexicanus consperens
—Canon Wren—

Pretty well distributed over the Gila River Reserve.

May 31st 2 ms. West of Chloride, Chloride Creek, Sierra Co. Elev. 6300. nest near canyon bed up under hanging rock, in pocket well protected. Nest made of coarse sticks, lined with grass and feathers. very young birds. They are busy feeding the youngsters still the male finds time to hollow shrill, occasionally.

Certhia familiaris montana
Rocky Mt. Creeper

Resident, scattered, no place common, In San Mateo Forest Reserve, and Gila River Reserve. I have observed it constantly, in these districts, never found nest or young. The birds are constantly slipping about over the bodies of trees, quiet as the ants.

Sitta carolinensis nelsoni
Slinder-billed [*sic*] Nuthatch

A very abundant Bird—Resident. In the Gila River and San Mateo Forest Reserves. A constant worker for food.

June 3rd Building nest in old wood-pecker hole, Monument Pass Black Range, Sierra Co. Elev. 8000.

July 11th observed near Glorieta.

July 16th Observed in the Jemez National Forest Reserve, North of Gallina River.

July 25th Seen in Jicarilla Reserv. At Stinking Lake, and Horse Lake.

This is the white-breasted nuthatch, as it is called in *New Mexico Birds* (Ligon, 1961). Florence Merriam Bailey uses the name "slender-billed" in her 1902 *Handbook of Birds of the Western United States*, giving it separate subspecies status. In *Birds of New Mexico* (1928), she has switched to "Rocky Mountain nuthatch" for this species.

Sitta pygmaea
—Pigmy Nuthatch—

Abundant in all the Mts. where there is pine.

June 3rd Monument Pass, Bird working on nest 8 ft. up in oak, old wood-pecker hole, nest made of grass, no eggs. Not migratory.

Aug. 19th Near Thoreau, McKinley Co. (San Antonio Pass.)

Auriparus flaviceps
Verdin

Coming East from Gila Reserve, first noted—

June 9th Cotton-wood Spring Cuchillo Creek (cuchillo.)

June 13th Abundant and nesting San Andrea Mts. To Summit (Sulphur Pass) Elev. about 6000.

June 15th Many nests in Mesquite over Tularosa Flats.

June 17th West side Sacramento Mts. Near High Rolls, Elev. 6400.

Myadestes townsendi
Tow[n]send's Solitaire

One record, Specimen in Kelly Canyon, San Mateo Mts. Socorro Co. Elev. about 6500.

Nov. 27th The bird was softly singing in some bushes. had several cedar berries in its throat, the Blue Berries off red cedar.

Ligon obviously collected this bird but provided no specimen number. He seemingly wasn't above collecting a bird simply to identify it.

Planesticus migratorius propinguris
Western Robin

Constant Resident, Gila River Forest Reserve.

May 18th Nest on Chloride Creek, 6 miles west of Chloride. Sierra Co. Nest 30 ft. up in Mt. Cotton-wood. 4 fresh eggs.

June 1st Nests on all watered canyons. Nest in Monument Pass. Sierra Co. Elev. 8000.

June 17th Nest in Canyon, ½ mile West of Cloudcroft, Otero Co.

June 10th Young out of nest, in Bosque, Rio Grande, near Palomas Springs

June 20th Com. on Penasco River

July 10th At Anton Chico, Pecos Valley.

July 12th In Santa Fe.

July 15th Some, not com. Jemez Forest Reserve.

July 25th Com. at Lakes in Jicarilla Reservation. Rio Arriba Co.

Aug 18th San Antonio Pass, North of Thoreau, McKinley Co. 16ms.

Sialia currcoides
Mountain Bluebird

Resident, tho' rare in Winter, Gila Forest Reserve

May 23rd Nest 4 ms. above the V + T Ranch. Socorro Co. 5 fresh eggs. Elev. 7200. Also 2 nests in Cliff, with young birds.

June 19th Com. Sacramento Mts. Nesting-young—James Canyon, Otero Co.

July 11th Com. about Glorieta.

July 16th Abundant Jemez Reserve.

July 25th Abundant over Jicarilla Reservation.

Aug. 19th Com. (abundant) North of Thoreau McKinley Co. for 20 miles.

Sialia mexicana bairdi
Chestnut-Backed Bluebird

Constant Resident, and very abundant all over Gila River Reserve.

May 29th 6 ms. West of Monument Pass. Sierra Co. Nest in dead Oak snag. Made of grass. 5 fresh eggs.

June 4th 2 nests, in one dead pine Snag, Haut [Hoyt] Creek, Socorro Co. Elev. 6500.

June 10th Nests all over Gila Reserve in Pine.

In *New Mexico Birds* (Ligon, 1961), it is called western bluebird.

I wonder when the word "snag" came into common usage for standing dead trees. Ligon recognizes them as key nesting habitat for some species. In recent years, snag protection has become a serious component of natural resource management in national forests.

Selasphorus rufus
[Rufous hummingbird] (no. 53)

Aug. 1st I find this Humming bird quite com. here, feeding of flowers. No. 9. That grow in abundance about. This is my first observation of the bird. It seems to be the boss among the Humming bird keeping other Species out of its way.

[A note written in pencil here says "same as page 154," referring to the Rufous Hummingbird.]

(no. 54)

Aug. 1st I observe this Humming Bird quite com. with, or near no. 53. Sucking the same flowers. The birds, as no. 53, was are very fat. This bird is quite com. in the Gila Reserve. Socorro and Sierra Co's. I found it nesting on the head of the East Gila River, in cotton-wood.

May 16th Chloride Creek, 1½ miles West of Chloride, Sierra Co., I found nest in bed of Canyon. 1 fresh egg. Nest in Cotton wood, about 30 feet up. Elev. 6300. The birds were very abundant.

—Note—

I will state: There is a chance of me being mistaken about the Specimen, and these breeding birds being different. I secured the female that had nest and one egg. She was identically the same in marking, on the back as this one. also had the white tips of under tail feathers. But she was lighter beneath and according to my record had a little longer bill.

In *New Mexico Birds* (1961), Ligon states that up to 1958 no record existed of the rufous hummingbird nesting in New Mexico. If so, then the bird he saw on May 16 must have been of a different species. Yet Cooke, or whoever was handling the specimens at the US Biological Survey, classfied both specimens as rufous hummingbird. As late as 1928, Florence Merriam Bailey in *Birds of New Mexico* says there is no record of the rufous nesting in New Mexico. Yet Ligon mentions a nest above. Bailey does not acknowledge Ligon's record of this species. New Mexico is not considered within the breeding range of the rufous hummingbird.[51] The nest Ligon found must have been of another species.

Steganopus tricolor
Wilson's Phalarop.

Apr. 8th V + T Lake, Socorro Co. Elev. 7000.
Apri. 29th 5 V + T Lake.
June 28th 25 ms. North of Roswell, 7 in Newly filled, lake. 2 Specimens here.

Gallinago delicate
—Jack Snipe—

Observed throughout winter on Alamosa River Sierra Co. and in Gila Reserve-Beaver Creek.
Apr. 1st. 1 V + T Lake, Socorro Co.
May 6th 1 Palomas Springs, Sierra Co.
Aug. 11th One at Stinking Lake-Rio Arriba Co., Wilson's or common snipe.

Cyrtonyx montezumae mearnsi
Mearn's Quail.

—Range—

Guadalupe Mts. rather common.
Sacramento Mts. Com. in James Canyon East of Cloudcroft, to Mayhill. And North into Tula Rosa Canyon.
San Andrea Mts. West of Alamogordo.
San Mateo Mts. on Western Slope, it is Com.—this in Sierra and Socorro Co's.
Black Range, and throughout the Gila River Reserve, to Elev. of 9000. and constant, about where found.
I have found it most abundant in the Black Mts. between East and Middle Gila. Socorro Co. It is found here, usually about 6 in a bunch. From 2 to —12, is the range of the no's. often in mid-winter I observe 2 of the birds—a pair, to-gether. It is well distributed, but no where abundant.
By May 15th they are generally paired out, but I believe it is late in June before they lay. As young are always late hatching off.
Its Food, Consists of small herbs that it scratches from the ground with its long sharp claws. Also, at times it makes an exclusive diet of Pinon nuts, and acorns are a favorite food.

By 1927, in *Wildlife of New Mexico*, Ligon was noting the reduced numbers and range of the Mearns quail.

Melospiza melodia montana
[Song Sparrow] (no. 55)

Aug. 2nd A fairly common bird in the rank grasses along the lake Shores, at Stinking lake. I have observed it no other place.

Sings sweetly in early morning and late P.M.

Petrochelidon lumifrons
Swallow. No. 8.

First observed—

April 1st 5 at V + T Ranch, Gila Reserve, Socorro Co. N. Mex. Elev. about 7000

June 3rd Find them busily nest building on Head East Gila. Elev. 6500

June 6th 1 mile below V + T Headquarter ranch. Colony nesting 60 occupied nests in one wad, jammed under one projecting rock, to side of canyon, 30 feet up. All old nests re-occupied. Above the V + T Ranch three to 3½ ms. is another great breeding sight. Mostly old nests being used, on account, I believe, a dry Summer,—Spring rather, no mud nearer than a mile.

June 7th for miles up East Gila and into Haut [Hoyt} Creek, hardly out of sight of nesting birds. Many using old half-wrecked nests many here, building new nests.

Totanus melanoleucus
[Greater Yellowlegs] (Specimen no. 59)

June 15th I found two pr of these birds at the Mal Pai Springs. 25 ms. North-West of Tularosa. From their action I am confident they were breeding birds. I saw no more until—

Aug. 7th 2 at Dulcie Lake, South of Dulcie, 4 ms. Jicarilla Res. Elev. 6700. These were not breeding birds, Specimen secured contained, in its mouth and throat, water-dog 2 in. long.

Nycticorax nycticorax naevuis
[Black-Crowned Night Heron] (no. 62)

July 30th These birds are fairly common at Stinking Lake, about 1/3 of what is recorded as (41. no) are these, making estimate of 8 or 9 of the birds, but I am confident there are more of each than given here. These are generally with no. 41.

This is another puzzling entry. Ligon seems to think that two species of these herons were present at Stinking Lake. The US Biological Survey identification for both specimens (nos. 62 and 41) indicates that they were both black-crowned night-heron.

Agelaius phoeniceus
Sonora Red-wing. (Indiv. no 74)

May 9th When I made my first visit of the season, to Palomas Springs, Sierra Co. I found these Red wing fairly com—just begun to build their nests in the Tula Grass.

June 11th I found many nests, birds just hatching. one nest in short grass near the ground in Swampy place. 4 very small young. I did not see the female bird, but as I drew near, male kept constantly over me, and when I found the nest, he remained only a few feet above my head, uttering his notes of greatest alarm. Some young were out of nests. Perhaps 20 breeding Prs.

Hydrochelidon nigra surinamerisis
[American black tern] —no. 66—

Aug. 11th This is a fairly Com. bird at Stinking Lake, Flies over Lake in Company, Generally, with No. 67. Always seen over west side of main Lake. Specimen was shot from boat.

While the Specimen, I think is a young bird,—this season. I am not prepared to say where it was hatched. I could not determin[e] what sex, and its bones seemed tinder [*sic*].

This genus does not appear either in *New Mexico Birds* (Ligon, 1961) or *Birds of New Mexico* (F. Bailey, 1928). Florence Merriam Bailey shows it as the American black tern in her *Handbook of Birds of the Western United States* (1902). In *Birds of New Mexico*, she gives the genus as *Chilidonias*. Ligon uses this genus in *New Mexico Birds*, but does not mention his Stinking Lake records.

Same as page 165 [This is written in pencil at the top of the page, referring to the American black tern.] —no. 67—

I have observed these bird each time I go to West Side of main Lake. Always flying about over the water. Today there was in the bunch about 25, perhaps $^{2}/_{3}$ of this bird and $^{1}/_{3}$ —66. When I shot this one, and it fell in the water, the others hovered over it hollowing, paying no attention to me. I do not know wheather these bird nest here or not. As I am not familiar with them. I do not know what character of nesting sight they choose.

The end

—Index—

[The page numbers shown here are pages in the breeding bird report handwritten notebook.]

There is nothing in the journal below this.

One species conspicuously missing in the diary and breeding bird report is the loggerhead shrike. While doing aplomado falcon surveys on the Jornada del Muerto during the spring of 2009, I found these to be abundant and, by their very nature, conspicuous. Ligon does not mention them. In view of his long experience on the Jornada, his tendency to note the more conspicuous species, and his tendency to moralize about the behavior of species, it seems inconceivable that he would not have mentioned shrikes had they been present. It is currently considered a species of concern, having declined in numbers since the 1970s, continent wide. However, it may well be more abundant now than it was in 1913, at least in New Mexico. Apparently, Ligon's first mention of the species was in 1915, when he saw it between Socorro and Albuquerque (Ligon, 1961).

Appendix Table 1

Binomials Used by Ligon Compared with Current Common Names and Binomials

Birds

Common name used by Ligon[a]	Binomial in breeding bird report	AOU[b] Check-list	Current binomial[c]	Comments, and current common name if different
Spotted sandpiper	*Actitus macularius Actitus Actitus macularius*	close	*Actitis macularius*	1910 AOU Check-list uses *A. macularia*
White-throated swift	*Aeronantes melanolencus*	yes	*Aeronautes saxatalis*	
Redwing	*Agelaius phoeniceus*	yes	*Agelaius phoeniceus*	Red-winged blackbird
Golden eagle	*Aguila chrysaetos*	yes	*Aquila chrysaetos*	
Mallard	*Anas platyrhynchos*	yes	*Anas platyrhynchos*	
Woodhouse jay	*Aphelocoma woodhousei*	yes	*Aphelocoma californica*	Western scrub-jay
Lewis woodpecker	*Asyndesmus lewisi*	yes	*Melanerpes lewis*	Lewis's woodpecker
Verdin	*Auriparus flaviceps*	yes	*Auriparus flaviceps*	
Stephens whip-poor-will	*Autrostomus Mexicanus macromystax*	yes	*Caprimulgus arizonae*	Mexican whip-poor-will
Great horned owl	*Bubo virginianus pallescens*	yes	*Bubo virginianus*	
Swainson hawk	*Buteo swainsoni*	yes	*Buteo swainsoni*	Swainson's hawk
Western red-tail	*Buteo borealis calurus*	yes	*Buteo jamaicensis*	Red-tailed hawk
Scaled quail	*Callipepla squamata*	yes	*Callipepla squamata*	
House finch	*Carpodacus mexicanis frontatis*	yes	*Carpodacus mexicanus*	
Turkey vulture	*Cathartes aura septentrionalis*	yes	*Cathartes aura*	
White-throated wren	*Catherpes mexicanus consperens*	yes	*Catherpes mexicanus*	Canyon wren after 1957
Brown creeper	*Certhia familiaris montana*	yes	*Certhia americana*	
Belted kingfisher	*Ceryle alcyon*	yes	*Megaceryle alcyon*	
Gadwall	*Chaulelasmus streperus*	yes	*Anas strepera*	
Lark sparrow	*Chondestes grammacus strigatus*	yes	*Chondestes grammacus*	
Texas nighthawk	*Chordeiles accutipennis texensis*	yes	*Chordeiles acutipennis*	Lesser nighthawk
Nighthawk	*Chordeiles virginianus henryi*	yes	*Chordeiles minor*	Common nighthawk
Yellow-billed cuckoo	*Coccyzus americanus occidentalis*	yes	*Coccyzus americanus*	
Red-shafted flicker	*Colaptes cafer collaris*	yes	*Colaptes auratus*	Northern flicker

(continued)

Birds (*continued*)

Common name used by Ligon[a]	Binomial in breeding bird report	AOU[b] Check-list	Current binomial[c]	Comments, and current common name if different
Bobwhite	*Colinus virginianus texanus*	yes	*Colinus virginianus*	Northern bobwhite. Ligon also mentions the masked bobwhite, *C.v. ridgwayi*, in correspondence. The current AOU Check-list does not show it as a separate subspecies.
Bandtailed pigeon	*Columba fasciata*	yes	*Patagioenas fasciata*	Band-tailed pigeon
Eared grebe	*Colymbus nigricollis californicus*	yes	*Podiceps nigricollis*	
Crow	*Corvus brachyohynchos hisperis*	yes	*Corvus brachyrhynchos*	American crow
Raven	*Corvus corax sinuatus*	yes	*Corvus corax*	Common raven
White-necked raven	*Corvus cryptoleucus*	Yes	*Corvus cryptoleucus*	Chihuahuan raven
Long-crested jay	*Cyaanocitta stelleri diadeniata*	yes	*Cyanocitta stelleri*	Steller's jay
Pinyon jay	*Cyanocephalus cyanocephalus*	yes	*Gymnorhinus cyanocephalus*	
Mearn's quail	*Cyrtonyx montezumae mearnsi*	yes	*Cyrtonyx montezumae*	Montezuma quail
Hairy woodpecker	*Dryobates villosus*	yes	*Picoides villosus*	
Purple grackle	*Duphagus cyanocephalus*	yes	*Euphagus cyanocephalus*	Brewer's blackbird
Ruddy duck	*Erismatura jamaicensis*	yes	*Oxyura jamaicensis*	
Aplomado falcon	*Falco fusco-caerulescens*	yes	*Falco femoralis*	
Prairie falcon	*Falco mexicanus*	yes	*Falco mexicanus*	
American sparrow hawk	*Falco sparverius phalaeria*	yes	*Falco sparverius*	American kestrel
Coot	*Fulica americana*	yes	*Fulica americana*	American coot
Wilson's snipe	*Gallinago delicata*	yes	*Gallinago delicata*	
California cuckoo	*Geococcyx californianus*	yes	*Geococcyx californianus*	Greater roadrunner
Maryland yellowthroat	*Geothlypis trichas occidentalis*	yes	*Geothlypis trichas*	Common yellowthroat
Great blue heron	No binomial given	no	*Ardea herodias*	
Bald eagle	*Haliaeetus leucocephalus*	yes	*Haliaeetus leucocephalus*	
Cactus wren	*Heleodytes brunneicapillus couesi*	yes	*Campylorhynchus brunneicapillus*	

(*continued*)

Birds (*continued*)

Common name used by Ligon[a]	Binomial in breeding bird report	AOU[b] Check-list	Current binomial[c]	Comments, and current common name if different
Black-necked stilt	*Himantopus mexicanus*	yes	*Himantopus mexicanus*	
Barn swallow	*Hirundo erythrogastra*	yes	*Hirundo rustica*	
Black tern	*Hydrochelidon nigra surinamerisis*	yes	*Chlidonias niger*	
Bullock's oriole	*Icterus bullocki*	yes	*Icterus bullockii*	
Scott's oriole	*Icterus parisorum*	yes	*Icterus parisorum*	
Little brown crane	No binomial given	no	*Grus canadensis*	Considered a small subspecies of sandhill crane.
Gambel's quail	*Lorphortyx gambeli*	yes	*Callipepla gambelii*	
Redhead	*Marila americana*	yes	*Aythya americana*	
Redheaded woodpecker	*Melanerpes erythrocephalus*	yes	*Melanerpes erythrocephalus*	Red-headed woodpecker
Wild turkey	*Meleagris gallopavo merriami*	yes	*Meleagris gallopavo*	***Merriami*** is the subspecies found in the southwestern United States.
Baird's woodpecker	*Melinerpes formicivorus*	yes	*Melinerpes formicivorus*	Florence Bailey calls this bird the Mearn's woodpecker. I do not find it referred to as Baird's in any other source. Ligon calls it the Acorn woodpecker in *New Mexico Birds*.
Song sparrow	*Melospiza melodia montana*	yes	*Melospiza melodia*	
Mawkingbird	*Mimus polyglottos leucopterus*	yes	*Mimus polyglottos*	Northern mockingbird. Ligon consistently spells common name "mawkingbird."
Dwarf cowbird	*Molothrus ater obscurus*	yes	*Molothrus ater*	Ligon calls it "dwarf" cowbird. Listed in current AOU Check-list as brown-headed cowbird.
Townsend's solitaire	*Myadestes townsendi*	yes	*Myadestes townsendi*	
Western wood pewee	*Myiochanes richardsoni*	Yes	*Contopus sordidulus*	Western wood-pewee
Clarke's nutcracker	*Nucifraga columbiana*	yes	*Nucifraga columbiana*	Clark's nutcracker

(continued)

Birds (*continued*)

Common name used by Ligon[a]	Binomial in breeding bird report	AOU[b] Check-list	Current binomial[c]	Comments, and current common name if different
Long-billed curlew	*Numenius americanus*	yes	*Numenius americanus*	
Black crowned night heron	*Nycticorax nycticorax naevuis*	yes	*Nycticorax nycticorax*	Black-crowned night-heron
Horned lark	*Otocoris alpestris leucolaema*	yes	*Eremophila alpestris*	
Flammulated screech owl	*Otus flammeolus*	yes	*Otus flammeolus*	Flammulated owl
Kildeer	*Oxyechus vociferus*	yes	*Charadrius vociferus*	Killdeer
House sparrow	*Passer domesticus*	yes	*Passer domesticus*	
Cliff swallow	*Petrochelidon lunifrons*	yes	*Petrochelidon pyrrhonota*	
Poor will	*Phalaenoptilus nuttalli*	yes	*Phalaenoptilus nuttallii*	Common poorwill
Magpie	*Pica pica hudsonia*	yes	*Pica hudsonia*	Black-billed magpie
Robin	*Planesticus migratorius propinguris*	yes	*Turdus migratorius*	American robin
Pie-billed grebe	*Podylimbus podiceps*	yes	*Podilymbus podiceps*	Pied-billed grebe
Purple martin	*Progne subis*	yes	*Progne subis*	
Vermilion flycatcher	*Pyrocephalus rubinius mexicanus*	yes	*Pyrocephalus rubinus*	
Blue-winged teal	*Querquedula discors*	yes	*Anas discors*	
Rock wren	*Salpinctes obsoletus*	yes	*Salpinctes obsoletus*	
Black phoebe	*Sayornis nigricans*	yes	*Sayornis nigricans*	
Scarlet ibis	No binomial given		*Eudocimus ruber*	Identity of bird Ligon saw remains uncertain.
Rufous hummingbird	*Selasphorus rufus*	yes	*Selasphorus rufus*	
Mountain bluebird	*Sialia currucoides*	yes	*Sialia currucoides*	
Western bluebird	*Sialia mexicana bairdi*	yes	*Sialia mexicana*	
White breasted nuthatch	*Sitta carolinensis nelsoni*	yes	*Sitta carolinensis*	White-breasted nuthatch
Pygmy nuthatch	*Sitta pygmaea*	yes	*Sitta pygmaea*	
Burrowing owl	*Speotyto cunicularia hypogaea*	yes	*Athene cunicularia*	
Black-chinned sparrow	*Spizella atrogularis*	yes	*Spizella atrogularis*	
Wilson's phalarope	*Steganopus tricolor*	yes	*Phalaropus tricolor*	

(*continued*)

Birds (*continued*)

Common name used by Ligon[a]	Binomial in breeding bird report	AOU[b] Check-list	Current binomial[c]	Comments, and current common name if different
Western meadowlark	*Sturnella neglecta*	yes	*Sturnella neglecta*	
Williamson's sapsucker	*Syhyrapicus thyroideus*	yes	*Sphyrapicus thyroideus*	
Violet-green swallow	*Tadycineta thalassina lepida*	close	*Tachycineta thalassina*	1910 AUO Check-list shows *Tachycynata*.
Curve-billed thrasher	*Toxostoma curvirostre*	yes	*Toxostoma curvirostre*	
Greater yellowlegs	*Totanus melanoleucus*	yes	*Tringa melanoleuca*	
House wren	*Troglodytes aedon parkinansis*	yes	*Troglodytes aedon*	
Cassin's kingbird	*Tyrannus vociferansi*	yes	*Tyrannus vociferans*	
Yellow-headed blackbird	*Xanthocephalus xanthocephalus*	yes	*Xanthocephalus xanthocephalus*	
Turtle dove	*Zenaidura macroura marginella*	yes	*Zenaida macroura*	Mourning dove
	Not mentioned by Ligon		*Zenaida asiatica*	White-winged dove
White-crowned sparrow	*Zonotrichia leucophrys*	yes	*Zonotrichia leucophrys*	
Vero	No binomial given	no	*Vireo* spp., probably *V. plumbeus* or *V. gilvus*	Several vireo species occur in the area. This is probably plumbeous or warbling vireo.
Hermit thrush	Not mentioned by Ligon		*Catharus guttatus*	
Pygmy owl	Mentioned in diary but not in breeding bird report		*Glaucidium gnoma*	Northern pygmy owl
	Not mentioned by Ligon		*Anas clypeata*	Northern shoveler
	Not mentioned by Ligon		*Anas crecca*	Green-winged teal
Black headed grosbeak	No binominal given		*Pheucticus melanocephalus*	Black-headed grosbeak
Tanager	No binomial given		*Piranga ludoviciana*	Western tanager. This is the only tanager that might have been mistaken for the black-headed grosbeak.

(*continued*)

Birds (*continued*)

Common name used by Ligon[a]	Binomial in breeding bird report	AOU[b] Check-list	Current binomial[c]	Comments, and current common name if different
Not noted by Ligon	No binomial given		*Ictinia mississippiensis*	Mississippi kite
Cooper's hawk	No binomial given			identified erroneously and entry changed to marsh hawk.
Marsh hawk	No binomial given		Circus cyaneus	Northern harrier. Mentioned in diary but not included in breeding bird report.
Not present in Ligon's time	Not present in Ligon's time		*Streptopelia decaocto*	Eurasian collared dove
Not noted by Ligon			*Icteria virens*	Yellow-breasted chat
Not noted by Ligon			*Pipilo maculatus*	Spotted towhee
Not noted by Ligon			*Aimophila cassinii*	Cassin's sparrow
Not noted by Ligon			*Empidonax traillii*	Willow flycatcher
Gull	No binomial given		Species unknown	Species unknown
Plover	No binomial given		Species unknown	Species unknown
Avocet	No binomial given		*Recurvirostra americana*	American avocet
King bird	No binomial given		*Tyrannus* sp.	Not mentioned in breeding bird report; discussed in 1918 report for Pecos Valley. Ranges of Cassin's, eastern, and western kingbirds overlap here.
Blue grosbeak	No binomial given		*Passerina caerulea*	Blue grosbeak. Not mentioned in 1913 breeding bird report; noted in 1918 report for Pecos Valley.
Crested flycatchers	No binomial given		*Myiarchus crinitus*	Great crested flycatcher. Not noted in 1913 breeding bird report; noted in 1918 report for Pecos Valley.
Duck hawk	No binomial given		Probably *Falco peregrinus*	Probably peregrine falcon. Noted as present at Stinking Lake but not given in species accounts.

Mammals

Common name used by Ligon	Binomial used by Ligon if present	Current binomial[d]	Comments; current common name if different
Rock squirrel	None	*Spermophilus variegatus*	Rock squirrel
Chipmonk	None	*Eutamias dorsalis; Eutamias quadrivitattus*	Cliff and Colorado chipmunks both occur in area. This could also have been golden-mantled ground squirrel (see below).
Abert's squirrel	None	*Sciurus aberti*	Abert's or tassle-eared squirrel
Golden-mantled ground squirrel	Not mentioned by Ligon	*Spermophilus latera*	See notes on chipmunks above.
Black-tail deer	None	*Odocoileus hemionus*	Mule deer
Elk	Not present in 1913	*Cervus elaphus*	Rocky Mountain elk. Reintroduced in 1950s. Merriam's elk noted by Ligon as extirpated by 1880s.
Antelope	None	*Antilocapra americana*	Pronghorn
Bighorn	None	*Ovis canadensis*	Bighorn. Not mentioned in 1913 breeding bird report.
Bison	None	*Bos bison*	Noted in 1918 report for Pecos Valley. Domestic herd in Pecos Valley.
Prairie dog; Mountain prairie dog	None	*Cynomys ludovicianu; C. gunnisoni*	Ligon notes two species. Those he saw on the Jornada del Muerto and in the mid--Pecos Valley grasslands were the black-tailed prairie dog. As he moved northward of Santa Rosa, he began to see the Gunnison's prairie dog.
Cotton-tail	None	*Sylvilagus floridanus*; *S. auduboni*; *S. nuttali*	Ligon did not differentiate among these species but passed through potential habitats and range of all three.
Jackrabbit	None	*Lepus californicus*	Black-tailed jackrabbit
None	Not mentioned by Ligon		Oryx[e] This species was not present in 1913.

(continued)

Mammals (*continued*)

Common name used by Ligon	Binomial used by Ligon if present	Current binomial[d]	Comments; current common name if different
Not mentioned by Ligon	None	*Lepus townsendi*	White-tailed jackrabbit. Erroneously stated as present at Brantley Lake by New Mexico State Parks in 2008 Brantley Lake State Park brochure.
Badger	None	*Taxidea taxus*	Badger
Coyote	None	*Canis latrans*	Coyote
Beaver	None	*Castor canadensis*	Beaver
Lobo wolf	None	*Canis lupus*	Gray wolf

Fish, Reptiles, and Amphibians

Common name used by Ligon	Binomial used by Ligon if present	Current binomial	Comments; current common name if different
Big mouth sucker	None given	*Catostomus* spp.	Species unknown
Trout	None given	*Salmo* spp.	Species unknown
Salamander	None given	*Ambystoma tigrum*	Tiger salamander
Not given	None given	*Cyprinodon tularosa*	White Sands pupfish
Rattle snake	None given	*Atrox* spp.	Species unknown
Bullfrog	None given	*Rana catesbeiana*	Bullfrog

Plants[f]

Common name used by Ligon	Binomial used by Ligon if present	Current binomial	Comments; current common name if different
Oak	None given	*Quercus* spp.	Ligon was variously in range of Gambel's oak, turbinella oak, and gray oak.
Quaking asp	None given	*Populus tremuloides*	Quaking aspen
Mt. cottonwood	None given	*Populus angustifolia*	Narrowleaf cottonwood
Wild flags	None given	Not known	Uncertain what plant Ligon is referring to.
Oak	None given	*Quercus gambelii*	Gambel oak. Ligon mentions oaks but does not specify species. This is one of several in the area he traversed.
Not mentioned	None given	*Pseudotsuga macrocarpa*	Douglas fir. Ligon mentions firs but does not specify Douglas fir. Both Douglas fir and white fir are present in area.
Yellow pine	None given	*Pinus ponderosa*	Ponderosa pine. Ligon uses "pine" mostly, without giving species. White pine also present in area.
Juniper; Cedar; Red cedar	None given	*Juniperus scopulorum; J. deppeana; J. coahuilensis; J. osteosperma; J. monosperma; J. communis*	Rocky Mountain, alligator, redberry, Utah, oneseed, and common junipers all possible in area covered by Ligon. Not sure which of these trees Ligon considered juniper, cedar, or red cedar.
Pinyon	None given	*Pinus edulis; P. monophylla*	Twoneedle and singleleaf pinyons both possible in the area Ligon covered. He does not differentiate between the two.
Cottonwood	None given	*Populus fremontii; P. deltoides*	Fremont and Eastern cottonwoods both possible in region.
Walnut	None given	*Juglans major*	Arizona walnut
Willow	None given	*Salix* spp.	There are several willows in region, too many to list here. Ligon does not differentiate.

(continued)

Plants[f] (*continued*)

Common name used by Ligon	Binomial used by Ligon if present	Current binomial	Comments; current common name if different
Box elder	None given	*Acer negundo*	Boxelder
Creosote	None given	*Larrea tridentata*	Creosote bush
Greasewood	None given	Unknown	Not sure what Ligon refers to here. The other common desert shrub in area is tar bush. This is a commonly used name for creosote bush, but he distinguishes between creosote and greasewood.
Mesquite brush	None given	*Prosopis glandulosa; P. pubescens; P. velutina*	Honey, screwbean, and velvet mesquites all possible in region.
Spanish dagger	None given	*Yucca harrimaniae*	Spanish bayonet. Present in region, although Ligon may have been referring to some other yucca-like plant.
Mescal	None given	Uncertain	Ligon may have been referring to the mescal bean (mountain laurel) or to a species of agave here.
Shingle grass sotol	None given	*Probably Dasylirion wheeleri*	Common stool
Jointed cactus	None given	*Cylindropuntia* spp.	Species uncertain
Candle cactus	None given	*Cylindropuntia kleiniae*	Candle cholla
Soapweed	None given	*Yucca elata*	Soapweed yucca
Ash	None given	Probably *Fraxinus velutina*	Velvet ash
Sage brush	None given	*Artemisia tridentata*	Big sagebrush. Present on Jicarilla Apache Indian Reservation. Not sure what Ligon was calling sage brush when crossing Jornada del Muerto.

(continued)

Plants[f] *(continued)*

Common name used by Ligon	Binomial used by Ligon if present	Current binomial	Comments; current common name if different
Not mentioned	None given	*Atriplex canescens*	Fourwing salt bush. Fairly common throughout region Ligon covered. This may be the species he was calling sage bush in southern New Mexico.
Not mentioned	None given	*Lycium berlandieri*	Berlandier's wolfberry
Salt grass	None given	*Distichlis spicata*	Saltgrass
Spruce; Blue spruce	None given	*Picea pungen; P. engelmannii*	Blue spruce; Engelmann spruce. Both possible for region covered.
Moss	None given	Unknown	Unknown
Sleepy grass	None given	*Stipa robusta*	Sleepygrass
Tabosa	None given	*Pleuraphis mutica*	Tabosagrass
Grama grass	None given	*Bouteloua* spp.; *B. gracilis; B. curtipendula; B. eriopoda*	Several gramas in region. Blue grama, sideoats grama, and black grama most common.
Cherry	None given	*Prunus emarginata*	Bitter cherry
Tula grass	None given	*Probably Schoenoplectus acutus*	Tule

[a] The common name used by Ligon was apparently drawn from Florence Merriam Bailey's *Handbook of Birds of the Western United States* (1902).

[b] American Ornthologists' Union

[c] The American Ornithologists' Union, "Check-list of North American Birds," http://www.aou.org/checklist/north/index.php.

[d] "Wilson and Reeder's Mammal Species of the World," http://www.bucknell.edu/MSW3/search.asp; American Society of Mammologists, "Mammals of New Mexico," http://www.mammalsociety.org/statelists/newmexico.html; Findley et al., 1975.

[e] Burkett, D. W. 1999. *Comprehensive Oryx Management Plan*. MEVATEC report no. 400A2/99/002F, March. Prepared by MEVATEC Corporation for White Sands Missile Range and the New Mexico Department of Game and Fish. U.S. Department of the Army, CSTE-DTC-WS-ES-ES.

[f] Plant binomials are taken from the USDA National Resources Conservation Service PLANTS database, http://plants.usda.gov.

Appendix Table 2

Specimens Collected by Ligon during the 1913 Breeding Bird Survey

Species	Gender	Age	Date	Ligon no.	USNM* no.	Catalog location	Diary location
House wren	Unknown	Adult	Probably 6/3	1	Unknown	Unknown	Probably Chloride Canyon, Black Range
Comment: This specimen does not appear in the Smithsonian files. It is recorded in his report and is, apparently, the first specimen he collected on his 1913 survey. Possibly mentioned in NMB,[1] p. 209.							
Flammulated screech owl			Between 6/3 and 6/7	4	Unknown	Unknown	Unknown
Comment: Ligon does not mention this species in the diary, although he acknowledges collecting eggs for it in his October 17 correspondence with E. W. Nelson of the U.S. Biological Survey. He has an entry in his report wherein he states, "I have only one record of this owl," where he lists specimen no. 4. It does not occur among the Smithsonian files. By numerical sequence, it must have been taken in the Black Range or an upper Gila River tributary. In NMB, Ligon mentions a nest thirty miles west of Chloride. This may be the source of this specimen.							
Cliff swallow	Unknown	Possibly eggs	Probably 6/7	8	Unknown	Unknown	Probably mouth of Haut [Hoyt] Creek
Comment: Not in Smithsonian files. Ligon's diary discusses a colony of cliff swallows at the mouth of Haut [Hoyt] Creek. He mentions nests with two, three, and four eggs. This entry is of particular interest, because the breeding birds report uses the binomial *Petrochelidon lunifrons*, undoubtedly written in later by Wells W. Cooke. Florence Merriam Bailey uses the above binomial for cliff swallows in HOBWUS,[2] but by the time BONM[3] was published, she was using *albifrons* as the species designation. By the time Ligon wrote NMB, he was using *pyrrohonta* to designate the species.							
Horned lark			Probably 6/9	9	Unknown	Unknown	Between Cuchillo and Winston
Comment: Not in Smithsonian files.							
Baltimore oriole	Female	Adult	6/10	10	366141	Elephant Butte, Sierra Co.	Cottonwood Spring, Cuchillo Creek, 12 mi. west of Elephant Butte
Comment: Smithsonian record. Also shown in breeding birds report. Cottonwood Spring no longer exists. It was near the present site of a flood control dam in Cuchillo Creek. Wells W. Cooke entered it as *Icterus bullocki* in the breeding birds report; the Smithsonian form calls it *Icterus galbula bullocki*. Florence Merriam Bailey calls it *bullocki* in both HOBWUS and BONM.							

(continued)

Species	Gender	Age	Date	Ligon no.	USNM* no.	Catalog location	Diary location
Spotted sandpiper			Probably 6/11	11	Unknown	Unknown	Probably Elephant Butte or Palomas Springs
Comment: This specimen does not show up in the Smithsonian files. However, it was confirmed in pencil in the margin of the report by Wells W. Cooke, indicating that he had seen the specimen. This suggests that some of Ligon's specimens have disappeared from the Smithsonian since he submitted them.							
Sonoran redwing			Probably 5/9	JSL74	Unknown	Unknown	Probably Palomas Springs
Comment: Not in Smithsonian files. This specimen was collected before Ligon began his official survey. He is using his personal specimen numbering system, which shows that he had been collecting for some time prior to beginning the survey.							
Baltimore oriole	Male	Adult	5/11	JSL 75	366140	Sierra Co.	
Comment: This information is from the Smithsonian record; the specimen is not in Ligon's report. Ligon was at Palomas Springs on May 9. This specimen was probably taken on the Rio Grande, although he might have reached Cottonwood Spring en route to Chloride.							
American kestrel	Male	Adult	5/12	JSL76	367162	New Mexico, between Palomas Creek and Chloride	
Comment: This information is from the Smithsonian record. This species, while mentioned in the diary, is not given an entry in Ligon's breeding birds report. The date places him either in Palomas Springs or en route to, or at, Chloride.							
Vermillion flycatcher			Probably late May, early June	JSL85	Unknown	Unknown	Probably Chloride Creek
Comment: Not in Smithsonian files. Numbering places its date of collection between 5/12 and 6/1, 1913, with Ligon at Chloride. A puzzling entry in the report states: "(This specimen will be sent in later to have this record verified) Stokley Ligon Aug. 10th, 1913." If he took the specimen at Chloride prior to beginning the survey, he probably did not have it along in August. He wrote the report before leaving Stinking Lake. One entry in the report suggests he may have collected this on May 24, 1913, at V + T Ranch.							
Black phoebe			6/1	JSL88			2 mi. west of Chloride
Comment: Not in Smithsonian files; mentioned in diary entry for 6/1, but not in breeding birds report.							

(continued)

Species	Gender	Age	Date	Ligon no.	USNM* no.	Catalog location	Diary location
Western wood pewee	6/1	JSL89					2 mi. west of Chloride
Comment: Noted as collected in diary, but not mentioned in breeding birds report; not in Smithsonian files. Ligon notes counting eggs in nest.							
Curve billed thrasher			6/1	JSL90			½ mi. east of Chloride
Comment: Not in Smithsonian files. Ligon notes nest.							
Vireo			6/1	JSL91			2 mi. west of Chloride
Comment: Not in Smithsonian files. Ligon notes collecting the bird on 6/1. No entry in breeding birds report for virios.							
Mallard		Chick	6/6	None	365040		V + T Ranch
Comment: This information is from the Smithsonian files; location is from diary.							
Mallard		Chick	6/6	None	365041		V + T Ranch
Comment: This information is from the Smithsonian record; location is from diary.							
Yellowthroat			Probably 6/11	12	Unknown	Unknown	Probably Palomas Springs vicinity
Comment: No record in Smithsonian; shown in breeding birds report. By numerical sequence, Ligon was on the Rio Grande.							
Redwing blackbird			6/11 or 6/15	15	Unknown	Unknown	Palomas Springs vicinity or Malpais Spring
Comment: It is impossible to determine exactly the date or location of this specimen. Specimens 13 and 14 are missing and do not show up in breeding birds report or diary. This could have been taken before Ligon left the Rio Grande, or it could have been taken at Malpais Spring.							
Swallow (*lumifrons*)			6/19	15--16	Unknown	Unknown	Peñasco River east of Mayhill
Comment: The overlap of the number with the above entry is confusing. However, these are not in the Smithsonian files and are mentioned only in the breeding birds report. Ligon notes killing three swallows with rocks on this date east of Mayhill.							

(*continued*)

Species	Gender	Age	Date	Ligon no.	USNM* no.	Catalog location	Diary location
Cassin's kingbird			6/20	18	Unknown	Unknown	Lower Peñasco River
Comment: Not in Smithsonian files; noted in breeding birds report.							
Horned lark			Probably 6/21	19	Unknown	Unknown	Probably between Hope and Artesia
Comment: Not in Smithsonian files; noted in breeding birds report.							
Redwing			6/24	20	Unknown	Unknown	Seven Rivers Valley
Comment: Not in Smithsonian files; noted in breeding birds report.							
Western wood pewee[4]		Male	adult	7/5	25	365542	12 mi. above Santa Rosa on Pecos River North of Santa Rosa
Comment: Smithsonian record.							
Horned lark		Eggs	7/6	8E/13,185	B33249	10 mi. northwest of Santa Rosa	North of Santa Rosa
Comment: Smithsonian record. Here, Ligon introduces another numbering system for eggs. I'm not sure what the numbers signify.							
Lewis's woodpecker			Probably 7/15	28	Unknown	Unknown	Chama River
Comment: No Smithsonian record; in breeding birds report only.							
Spotted sandpiper			7/15	31	Unknown	Unknown	Chama River
Comment: No Smithsonian record; in breeding birds report only.							
Crow			Probably 7/15	32	Unknown	Unknown	Chama River
Comment: No Smithsonian record; in breeding birds report only. Diary leaves impression that this bird could have been collected on 7/13, but the sequence supports 7/15.							

(continued)

Species	Gender	Age	Date	Ligon no.	USNM* no.	Catalog location	Diary location
Hairy woodpecker			7/17	33	Unknown	Unknown	7 mi. south of Stinking Lake
Comment: No Smithsonian record; in breeding birds report.							
Eared grebe	Unknown	Adult	7/17	34	240176	Stinking Lake	Stinking Lake
Comment: Smithsonian record.							
Mallard	Unknown	Adult	7/17	35	240231	Rio Arriba Co.	Stinking Lake
Comment: Smithsonian record.							
Mallard		Eggs	7/17	4E/13,189	840128	Lake Burford	Stinking Lake
Comment: Smithsonian record.							
Pied-billed grebe	Female	Adult	7/18	36	240177	Forester Is.[5] Alaska	Stinking Lake
Comment: This record is mysteriously muddled in the Smithsonian report. It says the specimen was taken in Alaska, but this would have been impossible. In his breeding birds report, Ligon mentions this specimen number at Dulce Lake. However, the number sequence and date assure that he was at Stinking Lake. The specimen number is mentioned in association with "grebe" in the report, without a mention of which species. Ligon notes about fifty pied-billed grebes at Stinking Lake, so it was undoubtedly collected there on 6/18.							
Ruddy duck	Female	Adult	7/18	37	240235	Stinking Lake	Stinking Lake
Comment: Smithsonian record.							
Redhead	Female	Adult	7/21?, possibly 7/20	38	237240	Stinking Lake	Stinking Lake
Comment: The Smithsonian file shows this specimen taken on 7/21, as does Ligon's report. This places it numerically out of sequence. He mentions collecting two ducks of unstated species on 7/20, and I suspect this was one of them.							
Eared grebe		Eggs	7/20	Ligon F2/13	B33251	Stinking Lake	Stinking Lake

(continued)

Species	Gender	Age	Date	Ligon no.	USNM* no.	Catalog location	Diary location
Blue-winged teal	Female	Adult	7/20	40	240233	Stinking Lake	Isolated lake northeast of Stinking Lake
Black-crowned night-heron	Male	Immature	7/20	41	240234	New Mexico	Isolated lake northeast of Stinking Lake
Comment: Smithsonian record. Ligon's entry in the report for this specimen number is confusing. In his diary, he mentions collecting a heron on 7/20. He assigns this specimen number to great blue heron.							
			Unknown	42			
Comment: Not in Smithsonian files; no record in diary.							
Redwing			Unknown	43			Stinking Lake
Comment: Not in Smithsonian files; mentioned in breeding birds report summary.							
Yellow-headed blackbird			Unknown	44			Stinking Lake
Comment: Not in Smithsonian files; mentioned in breeding birds report summary.							
Redhead		Chick	7/21	None; perhaps meant to be 45	365020	Stinking Lake	Stinking Lake
Comment: Ligon is again inconsistent in his personal numbering system. This is a chick collected along with no. 38 above. In his diary, he notes shooting the mother of a brood.							
Coot		Young	7/21–24	46		Unknown	Unknown
Comment: Not in Smithsonian files. Noted in breeding birds report species account, but does not mention when or where it was collected.							
Yellow-headed blackbird		Probably young	Probably 7/30	47			
Comment: Not in Smithsonian files; noted in breeding birds report summary.							

(continued)

Species	Gender	Age	Date	Ligon no.	USNM* no.	Catalog location	Diary location
Yellow-headed blackbird		Young	Probably 7/30	48			
Comment: Not in Smithsonian files. Ligon mentions shooting into a flock of about fifty and killing several. Number 48 was originally placed under redwing entry in report. However, Ligon noted uncertainty in the identification, and Wells W. Cooke annotated the report, placing this specimen in yellow-headed. Thus, Cooke apparently saw this specimen, but it did not exist in Smithsonian files in 2008.							
Blue-winged teal	Male	Adult	7/30	49	240234	Rio Arriba Co.	Isolated lake to northeast
Comment: In Smithsonian files.							
Redhead	Male	Adult	7/31	50	240238	Stinking Lake	Stinking Lake
Comment: In Smithsonian files. Ligon mentions shooting one duck in diary on this day. He does not mention the specimen number in his report.							
			Unknown	51			
Comment: No mention of specimen in breeding birds report; not in Smithsonian files. Fate unknown.							
House wren			Probably 8/1	52	Unknown	Unknown	Stinking Lake
Comment: Not in Smithsonian files; noted in breeding birds report.							
Rufous hummingbird			8/1	53	Unknown	Unknown	Stinking Lake
Comment: Not in Smithsonian files; noted in breeding birds report along with no. 54, below.							
Rufous hummingbird		Female	Adult	8/1	54	365753	Stinking Lake
Comment: In Smithsonian files; mentioned in breeding birds report.							
Mallard		Eggs	8/1	Ligon	F8/13	B33250	Stinking Lake
Comment: In Smithsonian files.							
Song sparrow			8/2	55	Unknown	Unknown	Unknown
Comment: Not in Smithsonian files; noted in breeding birds report.							
			Unknown	56		Unknown	
Comment: Not in Smithsonian files; no mention in diary or breeding birds report.							

(continued)

Species	Gender	Age	Date	Ligon no.	USNM* no.	Catalog location	Diary location
Purple grackle?	Unknown		Probably 8/3	57			Probably Rock Lake
Comment: Not in Smithsonian files. Noted in breeding bird report as purple grackle, but Wells W. Cooke later gives it the binomial of Brewer's blackbird.. Ligon mentions a large number of blackbirds at Rock Lake on 8/3.							
Great blue heron	Male	Adult	8/7	58	242488	NM	Dulcie Lake
Comment: In Smithsonian files; mentioned in breeding birds report as collected.							
Greater yellowlegs			8/7	59	Unknown	Unknown	Dulcie Lake
Comment: Not in Smithsonian files; mentioned in breeding birds report.							
Lark sparrow			Unknown	61	Unknown	Unknown	Unknown
Comment: Not in Smithsonian files; mentioned in breeding birds report, but date of collection not shown.							
Black-crowned night-heron	Female	Adult	8/10	62	240245	Clear Lake	Clear Lake
Comment: Diary says this specimen was from Clear Lake; Smithsonian file says Stinking Lake.							
Pied-billed grebe		Chick	8/10	63	365323	NM	Clear Lake
Comment: In Smithsonian files; noted in diary and report.							
			Unknown	64			
Comment: Not in Smithsonian file; not mentioned in breeding birds report. Fate unknown.							
Ruddy duck		Chick	8/10	None; possibly 64	365030	New Mexico	Clear Lake
Comment: In Smithsonian files; mentioned in breeding birds report.							
Gadwall	Female	Adult	8/10	65	240235	Stinking Lake	Stinking Lake
Comment: In Smithsonian files; noted in diary and breeding birds report.							
Black tern			8/11	66	Unknown	Unknown	Unknown
Comment: Not in Smithsonian files. Wells W. Cooke entered trinomial, *Hydrocelidon nigra surinamerisis*, in breeding birds report. No mention in diary.							

(continued)

Species	Gender	Age	Date	Ligon no.	USNM* no.	Catalog location	Diary location
Unknown			8/11	67	Unknown	Unknown	Unknown
Comment: Not in Smithsonian file; mentioned in breeding birds report. Said to fly with black terns. Fate of specimen unknown.							
Eared grebe		Chick	8/11	68	365324	New Mexico	Stinking Lake
Comment: In Smithsonian files.							
Great blue heron	Male		8/12	69	242449	New Mexico	Stinking Lake
Comment: In Smithsonian files, and in diary and breeding birds report.							

* USNM = United States National Museum, the former name of the Smithsonian Institution.

[1] NMB = *New Mexico Birds* (Ligon, 1961)

[2] HOBWUS = *Handbook of Birds of the Western United States* (F. Bailey, 1902)

[3] BONM = *Birds of New Mexico* (F. Bailey, 1928)

[4] This number is given in the breeding birds report under Cassin's kingbird.

[5] This is obviously an error on the USNM form.

NOTES

1. Ligon's field diary, "Field Diary, S. Stokley Ligon," and breeding bird report, "Breeding Birds of New Mexico," are in the United States Fish and Wildlife Service Field Reports, 1860–1961, record unit 7176, box 75, folder 1, Smithsonian Institution Archives. J. Stokley Ligon Special Reports 1913.

2. Jackson, n.d. Two-page documentation of Ligon's camera on file at the New Mexico Department of Game and Fish, Santa Fe.

Ligon used the 5" × 7" format, presumably this Black Beauty camera, through 1913. His later glass plates are 3¼ by 5½—standard postcard size. In his photographic journals, he mentions a Premo camera. This brand was made by Kodak and, among other formats, was made to take postcard-sized photographs. The fate of this second camera is unknown, but Ligon used it until at least January 1921.

In December 2009, James Enyeart (pers. comm.) inspected the camera at the Santa Fe Office of the New Mexico Department of Game and Fish and provided the following information. The camera bears the brand name of Black Beauty. The camera is a 5" × 7" dry plate camera and could only have been used to make glass plate negatives. It has an Anastigmat Lens, 5" × 7", serial number 7776, which matches the camera body serial number. This means the camera is the original instrument without any changes or adaptions. It was not a "view camera," but would have been defined as a "field camera" because it folded up into a self-contained unit.

The Black Beauty camera was manufactured by the Seneca Camera Co. of Rochester, New York, which was founded in 1899 and incorporated in 1900. It was the largest independent maker of cameras by 1910. However, there may have been other makers of the Black Beauty camera; the 1895 Montgomery Ward catalogue lists cameras, plates, and processing supplies in the contents. Additionally, the catalogue offered for sale a Style No. 10, which was a 5" × 7" field camera, for $12.50 and dry plates for $0.65 each.

3. J. Stokely Ligon to E. W. Nelson, Aug. 19, 1928, National Personnel Records Center, US National Archives and Records Administration, St. Louis, MO.

4. From a letter in the Ligon personnel files, National Personnel Records

Center, US National Archives and Records Administration, St. Louis, MO, for which the first page is missing. This was probably written to Vernon Bailey and may have been a rather oblique letter of application for the bird survey position.

5. Blachly, 1952.

6. J. Stokely Ligon to E. W. Nelson, Aug. 19, 1928, National Personnel Records Center, US National Archives and Records Administration, St. Louis, MO.

7. The full collection of float-trip photographs is in an album owned by Stokley's nephew, David R. Ligon of Las Cruces, New Mexico. A few of these photographs also show up among uncataloged glass plate negatives in the J. Stokley Ligon Collection at the Denver Public Library. Ligon made at least two, possibly three, float trips on the Pecos River.

8. Blachly, 1952.

9. Janice Sabec, Trinity University Library, San Antonio, e-mail correspondence regarding Ligon attendance records and early Trinity University catalogs, 2008.

10. Trinity University, 1898.

11. Stokley's uncle, L. A. Renick, had a well-drilling business on the Jornada del Muerto by 1905, and David R. Ligon noted that the Ligon males were traveling to the area and into the San Mateo Mountains on hunting expeditions as early as 1903. Ligon may have visited the Bar Cross Ranch before 1907, but we have no record of him working there before that year.

12. Harry C. Oberholser, unpublished section of *Birds of Texas* manuscript, "Investigations by the United States Biological Survey. Field Operations," microfilm, University of Texas Press Manuscripts, 1919, 1944, 1950–, Archives and Manuscripts, Briscoe Center for American History, University of Texas, Austin.

13. United States Fish and Wildlife Service Field Reports, 1860–1961, record unit 7176, Smithsonian Institution Archives. Vernon Bailey: box 72, folders 14, 15, 16; E. A. Goldman: box 73, folder 31.

14. J. Stokley Ligon files, Denver Public Library; Blachly, 1952.

15. "Ranch Life on the Jornada," photograph album, Ligon Collection, Harry Ransom Center, University of Texas, Austin.

16. "San Mateo–Black Range Hunts," photograph album, Ligon Collection, Harry Ransom Center, University of Texas, Austin.

17. Ligon's movements can be traced in two small pocket notebooks that record locations and dates of his photographs. J. Stokley Ligon Collection, Denver Public Library.

18. Quoted with the permission of Mr. and Mrs. Donald Edmund of Chloride, New Mexico. Schmidt's book (1977) has been re-issued by the Edmunds.

19. Henry A. Schmidt Photography Collection, Center for Southwest Research, University of New Mexico, Albuquerque.

20. J. S. Ligon, unpublished photograph notebooks. J. Stokley Ligon Collection, Denver Public Library.

21. National Personnel Records Center (NPRC), US National Archives and Records Administration, St. Louis, MO.

22. Ibid.

23. "Albuquerque Transportation History," Wheels Museum, http://www.wheelsmuseum.org/011505.html.

24. United States Fish and Wildlife Service Field Reports, 1860–1971, record unit 7176, box 72, folders 14, 15, 16, Smithsonian Institution Archives.

25. United States Fish and Wildlife Service Field Reports, 1860–1961, record unit 7176, box 73, folder 31, Smithsonian Institution Archives.

26. NPRC.

27. NPRC.

28. Tow is flax or hemp fiber used for weaving.

29. Photographs courtesy of Michael Campbell Photography, Washington, D.C.

30. *Rio Grande Republican*, Las Cruces, NM, July 20, 1909. "L. A. Rennick [*sic*], a former resident of Las Cruces now located in the north end of San Andreas, where he has a fine ranch, spent today in Cruces."

31. Vernon Bailey to Ligon, June 7, 1913. Letter mailed to Engle in which Cooke's list of important birds and a circular of general directions for field work were included. National Personnel Records Center, US National Archives and Records Administration, St. Louis, MO.

32. John Hubbard, pers. comm., 2008.

33. *Oxford English Dictionary*, http://www.oed.com.

34. John Hubbard, pers. comm., 2008.

35. This group included Patty Woodruff; Mara Weisenberger, San Andres National Wildlife Refuge; Dave Anderson and Trish Griffin, White Sands Missile Range; Dave Griffin, private biologist; and Joe Truett, Turner Endangered Species Fund.

36. Entering the mountain via the Rhodes Pass Road, we passed the still-active Woolf Ranch, then the site of Eugene Manlove Rhodes's grave and the abandoned Miller Ranch. We turned south through valleys running east of and parallel to the mountain crest, and en route to the head of Sulphur Canyon, we passed the Walson Place and another Woolf Ranch headquarters. Finally, after leaving Sulphur Canyon and heading on into Green Valley, we passed the Crockett Ranch. None of these, apparently, were present in 1913.

37. Dave Anderson, White Sands Missile Range, pers. comm., Dec. 18, 2007.

38. Dave Anderson of the White Sands Missile Range informs me that a species of sand sage occurs in the area, but it is not large enough or abundant enough to be of serious note.

39. HDR Engineering, Inc. (n.d.), pp. 60, 64.

40. "Historical Note, Inventory of the New Mexico Department of Game and Fish archives, 1905–ongoing," New Mexico Commission of Public Records State Records Center and Archives, http://rmoa.unm.edu/docviewer.php?docId=nmar1981-057.xml.

41. National Personnel Records Center (NPRC), US National Archives and Records Administration, St. Louis, MO

42. Ibid.
43. Ibid.
44. Ibid.
45. United States Fish and Wildlife Service Field Reports, 1860–1961, record unit 7176, box 75, folder 2, Smithsonian Institution Archives.
46. "Albuquerque Transportation History," Wheels Museum, Albuquerque, NM, http://www.wheelsmuseum.org/011505.html.
47. "Abiquiú Lake," Digital Abiquiu, http://www.digitalabiquiu.com/pages/tours/abiquiulake_t.html.
48. National Personnel Records Center, US National Archives and Records Administration, St. Louis, MO.
49. Florence Merriam Bailey was awarded an honorary LLD by the University of New Mexico in 1923. LLD degrees were also awarded to Elliot Barker (New Mexico State University, 1976) and Ligon (University of New Mexico, 1952).
50. C. Springer, US Fish and Wildlife Service, Albuquerque Office, e-mail correspondence, 2009.
51. Healy and Calder, 2006.

BIBLIOGRAPHY

Abernathy, Miles

2004 *Ride the Wind: The Amazing True Story of the Abernathy Boys*. Long Riders' Guild Press, http://www.horsetravelbooks.com/Welcome.htm.

Adams, Clarence Siringo

1986 *Tales and Trails along the Rio*. Old-time Publications, Roswell, NM.

Albert, Steven, Cynthia A. Ramotnik, and C. Gregory Schmitt

2004 Collared peccary range expansion in northwestern New Mexico. *The Southwestern Naturalist* 49:524–528.

Allred, Kelly W.

1993 The trail of E. O. Wooton. *New Mexico Resources*. Issue IX. College of Agriculture and Home Economics, New Mexico State University, Las Cruces.

American Ornithologists' Union

1913 Thirtieth Stated Meeting of the American Ornithologists' Union. *The Auk* 30:98.

Bailey, Florence M.

1902 *Handbook of Birds of the Western United States*. Houghton Mifflin, New York.

1928 *Birds of New Mexico*. New Mexico Department of Game and Fish in cooperation with the State Game Protective Association and the Bureau of Biological Survey, Santa Fe.

Bailey, Vernon

1912 *Directions for Field Work of Assistants of the Biological Survey*. US Biological Survey publication form no. 69. Washington, D.C.

1931 *Mammals of New Mexico*. US Biological Survey North American Fauna no. 53. Washington, D.C.

Ball, Eve

1988 *Indeh: An Apache Odyssey*. University of Oklahoma Press, Norman.

Blachly, Louis

1952 Oral History of J. Stokley and Rose Ligon. Pioneers Foundation (New Mexico) Oral History Collection, Center for Southwest Research, University Libraries, University of New Mexico, tapes 194–200.

Brown, Bryan T., and Michael. W. Trosset

1989 Nesting-habitat relationships of riparian birds along the Colorado River in Grand Canyon, Arizona. *Southwestern Naturalist* 34(2):260–270.

Brown, David E., and Randall D. Babb

2009 Status of the porcupine (*Erithizon dorsatum*) in Arizona, 2000–2007. *Journal of the Arizona-Nevada Academy of Science* 41(2):36–41.

Brown, David E., and Neil B. Carmony

1990 *Aldo Leopold's Southwest*. University of New Mexico Press, Albuquerque.

Brown, Merle B.

1967 *Eight Rattles and a Button*. The Naylor Company, San Antonio, TX.

Calvin, Ross

1951 *Lieutenant Emory Reports*. University of New Mexico Press, Albuquerque.

Cameron, Jenks

1929 *The Bureau of Biological Survey*. Institute for Government Research Service Monographs of the United States Government no. 54. Johns Hopkins Press, Baltimore, MD.

Caton, John D.

1877 *The Antelope and Deer of North America*. Forest and Stream Pub. Co., New York.

Coues, Elliott

1874 *Birds of the Northwest: A Hand-Book of the Ornithology of the Region Drained by the Missouri River and its Tributaries*. US Government Printing Office, Washington, D.C.

Davis, Carolyn O.

2003 *Mogollon Mountain Man: Nat Straw 1856–1941*. Sanpete Publications, Flagstaff, AZ.

de Gouvenain, Roland C.

1996 Origin, history, and current range of saltcedar in the US *In* Joe DiTomaso and Carl E. Bell (eds.), *Proceedings of the Saltcedar Management Workshop*, US Forest Service, Rancho Mirage, CA, http://www.invasivespeciesinfo.gov/docs/news/workshopJun96/Paper1.html.

Degenhardt, William G., Charles W. Painter, and Andrew H. Price

1996 *Amphibians and Reptiles of New Mexico*. University of New Mexico Press, Albuquerque.

Desmond, Martha

2004 Effects of grazing practices and fossorial rodents on a winter avian community in Chihuahua, Mexico. *Biological Conservation* 116:235–242.

Dobie, Frank J.

1950 *The Ben Lilly Legend*. Little, Brown, and Co., Boston.

Easton, Robert, and MacKenzie Brown

1961 *Lord of Beasts: The Saga of Buffalo Jones*. University of Nebraska Press, Lincoln.

Evans, Dub
1951 *Slash Ranch Hounds.* University of New Mexico Press, Albuquerque.
Findley, James S., Arthur H. Harris, Don E. Wilson, and Clyde Jones
1975 *Mammals of New Mexico.* University of New Mexico Press, Albuquerque.
Flores, Rosie
1999 Ligon Family, *Pecos Enterprise,* June 29, 1999, Pecos, NM.
Ford, Fanny
1911 *The Natural Resources Survey of the Conservation and Natural Resources Commission of New Mexico.* Report no. I. New Mexican Printing Co., Santa Fe.
Glinski, Richard L., and Robert D. Ohmart
1983 Breeding ecology of the Mississippi kite in Arizona. *The Condor* 85: 200–207.
Hall, G. Emlen
2002 *High and Dry: The Texas–New Mexico Struggle for the Pecos River.* University of New Mexico Press, Albuquerque.
Hall, Martin H., and Jerry Thompson
2000 *Sibley's New Mexico Campaign.* University of New Mexico Press, Albuquerque.
Hallenbeck, Cleve
1950 *Land of the Conquistadores.* Caxton Printers, Ltd., Caldwell, ID.
HDR Engineering, Inc.
n.d. Preliminary New Mexico Extreme Precipitation Event Climatology. Prepared for New Mexico Office of State Engineers, Albuquerque, NM.
Healy, Susan, and William A. Calder
2006 *Rufous Hummingbird (Selasphorus rufus). In* A. Poole (ed.), "The Birds of North America Online," Cornell Lab of Ornithology, Ithaca, NY, http://bna.birds.cornell.edu/bna/species/053.
Herrick, C. L.
1900 The geology of the White Sands of New Mexico. *Journal of Geology* 8:112–128.
Hibben, Frank C.
1937 *A Preliminary Study of the Mountain Lion.* University of New Mexico Bulletin no. 318. University of New Mexico Press, Albuquerque.
Hildebrandt, Thomas D., and Ohmart, Robert D.
1982 *Final Report. Biological Resource Inventory (Vegetation and Wildlife), Pecos River Basin, New Mexico and Texas.* US Bureau of Reclamation contract no. 9-07-57-VO567. Tempe, AZ.
Hilliard, George
1996 *A Hundred Years of Horse Tracks: The story of the Gray Ranch.* High-Lonesome Books, Silver City, NM.
Hunter, William C., Robert D. Ohmart, and Bertin W. Anderson

1988 Use of exotic saltcedar (*Tamarix chinensis*) by birds in arid riparian systems. *The Condor* 90:113–123.

Hutchinson, W. H.

1956 *A Bar Cross Man*. University of Oklahoma Press, Norman.

Jackson, David G.

1961 The story of J. Stokley Ligon. *Texas Game and Fish* (Oct.):12–13, 29.

Jehl, Joseph R., W. Sean Boyd, Don S. Paul, and Daniel W. Anderson

2002 Massive collapse and rapid rebound: Population dynamics of eared grebes (*Podiceps nigricollis*) during an ENSO event. *Auk* 119:1162–1166.

Julyan, Robert

1998 *The Place Names of New Mexico*. University of New Mexico Press, Albuquerque.

Kamees, Larry, Tim Mitchusson, and Mark Gruber

2008 *New Mexico's Quail: Biology, Distribution, and Management Recommendations*. New Mexico Department of Game and Fish, Santa Fe.

Kemp, Ben W.

1968 *Cow Dust and Saddle Leather*. University of Oklahoma Press, Norman.

Kingsberry, John M.

1964 *Poisonous Plants of the United States and Canada*. Prentice Hall, Saddle River, NJ.

Klukhohn, Clyde

1927 *To the Foot of the Rainbow*. The Century Co., New York.

Knowles, Craig J.

2002 *Status of White-tailed and Gunnison's Prairie Dogs*. National Wildlife Federation, Missoula, MT and Environmental Defense, Washington, D.C.

Kofalk, Harriet

1989 *No Woman Tenderfoot*. Texas A&M University Press, College Station.

Lee, Susan E.

1960 *These Also Served*. Self-published, Los Lunes, NM.

Leopold, Aldo

1915 Stinking Lake. *The Pine Cone* (Christmas):1.

1918 Making Stinking Lake a game refuge. *Outers' Book–Recreation*. 58(4): 412–415.

1933 *Game Management*. Charles Scribner's Sons, New York.

Ligon, J. Stokley

1927 *Wildlife of New Mexico: Its Conservation and Management*. New Mexico State Game Commission, Santa Fe.

1946a *The Merriam's Turkey*. University of New Mexico Press, Albuquerque.

1946b *Upland Game Bird Restoration through Trapping and Transplanting*. New Mexico Game and Fish Commission, Santa Fe.

1961 *New Mexico Birds*. University of New Mexico Press, Albuquerque.

Livingston, M. F., and S. D. Schemnitz

1996 Summer bird/vegetation associations in tamarisk and native habitat along the Pecos River, southeastern New Mexico. *In* D. W. Shaw and D. M. Finch (tech. coords.), *Desired future conditions for southwestern riparian ecosystems: bringing interests and concerns together*, pp. 171–180. USDA General Technical Report RM-GTR-272. USDA Forest Service, Rocky Mountain Research Station, Fort Collins, CO.

Loeffler, Jack

2008 *Survival along the Continental Divide: An Anthology of Interviews*. University of New Mexico Press, Albuquerque.

Lovich, Jeffrey E.

1996 A brief overview of the impact of tamarisk infestation on native plants and animals. *In* Joe DiTomaso and Carl E. Bell (eds.), *Proceedings of the Saltcedar Management Workshop*, Rancho Mirage, CA, 13–15, http://www.invasivespeciesinfo.gov/docs/news/workshopJun96/Paper4.html.

McHugh, Tom

1972 *The Time of the Buffalo*. Alfred A. Knopf, New York.

Mearns, Edgar A.

1907 *Mammals of the Mexican Boundary*. Smithsonian Institution Bulletin no. 56. Smithsonian Institution, Washington, D.C.

Meine, Curt

1988 *Aldo Leopold: His Life and Works*. University of Wisconsin Press, Madison.

Meinzer, O. E., and R. F. Hare

1915 *Geology and Water Resources of the Tularosa basin*. US Geological Survey Water-Supply Paper 343. US Government Printing Office, Washington, D.C.

Miller, Robert Rush, and Anthony A. Echelle

1975 *Cyprinodon tularosa*, a new cyprinodontid fish from the Tularosa basin, New Mexico. *Southwestern Naturalist* 19:365–377.

Moffat, Riley Moore

1985 *Map Index to the Topographic Quadrangles of the United States, 1882–1940*. Western Association of Map Libraries, Santa Cruz, CA.

New Mexico Ornithological Society (NMOS)

http://www.nmbirds.org/

Oakes, Claudia L.

2000 History and consequence of keystone mammal eradication in the desert grassland: The Arizona black-tailed prairie dog (*Cynomys ludovicianus arizonensis*). PhD dissertation, University of Texas at Austin.

Oakes, Claudia, Nancy Kastning, Owen Williams, and David Barz

2004 *Black-tailed Prairie Dog Historic Colonies and Suitable Habitat on White Sands Missile Range, New Mexico*. Prepared by SWCA Environmental Consultants, Albuquerque, for Department of the Army, White Sands Missile Range.

Olmstead, Frederick R.

1857 *A Journey through Texas*. Dix, Edwards, and Co., New York.

Palmer, T. S.

1917 In memorium: Wells Woodbridge Cooke. *The Auk* 34(2):119–132.

Parker, Will

2001 *My Life as a Cowboy in the Sacramento Mountains: Memoirs of Will Parker.* Edited by Dawn Moore Santiago. *Pioneer* 5:1–2. Tularosa Basin Historical Society, Alamogordo, NM.

Phillips, Alan R., Joe T. Marshall, and Gale Monson

1964 *The Birds of Arizona.* University of Arizona Press, Tucson.

Phillips, David A. Jr., Kevin Palmer, and Christine S. VanPool

1994 *A study of the Elephant Butte Dam and Community Historic District, Sierra County, New Mexico.* SWCA Archeological Report no. 94–64 for US Bureau of Reclamation, Albuquerque.

Pittenger, John S., and Craig L. Springer

1999 Native range and conservation of the white sands pupfish (*Cyprinodon tularosa*). *The Southwestern Naturalist* 44(2):157–165.

Redford, Kent H., Keith Aune, and Eva Fearn

2009 The second recovery of bison. *The Wildlife Professional* (Fall):46–49.

Rhodes, May Davison

1938 *The Hired Man on Horseback.* Houghton Mifflin Co., Boston.

Robinson, Michael J.

2005 *Predatory Bureacracy: The Extermination of Wolves and the Transformation of the West.* University Press of Colorado, Boulder.

Roosevelt, Theodore R.

1914 *Through the Brazilian Wilderness.* C. Scribner's Sons, New York.

Rosenberg, Kenneth V., Robert D. Ohmart, William C. Hunter, and Bertin W. Anderson

1991 *Birds of the Lower Colorado River Valley.* University of Arizona Press, Tucson.

Russell, Stephen M., and Gale Monson

1998 *Birds of Sonora.* University of Arizona Press, Tucson.

Ruth, Maria M.

2005 *Rare Bird: Pursuing the Mystery of the Marbled Murelet.* Rodale Press, Emmaus, PA.

Schmidt, Raymond

1977 *New Mexico Recollections.* Self-published, Chloride, NM.

Shaw, Harley G.

1961 *Influence of Salt Cedar on White-Winged Doves in the Gila Valley.* Arizona Game and Fish Department Game Management Division Special Report. Phoenix, AZ.

Sheridan, Tom

1975 *The Bitter River: A Brief Historical Survey of the Middle Pecos River Basin.* Western Interstate Commission for Higher Education, Boulder, CO.

Sibley, David A.
2000 *The Sibley Guide to Birds*. Knopf, New York.
Smith, H. E.
1915 *The Grasshopper Outbreak in New Mexico during the Summer of 1913*. USDA bulletin no. 293. USDA, Washington, D.C.
Sonnichsen, C. L.
1960 *Tularosa: Last of the Frontier West*. University of New Mexico Press, Albuquerque.
Sullivan, James B.
1994 *A New Mexico Family: Tafoya-Sullivan and the Origins of Sierra County*. Burke Pub. Co., San Antonio, TX.
Sweet, John R.
2002 Men and varmints in the Gila wilderness, 1909–1936: The wilderness ethics and attitudes of Aldo Leopold, Ben Lilly, J. Stokley Ligon, and Albert Pickens towards predators. *New Mexico Historical Review* 77(3): 369–397.
Tiller, Veronica E. Valarde
2000 *The Jicarilla Apache Tribe: A History*. BowArrow Pub. Co., Albuquerque, NM.
Trinity University
1898 Trinity University Catalog. Trinity University Library, San Antonio, TX.
Truett, Samuel
2006 *Fugitive Landscapes*. Yale University Press, New Haven, CT.
Tschiffely, A. F.
1933 *Tschiffely's Ride: Ten Thousand Miles in the Saddle from Southern Cross to Pole Star*. Simon and Schuster, New York.
Wallace, Jeremy
2007 Shaping nature: J. Stokley Ligon and evolving ecological attitudes toward nature in twentieth-century New Mexico. Master's thesis, New Mexico State University.
Warren, Louis S.
1997 *The Hunter Game*. Yale University Press, New Haven, CT.
Waters, Frank
1942 *The Man Who Killed the Deer: A Novel of Pueblo Indian Life*. The Swallow Press, Denver, CO.
Wetherill, Marietta
1992 *Reflections on Life with the Navajos in Chaco Canyon*. Johnson Books, Boulder, CO.
Wetmore, Alexander
1918 Observations on the habits of birds at Lake Burford, New Mexico. *Auk* 37:221–247; 393–412.

Witham, T. G., and J. Maschinski
1996 Current hybrid policy and the importance of hybrid plants in conservation. *In* J. Maschinski, H.D. Hammond, and L. Holter (eds.), *Southwestern Rare and Endangered Plants: Proceedings of the Second Conference*, Flagstaff, AZ, Sept. 11–14, 1995, pp. 103–112. USD.A. Rocky Mt. Research Station, Fort Collins, CO.

INDEX

ABOUT THE AUTHORS

Harley Shaw grew up in Arizona and began working for the Arizona Game and Fish Department (AZGFD) in 1955, during his first summer out of high school. He completed a BS degree in wildlife management at the University of Arizona and a MS degree in wildlife management at the University of Idaho. From 1963 to 1990, he worked as a AZGFD research biologist, carrying out projects on mule deer, wild turkeys, mountain lions, and desert bighorns. His publications include *A Mountain Lion Field Guide* (Arizona Game and Fish, 1987), *Soul Among Lions* (University of Arizona Press, 2000), and *Stalking the Big Bird* (University of Arizona Press, 2004) and popular articles in *Arizona Wildlife Views*, *Horse & Rider Magazine*, *Rifle*, *Handloader*, *Rolling*, and *American Rifleman*. He wrote the research history chapter for *Cougar: Ecology and Conservation* (University of Chicago Press, 2005), which was given the edited book of the year award by The Wildlife Society. He has authored articles on mountain lions for the *The Journal of Wildlife Management*, the 1977 Predator/Prey Symposium sponsored by the American Society of Mammalogists, and the 1983 Wildlife/Livestock Interactions Workshop sponsored by the University of Idaho. He was one of thirteen members of a working group that wrote *Cougar Management Guidelines* (Wildfutures, Inc., 2005).

Since retiring from the AZGFD, Harley has continued to write, carry on contract research, and work with volunteer groups in establishing mountain lion population monitoring (track count) programs. He carried out a feasibility study for pronghorn reintroductions in Joshua Tree National Park and an assessment of research needs for pronghorn/predator relations in Arizona for the Arizona Pronghorn Foundation. He carried out a study of historic habitat change in the piñon-juniper habitats of northern Arizona. This work has led to coauthoring a catalog of early landscape photographs of the Prescott area and authoring *Wood Plenty, Grass Good, Water None: Featuring Twenty-Three Days with Lieutenant Amiel Weeks Whipple in His 1854 Exploration of the Upper Verde Water-*

shed (USDA, Forest Service, Rocky Mountain Research Station, 2006). He and his wife, Patty Woodruff, completed a general wildlife inventory for the Hubbell Trading Post at Ganado, Arizona, and have written an ecological history of that site. Over the past two years, Harley has presented papers at the Gila Symposium at New Mexico Western University and at the Arizona History Convention. He has hosted four annual mountain lion workshops at Ted Turner's Ladder Ranch.

Harley now lives in Hillsboro, New Mexico, where he is currently president of the Hillsboro Historical Society.

Mara Weisenberger has been a wildlife biologist for the US Fish and Wildlife Service at San Andres National Wildlife Refuge for the past eighteen years. During this time, she has served on temporary assignment on Kodiak Island, Alaska, for a brown bear study and at refuges in Colorado and Arizona. Recently, her San Andres assignments have included work at the Refuges Division in Washington, D.C., and as acting regional biologist for the Southwest Regional office in Albuquerque, New Mexico. A published author in scientific literature of the field, she holds a BA degree in psychology with a concentration in animal behavior and a MS degree in wildlife ecology from the University of Arizona. She resides in Las Cruces, New Mexico, with her husband and two children, who share her passion for wildlife and the outdoors.